eBay
QuickSteps

CAROLE MATTHEWS

JOHN CRONAN

McGraw-Hill/Osborne

New York Chicago San Francisco
Lisbon London Madrid Mexico City
Milan New Delhi San Juan
Seoul Singapore Sydney Toronto

McGraw-Hill/Osborne
2100 Powell Street, 10th Floor
Emeryville, California 94608
U.S.A.

To arrange bulk purchase discounts for sales promotions, premiums, or fund-raisers, please contact **McGraw-Hill/** Osborne at the above address. For information on translations or book distributors outside the U.S.A., please see the International Contact Information page immediately following the index of this book.

EBAY QUICKSTEPS

1234567890 WCK WCK 01987654

ISBN 0-07-225506-4

PUBLISHER / Brandon A. Nordin

VICE PRESIDENT AND ASSOCIATE PUBLISHER / Scott Rogers

ACQUISITIONS EDITOR / Roger Stewart

ACQUISITIONS COORDINATOR / Agatha Kim

SERIES CREATORS & EDITORS / Martin and Carole Matthews

TECHNICAL EDITORS / Carole Matthews, John Cronan

COPY EDITOR / Lisa McCoy

PROOFREADER / Chara Curtis

INDEXER / Kellen Diamanti

LAYOUT ARTISTS / Laura Canby, Bailey Cunningham

ILLUSTRATORS / Kathleen Edwards, Pattie Lee, Bruce Hopkins, Laura Canby

SERIES DESIGN / Bailey Cunningham

COVER DESIGN / Pattie Lee

As we have used eBay and focused our attention on the vast community it serves, we have become aware of the profound changes in how we buy and sell in this global economy. eBay represents a shift in tangible and intangible ways. Not only are millions of people conducting business at some level (from online garage sales to huge, global companies), but also we are thinking about the world in a very different way. No longer is that buyer in England a stranger or that seller of silk in Cambodia an unattainable source. We don't know whether our seller is tall, male or female, color-blind, or a soccer fan, but we do know whether he or she conducts business in an honorable way. What is this thing that combines materialism with such a sense of the essence of who we are? With that question in mind, we would like to dedicate this book to the millions of eBay users who have helped to transform the age-old practices of buying and selling into this vital and dynamic global economy.

Carole Matthews and John Cronan

About the Authors

Carole Matthews:

Carole Boggs Matthews has more than 30 years of computing experience. She has authored or co-authored over 60 books, including Microsoft Office PowerPoint 2003 QuickSteps, PhotoShop CS QuickSteps, and FrontPage 2003: The Complete Reference. Prior to her writing career, she co-founded and operated a computer business, developing tools to help others use computers in their businesses. An eBay user since 1998, Carole now applies that experience and many years of writing to eBay QuickSteps, bringing both business and computer knowledge to the book. Carole lives in Washington State with her husband Marty, son Michael, two cats, and the family dog.

John Cronan:

John Cronan has over 25 years of computer experience and has been writing and editing computer-related books for over 10 years. His recent books include Microsoft Office Excel 2003 QuickSteps and Microsoft Office Access 2003 QuickSteps. John and his wife Faye operate an antiques business in Washington State and frequent area auctions in search of merchandise they can "bring back to life." An eBay member since 1999, John couples his in-depth experience in writing books on software products with his antiques familiarity and eBay use to bring a unique perspective to eBay QuickSteps. John and Faye (and cat Little Buddy) reside in the historic mill town of Everett, WA.

Contents at a Glance

Acknowledgments

Although this book has only two names on the cover, it was really produced by a fantastic team of truly talented people. This team, the QuickSteps backbone, has again pulled together to produce a really great book in an incredibly short time. They did this by putting in endless hours, working selflessly with each other, and applying a great amount of skill.

Laura Canby, layout artist and prepress expert, has done her typical professional and wonderfully creative job, working many late and weekend hours. Thanks, Laura!

Lisa McCoy, copy editor, the newest member of the team, has contributed her great skill and a light touch to make our poor attempts at writing readable and accurate. Thanks, Lisa!

Bailey Cunningham, series designer and layout artist, stepped in to help with grace and skill. Her endless patience and great humor kept us sane and civil during long hours. Thanks, Bailey!

Chara Curtis, proofreader, did a great job of catching those slippery commas, bolding problems, and endless other dits and dats that escaped our eyes. Thanks, Chara!

Kellen Diamanti, indexer, confronting the bulk of her work at the tail end of the production cycle, bravely and gracefully created a wonderful and comprehensive index. Thanks, Kellen.

Keith Eyer, Layout artist and print specialist scanned, corrected, nudged and shuffled to get us to the printer on time. Thanks, Keith!

Roger Stewart, Editorial Director at Osborne, always standing behind us throughout the production process—even when the schedule looks bleak. Thanks, Roger!

To the many eBay users and businesses we contacted while writing this book who shared their experiences, suggestions, listing data, and other materials. Thanks to all for helping make this a better book!

Contents

1

2

Chapter 3   **Buying Strategies** 53

4

5

Introduction

QuickSteps books are recipe books for computer users. They answer the question "How do I...?" by providing a quick set of steps to accomplish the most common tasks with a particular program. The sets of steps are the central focus of the book. Sidebar QuickSteps provide information on how to do quickly many small functions or tasks that are in support of the primary functions. Sidebar QuickFacts supply information that you need to know about a subject. Notes, Tips, and Cautions augment the steps, but they are presented in a separate column to not interrupt the flow. Brief introductions are present, but there is minimal narrative otherwise. Many illustrations and figures, a number with callouts, are also included where they support the steps.

QuickSteps books are organized by function and the tasks needed to perform those functions. Each function is a chapter. Each task, or "How To," contains the steps needed for its accomplishment along with the relevant Notes, Tips, Cautions, and screenshots. Tasks are easy to find through:

- The Table of Contents, which lists the functional areas (chapters) and tasks in the order they are presented

- A How To list of tasks on the opening page of each chapter

- The index, which provides an alphabetical list of the terms that are used to describe the functions and tasks

- Color-coded tabs for each chapter or functional area with an index to the tabs in the Contents at a Glance

Conventions Used in this Book

eBay QuickSteps uses several conventions designed to make the book easier for you to follow. Conventions used include:

- An icon in the Table of Contents and in the How To list in each chapter references a QuickSteps or a QuickFacts sidebar in a chapter.

- **Bold type** is used for words or objects on the screen that you are to do something with, like click **Save As**, open **File**, and click **Close**.

- *Italic type* is used for a word or phrase that is being defined or otherwise deserves special emphasis.

- <u>Underlined type</u> is used for text that you are to type from the keyboard.

- SMALL CAPITAL LETTERS are used for keys on the keyboard, such as ENTER and SHIFT.

- When you are expected to enter a command, you are told to press the key(s). If you are to enter text or numbers, you are told to type them.

How to...

Chapter 1

Stepping into eBay

eBay is the world's largest online market. It is made up of sellers and buyers from all over the planet, not just your friendly neighborhood stores. You have the world at your fingertips—at exactly the right price. You can buy goods, or sell them, from businesses or individuals anywhere—and all from your own computer. eBay is both an exciting adventure for a novice buyer or seller and a place where business is conducted. eBay is easily accessible to all who have a computer and a sense of what to do.

This book provides an understanding of how a purchase or sale transaction works, from the seller getting the item on eBay to the buyer purchasing the item. You will learn to navigate around eBay and to buy and sell items. Finally, after learning how to protect yourself, you will see how to make eBay into a business for yourself. First off is a walk through a typical transaction, shown in Figure 1-1.

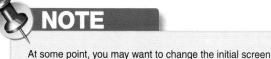

TIP

You may find that the page displayed in Figure 1-3 is what you see when you first bring up eBay. In this case, after exploring the areas you are most interested in, click **Home** to display the home page shown in Figure 1-2.

NOTE

At some point, you may want to change the initial screen that eBay displays. To bring up the page you want, save it as a Favorite by using your browser. On your browser menu, click **Favorites | Add To Favorites**, fill in the **Name** as you want it, and click **OK**. (In Netscape, you'll use Bookmarks instead of Favorites.)

Figure 1-3: You may initially see an alternative Welcome screen, for persons new to eBay, that contains beginning links for you to explore.

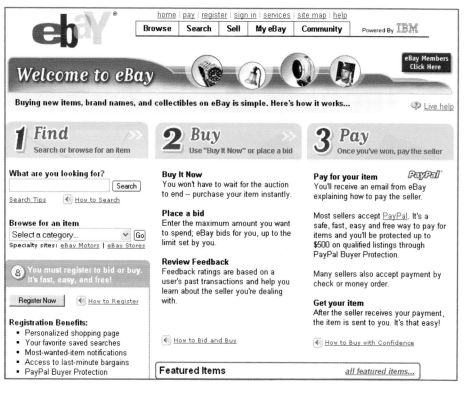

Browse eBay's Home Page

Your first stop is the home page, your base of operations when you start using eBay. From it, you can access any other location in eBay, get registered, and do anything else you need to do to get started. You get to the home page with these steps:

1. Open your browser.

2. Type www.ebay.com in the address bar, and press **ENTER**. The window displayed in Figure 1-2 opens.

Investigate Specialty Sites

Specialty Sites are links to eBay's own stores and sites.

1. From the home page, click one of the Specialty Sites links:

- Click **eBay Live** to find out about a conference that was held in June 2004. The conference provided a way for eBay participants to meet in person and attend workshops on how to be better at buying and selling on eBay. This link is time-sensitive and will be replaced at some time. However, eBay Live 2005 is being planned as we speak!

  Specialty Sites
  eBay Live!
  eBay Motors
  eBay Stores
  The Half Zone on eBay
  PayPal

- Click **eBay Motors** to display links to buying and selling everything from boats, motorcycles, autos, ATVs, and airplanes, to parts and accessories for them. Figure 1-4 shows the initial window.

Figure 1-4: In the eBay Motors store, you can buy all types of vehicles and their parts and accessories.

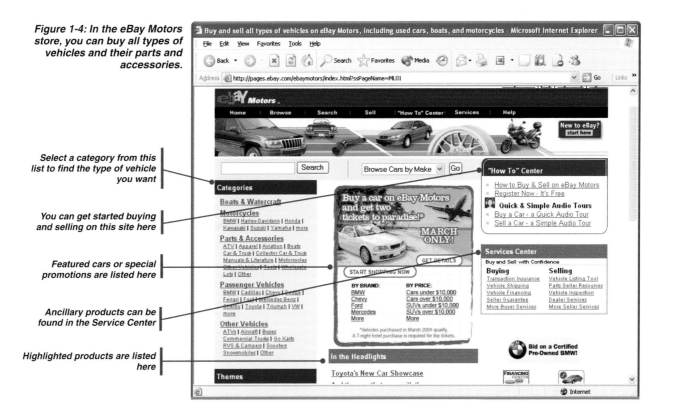

Select a category from this list to find the type of vehicle you want

You can get started buying and selling on this site here

Featured cars or special promotions are listed here

Ancillary products can be found in the Service Center

Highlighted products are listed here

NOTE

A feedback rating is a compilation of your feedback comments. A positive comment earns you 1 point; a negative comment loses you 1 point; a neutral comment has no effect. You must usually have a feedback rating of 10 to 30 points to be eligible for some auctions, such as the Buy It Now auction or the Buy It Now fixed-price auction. Comments are counted by eBay member; that is, two positives from the same member equals 1 point.

NOTE

eBay Anything Points allow you to get points for purchases you make. When you accumulate enough points, you can use them to purchase items. Sellers offering this feature are identified with the following ad on their View Item page. You can learn more about eBay Anything Points and register to participate when you click **Site Map** on the top links bar and select **eBay Anything Points** under Buyer Tools.

5 Anything *points* **per dollar** of the final price* for buyers who pay with **PayPal**

* Final price is closing eBay price and does not include fees such as shipping or tax.
For additional information about earning Points from sellers go to http://anythingpoints.ebay.com/earn.html
With the Points you earn, you can buy anything on eBay where PayPal is accepted!

- Click **eBay Stores** to find a store or create your own store in eBay. eBay Stores offers the same opportunities as the regular auctions; that is, auctions, Buy It Now fixed-price sales, and combo auctions with Buy It Now features (See Table 1-1). This is where you can find deals, if you are a buyer, or can create a storefront to list less-expensive items, if you are a seller. Since fees are lower for stores, the items are usually listed at lower prices than those for auctions. To open a store, you must have sold and had feedback on at least 20 items or be ID Verified (a way to guarantee to the buyer that you are who you say you are). Statistics seem to bear out that the eBay Stores sites get more traffic and higher-volume sales than the regular eBay items, especially with the links from items offered by the store in the regular sites and cross-promotion services that eBay offers. Chapter 10 talks more about eBay Stores.

- Click **the HalfZone on eBay** to find new and used books, music, movies and video games at reduced prices that are 50 percent or more off. These items are offered at fixed prices rather than auction prices, so it is more like shopping in a regular store. This is particularly nice for folks who don't want to bother with auctions.

- Click **PayPal** to sign up for a PayPal account. This feature is a way to facilitate purchases and sales. As a buyer, you can pay for items using several payment methods, and each purchase is insured for up to $500 USD. For sellers, PayPal allows customers to pay using a variety of credit or debit cards, automatically sends an invoice by e-mail, and facilitates using your transactions in money management software, such as Quicken or Money. It also facilitates and tracks shipping of the item to the customer. See Chapters 4 and 5 for additional information on PayPal.

2. Click **Home** on the menu bar to return to the home page, or click **Back** to display the previous page.

Look through Featured Items

The Featured Items listing gives you an opportunity to look at what is being promoted by sellers on eBay. Just click a title link to see the details of the auction or Buy It Now item.

TABLE 1-1: TYPES OF AUCTIONS

AUCTION	DESCRIPTION	REQUIREMENTS
Standard Auction	Follows a common auction format where a seller offers an item for sale and buyers bid on it. The highest bidder wins the right to purchase the item. There are variations to this format. For instance, a seller may require a hidden, minimum amount to be bid, known as a reserve price.	
Dutch Auction (also known as Multiple-Item Auction)	Allows you to sell multiple identical items. You can sell them in an online auction format, where each buyer has to bid higher, but all get it at the same lowest-bid price, or in a fixed-price format, where all items are sold for the same price.	You must be ID Verified or have a feedback rating of at least 30 and be registered for at least two weeks.
Private Auction	Allows the buyer to bid without revealing his or her user ID. Only the seller knows who the bidder is. This is done usually when the buyer might be embarrassed by the bid, such as with adult items.	
Buy It Now (Auction)	A combination auction that offers the item for a fixed price. If a buyer agrees to pay that price, the sale is made. If a buyer offers a lower price, however, the Buy It Now price is replaced with a normal auction format.	You must be ID Verified or have a feedback rating of at least 10 to offer a Buy It Now item.
Buy It Now (Fixed Price)	Offers the item for a given price, and there is no auction.	You must have a feedback rating of at least 30 and be a registered user for at least 14 days or be ID Verified.

There are restrictions for some items, such as adult items. Chapter 5 contains additional information on how to use this feature.

To explore Featured Items:

1. On the home page, scroll down until Featured Items is displayed.

> **Featured Items** *all featured items...*
> * The BEST 50 State Quarter Holder Coin Album Folder Book
> * Beautiful Lakeside Home

2. Click **All Featured Items** to the right of the section title to display all the Featured Items, not just the few that are rotated to the home page.

Explore Categories

Each item is identified as belonging to a *category*. A category is simply a system of names, within which an item may be found. For example, a diamond ring will probably be found in the broad category, Jewelry. In that category, however, are many other possibilities, such as antique, fashion, gold or silver, and so on. How well you can nail the category for your item is really important—both to buy and sell it. There are thousands of categories that are constantly being revised, so it is both very easy and very hard to find the category you want to use. Many categories are available, but the exact one may be harder to identify.

1. On the home page, find the top-level category that contains your item. Click the link. (Using the diamond ring example, you would most likely click "Jewelry & Watches.") Figure 1-5 shows the categories on the home page.

2. On the next layer, find the category that most closely matches what you want. Click that link. In our example, rings can be found in several subcategories, such as Fashion Jewelry, Men's, Rings, and Wholesale Lots. (In our example, clicking **Rings | Diamond** yields a screen displaying the beginning of 20,000 items.)

3. Continue to explore the categories until you find what you want. You may have to back up and start again or refine your browsing.

NOTE

Many items have an "item specific" or specialized search feature to help you locate the exact match. For instance, to narrow the search for a diamond ring, you can search by Ring Size, Carat, Cut, Metal, and Price Range. Chapter 2 talks more about the overall Search feature.

Rings

Gemstone
Any

Ring Size
Any

Carat
Any

Cut
Any

Metal
Any

Min Price   Max Price
[   ] to [   ]

☐ Combine with Basic Search

[Find]

Figure 1-5: Categories starts you on
your way to finding the item you want.

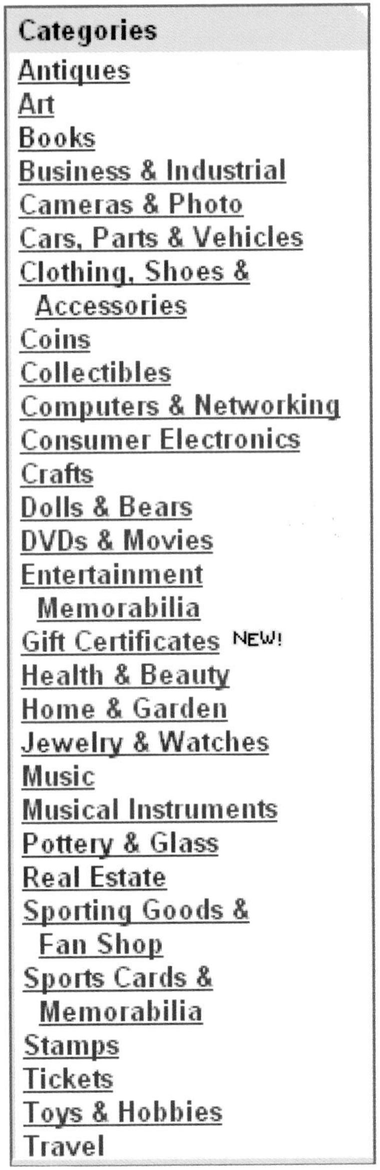

Categories

Antiques
Art
Books
Business & Industrial
Cameras & Photo
Cars, Parts & Vehicles
Clothing, Shoes &
  Accessories
Coins
Collectibles
Computers & Networking
Consumer Electronics
Crafts
Dolls & Bears
DVDs & Movies
Entertainment
  Memorabilia
Gift Certificates NEW!
Health & Beauty
Home & Garden
Jewelry & Watches
Music
Musical Instruments
Pottery & Glass
Real Estate
Sporting Goods &
  Fan Shop
Sports Cards &
  Memorabilia
Stamps
Tickets
Toys & Hobbies
Travel

Look for eBay Announcements

To see the latest changes and announcements on eBay:

1. Scroll to the second bottom links bar. If the links bar is unavailable, click **Home** on the top links bar first.

2. Click **Announcements** on the menu bar.

You will see about three months' worth of announcements.

Register as an eBay Member

Before you register you need:

- A valid e-mail address
- A User ID, which you create
- A password, which you enter
- To be at least 18 years of age

Register for eBay

To register to buy or sell items: (See Chapter 5 to create a seller's account.)

1. From the home page, click **Register Now**. You will see the Registration screen, as shown in Figure 1-6.

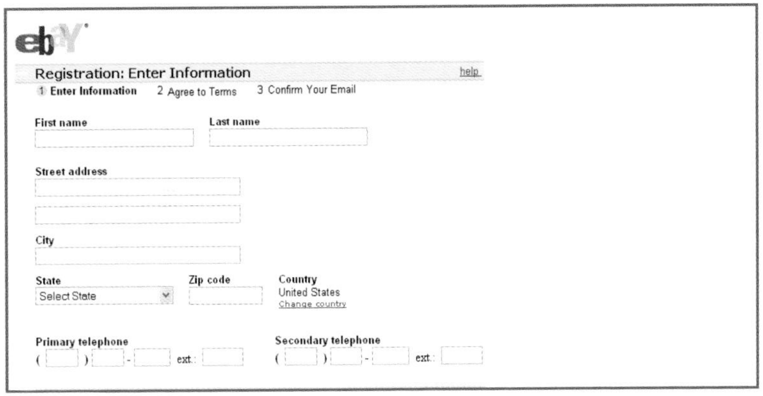

Figure 1-6:
When you
register
for eBay or
Half.com,
your first
task is to
enter your
name and
address
information.

ebY*

Registration: Enter Information   help
1 Enter Information   2 Agree to Terms   3 Confirm Your Email

First name   Last name

Street address

City

State   Zip code   Country
Select State   United States
                                      Change country

Primary telephone   Secondary telephone
(   )   -   ext: (   )   -   ext:

QUICK**FACTS**

USING A USER ID AND PASSWORD

CREATE A USER ID

In order to register with eBay, you must create a User ID. This is the name by which others on eBay do business with you and come to recognize you over time. To be more effective as a seller, your User ID can be one that identifies your business or products. As a buyer, you don't have the same considerations to worry about. In any case, it is your eBay name, so it ought to be one you like.

Your User ID must follow these rules:

- Be more than one character long
- Contain letters or numbers (but not "eBay" or the letter "e" followed by numbers)
- Cannot contain @, &, ', < or >, or more than one _ (underscore)
- Cannot contain spaces or tabs (but can contain a hyphen)
- Cannot be an e-mail address or web site, or contain any URLs
- Be unique in the eBay system

CREATE A PASSWORD

You will be asked to enter a password that verifies you are the valid user of your User ID. Since this password is an important one, you will want to follow these guidelines:

- Use a unique password for eBay. That is, do not use the same password that you use for other web sites or for your e-mail.
- Do not share the password with others.

2. Enter your name and address information and phone number into the text boxes, pressing **TAB** to advance to the next box.

3. Enter the following additional information, as shown in Figure 1-7:

- Type your e-mail address, press **TAB**, and enter the e-mail address again. Press **TAB**.

- Enter your new User ID (see the QuickSteps "Using a User ID and Password"). Press **TAB**.

- Enter your password in **Create Password**, press **TAB**, and enter the password again. Press **TAB**.

- Click the **Secret Question** down arrow to see the list of questions eBay may ask to verify your identity in case you forget your password or need to change it. Select the question you want to be your identifying one. Press **TAB**.

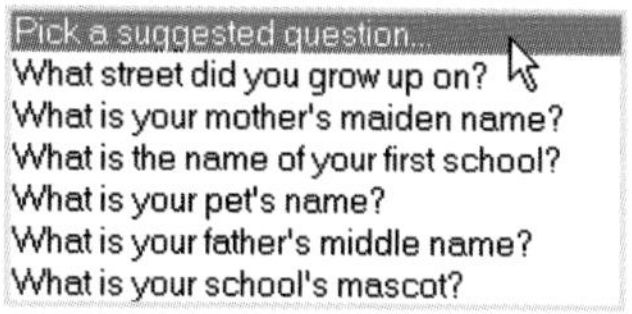

- Under **Secret Answer**, type your answer to the question you chose. Press **TAB**.

- Click the **Date Of Birth** down arrow, and choose the **Month** and **Day** of your birthday. Type the **Year**. Press **TAB**.

- Click **Continue**.

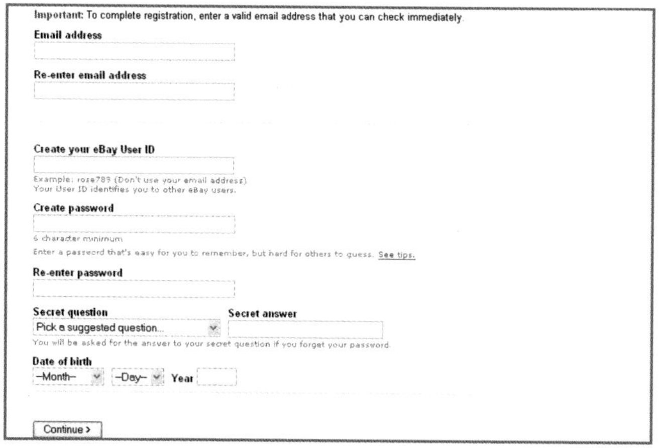

Figure 1-7: Your e-mail address, User ID, and password are entered during the registration process, along with a question to verify your identity.

1

TIP

eBay employees do not ask you for your password over the phone or via e-mail. If someone claims to be an eBay employee and asks for your password, you can be assured they are not who they say they are.

TIP

After registering, your User ID cannot be changed for 30 days.

NOTE

If you have an older User ID that uses an e-mail address, you may want to change it since e-mail addresses are no longer allowed as User IDs. This was changed to help prevent misuse of e-mail addresses and to protect against spam. If you haven't used the User ID for over a year and it was an e-mail address, you'll find that you have been assigned a temporary User ID, which can be changed to something else (you would have been sent an e-mail notifying you of this).

4. Read the User Agreement and Privacy Policy, as shown in Figure 1-8, or glance through them, noting the subjects covered, and print them using the Printer-Friendly User Agreement and Printer-Friendly Privacy Policy links. See "Read the User Agreement/e-Bay Policies" for additional information.

5. Enter this information:

   ● Click **I Am 18+ Years Old** to signal that you are old enough to trade on eBay.

   ● Click **I Understand That I Can Choose Not To Receive Communications From eBay** by changing the notification terms in My eBay after registration is complete.

6. Click **I Agree To These Terms**. (If you do not click this, you cannot register with eBay.)

7. The Confirm Your E-Mail window opens. At this point, eBay e-mails your registration confirmation to you at the e-mail address you provided.

Figure 1-8: The User Agreement must be agreed to before you can register with eBay.

Registration: Agree to Terms   ⑦ Need Help?

1 Enter Information   **2 Agree to Terms**   3 Confirm Your Email

Please read the User Agreement and Privacy Policy below.

```
User Agreement

THE FOLLOWING DESCRIBES THE TERMS ON WHICH EBAY OFFERS YOU ACCESS
TO OUR SERVICES.
```

Printer-friendly User Agreement

```
Privacy Policy

Your privacy is very important to us. We do not sell or rent your
personal information to third parties for their marketing purposes
without your explicit consent. Please read this privacy policy to
```

Printer-friendly Privacy Policy

Check the boxes and click **I Agree** to accept the User Agreement, Privacy Policy and incorporated terms.

☐ **I am 18+ years old.**
   21+ years old in some states.

☐ **I understand that I can choose not to receive communications from eBay.**
   After completing registration, I can change how eBay contacts me at any time by going to the Notification Preferences page in My eBay.

[**I Agree To These Terms >**]   I decline

2   3   4   5   6   7   8   9   10

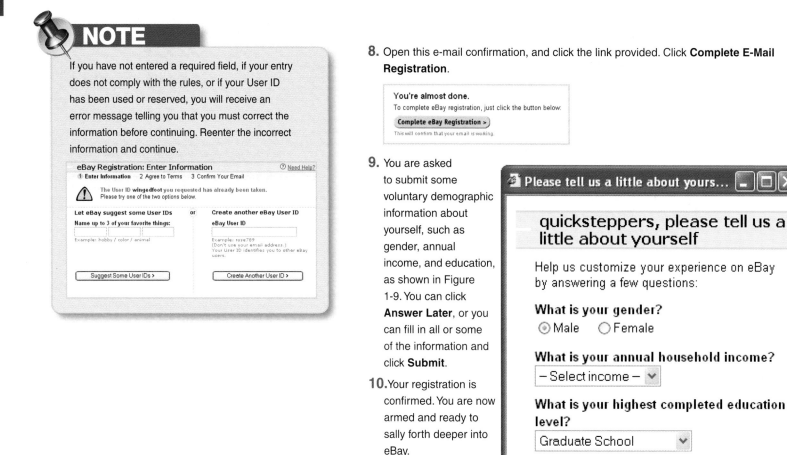

NOTE

If you have not entered a required field, if your entry does not comply with the rules, or if your User ID has been used or reserved, you will receive an error message telling you that you must correct the information before continuing. Reenter the incorrect information and continue.

eBay Registration: Enter Information   ⓘ Need Help?

1 Enter Information   2 Agree to Terms   3 Confirm Your Email

⚠ The User ID **wingedfoot** you requested has already been taken.
    Please try one of the two options below.

Let eBay suggest some User IDs   or   **Create another eBay User ID**

Name up to 3 of your favorite things: **eBay User ID**

[   ]   [   ]

Example: hobby / color / animal   Example: rose789
                                                (Don't use your email address.)
                                                Your User ID identifies you to other eBay
                                                users.

[Suggest Some User IDs >]   [Create Another User ID >]

8. Open this e-mail confirmation, and click the link provided. Click **Complete E-Mail Registration**.

> **You're almost done.**
> To complete eBay registration, just click the button below:
>
> [**Complete eBay Registration >**]
>
> This will confirm that your email is working.

9. You are asked to submit some voluntary demographic information about yourself, such as gender, annual income, and education, as shown in Figure 1-9. You can click **Answer Later**, or you can fill in all or some of the information and click **Submit**.

10. Your registration is confirmed. You are now armed and ready to sally forth deeper into eBay.

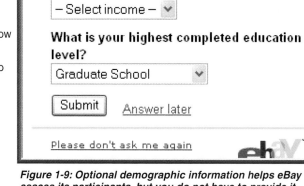

📄 **Please tell us a little about yours...**   [_][□][✕]

quicksteppers, please tell us a little about yourself

Help us customize your experience on eBay by answering a few questions:

What is your gender?

◉ Male   ○ Female

What is your annual household income?

[– Select income – ▾]

What is your highest completed education level?

[Graduate School   ▾]

[Submit]   <u>Answer later</u>

<u>Please don't ask me again</u>   eb**Y**

Figure 1-9: Optional demographic information helps eBay assess its participants, but you do not have to provide it.

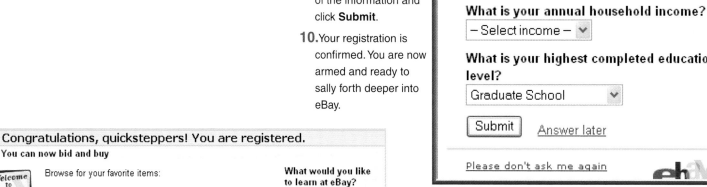

Congratulations, quicksteppers! You are registered.

You can now bid and buy

Welcome to eBay

Browse for your favorite items:

<u>Categories</u> - Select a category that matches your interests.
<u>eBay Stores</u> - Find items from eBay's top sellers.

Want to sell something? You need to <u>create a seller's account</u> on eBay.

What would you like to learn at eBay?
<u>How to find items</u>
<u>How to bid</u>
<u>Why eBay is safe</u>

UICKSTEPS

RESTORING YOUR PASSWORD

If you forget your password, or just want to change it, you can get a new password.

CHANGE YOUR PASSWORD

1. From the home page, click **My eBay**. (You may have to enter your password.) The My eBay window opens.

2. Scroll down to **My Account**, and click **Personal Information**.

3. On the Password item, click **Change**.

4. Type your current password, and click **Sign In**.

5. Enter your password in the New Password text box.

6. Press **TAB**. Reenter the new password.

7. Click **Change Password**.

8. Your new password is activated.

FORGET YOUR PASSWORD?

When you are prompted to enter your password and you have forgotten it, follow these steps:

1. Under the Password text box, click the **Forgot Your Password?** link. You are taken to the Forgot Your Password? screen.

2. Enter your eBay User ID in the text box, and click **Continue**.

Continued...

TIP

You have to use ID Verify to bid on items that cost more than $15,000 or to use the Buy It Now feature. If you are a seller, you cannot sell adult items without it.

Use ID Verify

eBay offers a service to verify that its U.S. (and U.S. territories) buyers and sellers are who they say they are. This gives others confidence that they are dealing with a real person, not a cyberspace phantom. To use ID Verify, you pay $5 to a third-party company whose business it is to verify identities. You supply some personal information and, once verified, you receive an ID Verify icon that is placed in your feedback profile.

1. From the top links bar, click **Services**.

2. Click **ID Verify** under General Services, and then click **Sign Up Now** at the bottom of the page.

3. On the ID Verify: Accept Terms screen, click **I Agree** after you read and agree to three conditions:

   - To pay $5 if you are granted an ID Verify designation (you don't pay if you don't pass)

   - Not to provide false information

   - Not to change your contact information for 30 days

4. Sign in with your User ID and password. Click **Secure Sign In**.

5. On the Verify Account Information page, verify that your contact information is correct. You also need to supply your social security number and driver's license number. Click **Continue** when finished.

6. Verify your information by scanning the Verify Account Information page. If the information is correct, click **Continue**. If it is incorrect, click **Back** and correct it.

7. You are asked some questions that only you know the answers to, including filling in credit card numbers, a past street address, and perhaps a mortgage amount. Click **Continue** when finished.

8. Review and verify your information.

9. After signing in one more time, you are informed that your ID Verify is successful, as shown in Figure 1-10.

RESTORING YOUR PASSWORD

(Continued)

3. On the Verify Identity screen, type the answer in the text box to the question that you specified when you first registered, such as your pet's name or the name of the street where you grew up. (If you have an older User ID and did not enter a secret question previously, you may not see this step.)

4. Enter your current ZIP code, your current telephone number, and your date of birth, and click **Continue**.

5. The Confirmation Step window opens, and you are notified that an e-mail has been sent.

6. Check your e-mail, and click the link in the e-mail that sends you to the Change Password window in eBay.

7. Enter your User ID, and click **Continue**. You are taken to the Change Password procedure, as described previously.

8. In the New Password text box, type your new password. Press **TAB**.

9. Reenter the password, and click **Change Password**.

10. If you don't have a secret question already, select a **Secret Question** and then type an **Answer to Secret Question**.

11. Your new password is activated.

NOTE

ID Verify is not a credit check, and if you do not pass the verification test, your credit will not be affected. Your credit information is used to prove that you are who you say you are, not whether or not you are creditworthy. eBay does not store or use any of the private information you supply.

Figure 1-10: The ID Verify Successful page immediately lets you know that you have passed the ID Verify procedure.

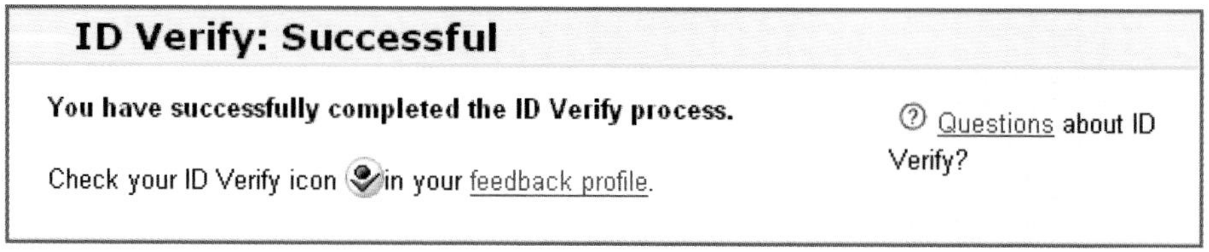

ID Verify: Successful

You have successfully completed the ID Verify process.

Check your ID Verify icon 💲in your feedback profile.

⑦ Questions about ID Verify?

10. Click **Feedback Profile** to see that the icon has been placed in your Member Profile.

11. Click **Home** to return to the home page.

Review the Rules and Policies

Before you register, you may want to take some time to review the User Agreement and Privacy Policy. They are fairly long, and you may be tempted to skip them altogether. However, I would encourage you to read them, or at least scan them, since they are binding legal contracts that you will be agreeing to. In addition, there are several other policies that you might be interested in.

Read the User Agreement/eBay Policies

The User Agreement outlines the terms and conditions under which you will interact with eBay. It describes the rules you will follow and what eBay's responsibilities are to you. It describes how misunderstandings and complaints are handled, among other issues.

1. From the home page, scroll down to the first bottom links bar, and click **Policies**. The window displayed in Figure 1-11 opens.

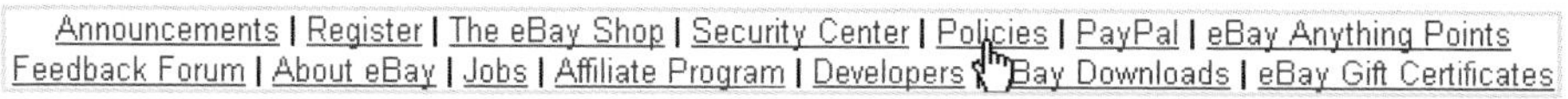

Announcements | Register | The eBay Shop | Security Center | Policies | PayPal | eBay Anything Points
Feedback Forum | About eBay | Jobs | Affiliate Program | Developers | eBay Downloads | eBay Gift Certificates

Prohibited and Restricted Items List:

- Academic Software
- Airline and Transit Related Items
- Alcohol (also see Wine)
- Animals and Wildlife Products
- Anti-circumvention Policy
- Artifacts
- Authenticity Disclaimers
- Autographed Items
- Batteries
- Beta Software
- Bootleg Recordings
- Brand Name Misuse
- Catalog and URL Sales
- Catalytic Converters and Test Pipes
- Charity or Fundraising Listings
- Comparison Policy
- Compilation and Informational Media
- Contracts and Tickets
- Counterfeit Currency and Stamps
- Counterfeit Items
- Credit Cards
- Downloadable Media
- Drugs & Drug Paraphernalia
- Electronics Equipment
- Embargoed Goods and Prohibited Countries
- Encouraging Infringement Policy
- Event Tickets
- Faces, Names and Signatures
- Firearms, Ammunition, Replicas, and Militaria
- Fireworks
- Food
- Freon and Other Refrigerants
- Government IDs and Licenses
- Hazardous, Restricted, and Perishable Items
- Human Parts and Remains

Figure 1-12: The Prohibited and Restricted Items List contains those items that cannot be sold on eBay.

Figure 1-11: Policies are issued to provide consistency and security to users.

2. Under Your eBay User Agreement, click **User Agreement**.

3. Click **User Agreement Frequently Asked Questions** for an overview.

4. Click **Home** to return to the home page.

Review Restricted Items

Certain items cannot be sold on eBay. These include alcohol, most animals, counterfeit or unauthorized replicas, tobacco, fireworks—the list goes on, as is partially seen in Figure 1-12.

1. From the home page, scroll down to the first bottom links bar, and click **Policies**.

2. Click **Prohibited And Restricted Items**.

3. Select the category containing the item in which you are interested.

4. Click **Home** to return to the home page.

Find Anything in eBay

The Site Map in eBay displays links to almost anyplace you want to go in eBay. To use it:

1. From the top links bar, click **Site Map**. The Site Map is displayed.
2. Scroll through the page until you find what you want. Click the link.

Customize with My eBay

The one part of eBay that is your domain, and where you interact with eBay both in buying and selling, is **My eBay**. This is where you track your purchases and sales. You can customize how eBay interacts with you and the information it displays. For instance, you can change the views offered or change personal information, such as your User ID, e-mail address, address information, shipping information, password, and About Me page.

Get to My eBay

Click **My eBay** on the menu bar. You may be asked to sign in, and then the My eBay page is displayed, as shown in Figure 1-13.

| Browse | Search | Sell | My eBay | Community |

Customize My eBay

You can customize nearly all the views, either by changing the information you see or by changing the order in which you see it. You can also change your personal information and preferences. Here's how you can customize views and information.

NOTE

Chapter 4 contains additional information on using My eBay to help manage your bidding activities. Chapter 7 leads you through organizing My eBay from a seller's perspective.

NOTE

You can use eBay Gift Certificates to buy a gift certificate for someone, which can be used to purchase items on eBay. To purchase one, select **Site Map** from the top linsk bar, scroll to **Buyer Tools**, and click **eBay Gift Certificates**.

Figure 1-13: My eBay is where you customize information and track your activity within eBay.

This is a list of the views
available in My eBay

This new user has a
feedback rating of 5

Click here to customize
the My Summary view

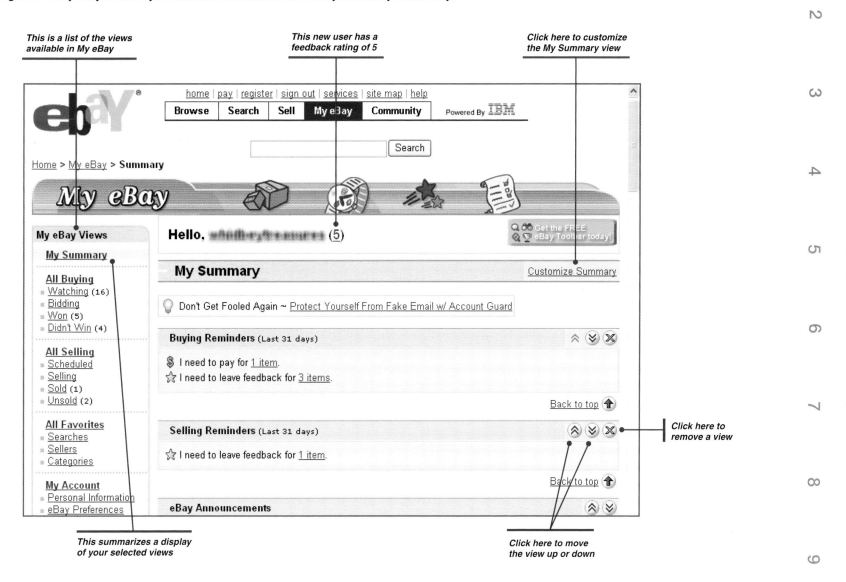

This summarizes a display
of your selected views

Click here to move
the view up or down

Click here to
remove a view

CUSTOMIZE THE MY SUMMARY VIEW

To select the views to display in My Summary:

1. Click **Customize Summary** on the My Summary title bar. The Customize My Summary dialog box is displayed, as shown in Figure 1-14.

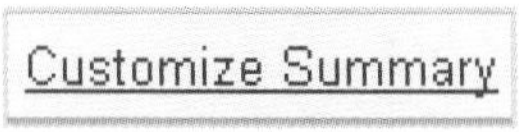
Customize Summary

Figure 1-14: Customize My Summary allows you to display the views you frequently use by switching between Available Views and Views to Display.

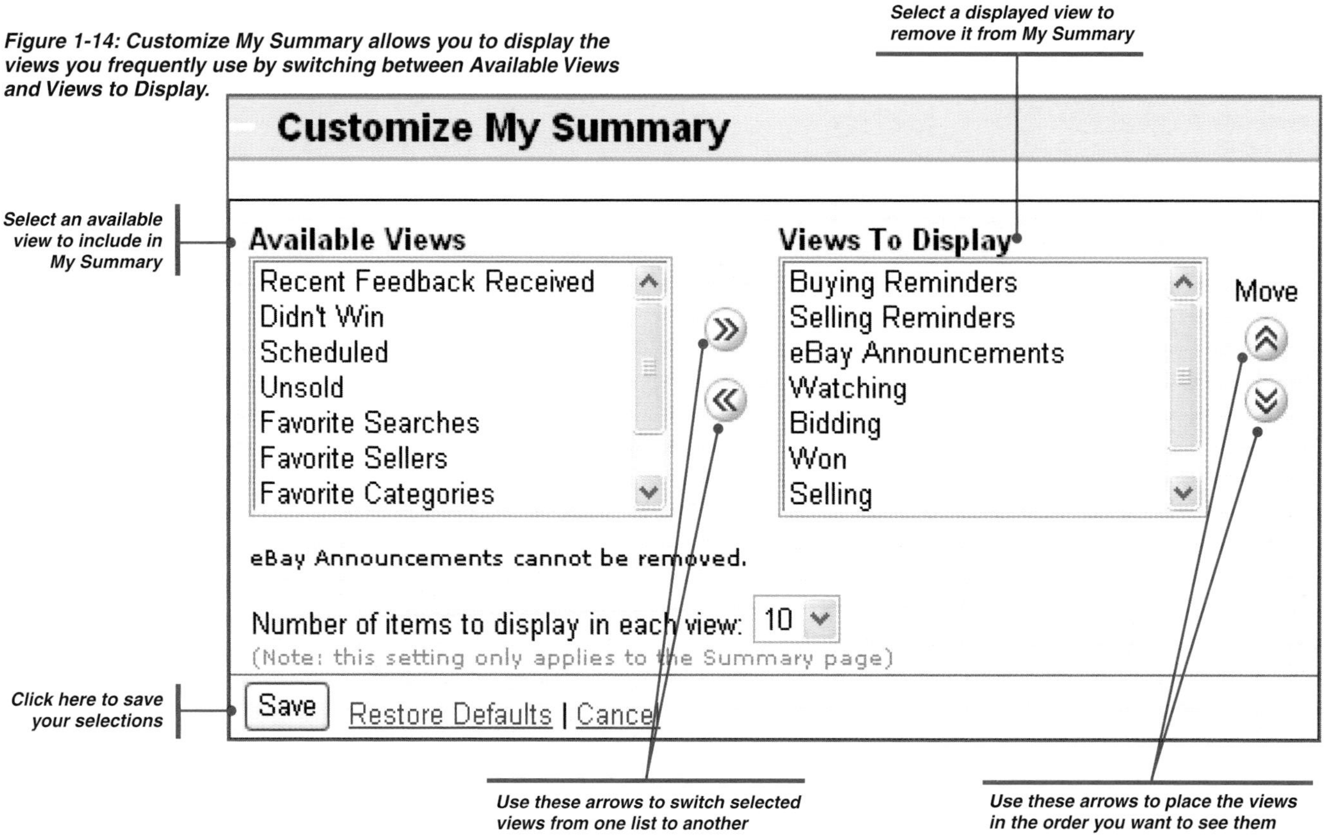
Select a displayed view to remove it from My Summary
Select an available view to include in My Summary
Click here to save your selections
Use these arrows to switch selected views from one list to another
Use these arrows to place the views in the order you want to see them
Customize My Summary
Available Views
Recent Feedback Received
Didn't Win
Scheduled
Unsold
Favorite Searches
Favorite Sellers
Favorite Categories
Views To Display
Buying Reminders
Selling Reminders
eBay Announcements
Watching
Bidding
Won
Selling
Move
eBay Announcements cannot be removed.
Number of items to display in each view: 10
(Note: this setting only applies to the Summary page)
Save
Restore Defaults | Cancel

Click **Restore Defaults** if you find you want the original My Summary views restored.

QUICKSTEPS

WORKING WITH MY EBAY VIEWS

When you are looking at a view, you can use it or change it in these ways:

SORT A VIEW

- To change the way a view is sequenced, click a column heading.
- To reverse the sort, click the column heading again.

☐ Title	Current Price ▲	Shipping Cost	Bids	Seller ID	Time Left	Action
☐ Franciscan Madeira Salad Plates - 4	$4.99	$12.30	0	angelakim1964 (192 ☆)	4d 17h 51m	Bid Now!

Click a column heading to change the sort

DELETE AN ITEM

To delete an item in a list:

1. Select the item to be deleted.
2. Click **Delete** (or **Remove** if that is what is on your view).

Delete

☐ Title

☑ Franciscan Madeira Salad Plates - 4

SHOW ONLY COMPLETED ITEMS IN A WATCHING OR ACTIVE VIEW

To show only the completed items in an Items I'm Watching list:

- Under the view title bar, click **Ended**.

Items I'm Watching (13 items)

Show: **All** | Active (3) | Ended (10)

- To show only the active items, click **Active**.
- To show both active and completed items in a view, click **All**.

- In the Available Views box, click the view you want to see in My Summary. Click the **right-pointing arrow** to move the selection to the Views To Display box.

- If there are views in the Views To Display box that you don't want in My Summary, select them and then click the **left-pointing arrow**.

- Arrange the Views To Display in the order you want to see them by clicking the **up and down arrows**.

Move

2. Click **Save** to save your changes.

CUSTOMIZE A MY EBAY VIEW

You can change the columns in a My eBay view to place the columns in the order you want to see them and to select which columns to include in the view.

1. Click **Customize** in the view title bar. The Customize *viewname* dialog box shown in Figure 1-15 is displayed, where *viewname* is the name of the My eBay view you are customizing. In this case, the My eBay view being modified is the Items I'm Watching view. Customize

2. Select from among these options to customize the view.

- To add a column from the Available Columns, select a column name, and click the **right-pointing arrow** to move it to the Columns To Display.

- To remove a column from the view, select a column from Columns To Display, and click the **left-pointing arrow** to remove it from the Columns To Display.

- To reorder the columns on the view, click the **up and down arrows** under Move.

- To show the item title above the details, select **Item Title On Its Own Row**.

- To display notes with the items, select **My Notes**.

- To display eBay notes, select **eBay Notes**.

- To display a picture on the listing, select **Pictures**.

- Click the **Items Per Page** down arrow, and select a number.

25 ▼	items per page
10	
25	
50	
75	
100	

3. Click **Save** to save your view changes.

Figure 1-15: The Customize dialog box allows you to select the columns you want in the view, add a separate row for the title, and add notes and pictures.

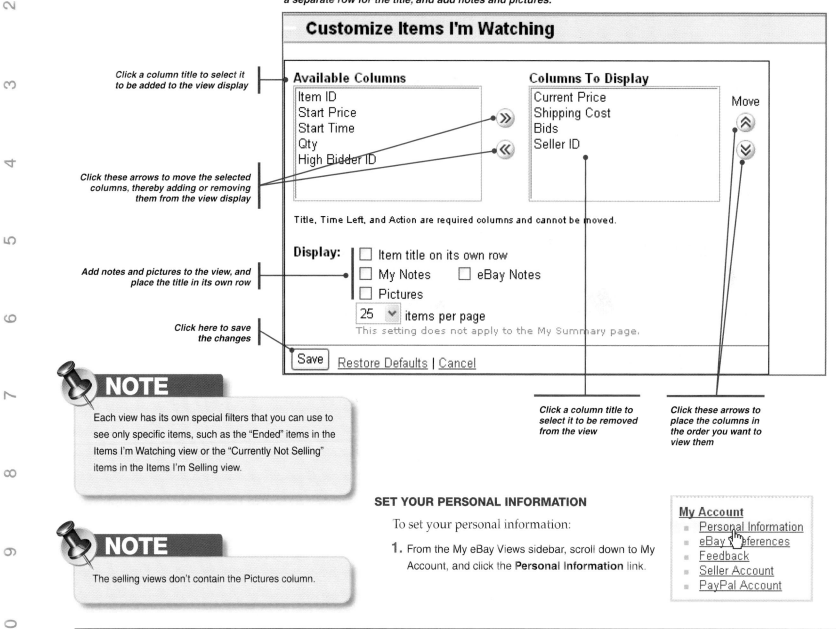

Click a column title to select it to be added to the view display

Customize Items I'm Watching

Available Columns

Item ID
Start Price
Start Time
Qty
High Bidder ID

Click these arrows to move the selected columns, thereby adding or removing them from the view display

Columns To Display

Current Price
Shipping Cost
Bids
Seller ID

Move

Title, Time Left, and Action are required columns and cannot be moved.

Display:

☐ Item title on its own row
☐ My Notes   ☐ eBay Notes
☐ Pictures

Add notes and pictures to the view, and place the title in its own row

25 ⌄ items per page

This setting does not apply to the My Summary page.

Click here to save the changes

Save   Restore Defaults | Cancel

Click a column title to select it to be removed from the view

Click these arrows to place the columns in the order you want to view them

NOTE

Each view has its own special filters that you can use to see only specific items, such as the "Ended" items in the Items I'm Watching view or the "Currently Not Selling" items in the Items I'm Selling view.

NOTE

The selling views don't contain the Pictures column.

SET YOUR PERSONAL INFORMATION

To set your personal information:

1. From the My eBay Views sidebar, scroll down to My Account, and click the **Personal Information** link.

My Account

- Personal Information
- eBay Preferences
- Feedback
- Seller Account
- PayPal Account

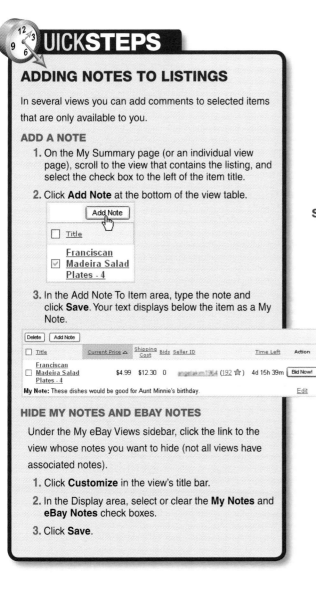

QUICKSTEPS

ADDING NOTES TO LISTINGS

In several views you can add comments to selected items that are only available to you.

ADD A NOTE

1. On the My Summary page (or an individual view page), scroll to the view that contains the listing, and select the check box to the left of the item title.

2. Click **Add Note** at the bottom of the view table.

> Add Note
> ☐ Title
> Franciscan
> ☑ Madeira Salad
> Plates - 4

3. In the Add Note To Item area, type the note and click **Save**. Your text displays below the item as a My Note.

Delete	Add Note						
☐ Title		Current Price △	Shipping Cost	Bids Seller ID		Time Left	Action
☐ Franciscan Madeira Salad Plates - 4		$4.99	$12.30	0	angelarm.1234 (192 ☆)	4d 15h 39m	Bid Now!
My Note: These dishes would be good for Aunt Minnie's birthday.							Edit

HIDE MY NOTES AND EBAY NOTES

Under the My eBay Views sidebar, click the link to the view whose notes you want to hide (not all views have associated notes).

1. Click **Customize** in the view's title bar.

2. In the Display area, select or clear the **My Notes** and **eBay Notes** check boxes.

3. Click **Save**.

---

2. From this page you can review and change:

- Your User ID, password, e-mail address, or wireless e-mail address (available through a wireless device, such as a PDA)

- Your About Me page

- Your billing and shipping information

- Your financial information, checking account, and credit card information

SET MY EBAY PREFERENCES

You can vary several aspects of how eBay interacts with you, for example, the initial My eBay page, how time is displayed, whether you want to retrieve removed items, or how Help content is displayed in My eBay.

1. From the My eBay Views sidebar, under My Account, click **eBay Preferences**.

2. Scroll down to My eBay Preferences, and choose from these options:

> **My eBay Preferences**
>
> | Default opening page: | All Buying ▾ |
> | Display time as: | ⊙ Time Left ○ End time/date |
> | Display help content in My eBay: | ☑ Yes |
> | Retrieve removed items: | ☐ Retrieve |
>
> Apply

- To change the initial page displayed, click the **Default Opening Page** down arrow, and select the view you want to see when My eBay is displayed. The default view will be My Summary.

- Select whether you want to see time displayed as Time Left or End Time/Date. The default is Time Left.

- To see Help content, select **Yes** next to Display Help Content In My eBay.

- To retrieve and display removed items, select **Retrieve**.

3. Click **Apply** to save the changes.

NOTE

Even though you selected the **Keep Me Signed In On This Computer Until I Sign Out** option, you will always be asked for your password when you are changing your personal account information.

QUICKSTEPS

SIGNING IN PERMANENTLY

You can be signed in automatically when you bring up eBay. When you are asked to sign in:

1. Enter your **eBay User ID**.
2. Enter your **password**.
3. Select **Keep Me Signed In On This Computer Unless I Sign Out**.
4. Click **Sign In**.

SET YOUR SIGN-IN ATTRIBUTES

To change your sign-in attributes:

1. From the My eBay Views sidebar, under My Account, scroll down and click **eBay Preferences**.

2. Scroll down to eBay Sign In Preferences, and click **Change**.

eBay Sign In Preferences		change
Keep me signed in until I sign out:	Yes	
Preferred sign in method:	eBay User ID and Password	
Display email addresses:	No	

3. Enter your User ID and password, and click **Sign In**.

4. On the Edit Your Sign In Options (shown in Figure 1-16), select from among these options:

- **Sign In options.** You can choose not to have to reenter your User ID and password when you are conducting transactions as a buyer. Select whether to be kept signed in on your computer until you sign out. If others use your computer, this is probably not a good idea.

- **Display Settings:** Select whether you want to be able to see the e-mail address of the person with whom you are conducting business.

- **Preferred Sign In Method:** Select between signing in using your eBay User ID and password or using your Microsoft Passport.

5. Click **Save Changes** to preserve your changes. A message is displayed stating that your changes have been updated. Click **My eBay Preferences Tab** to return to My eBay Preferences.

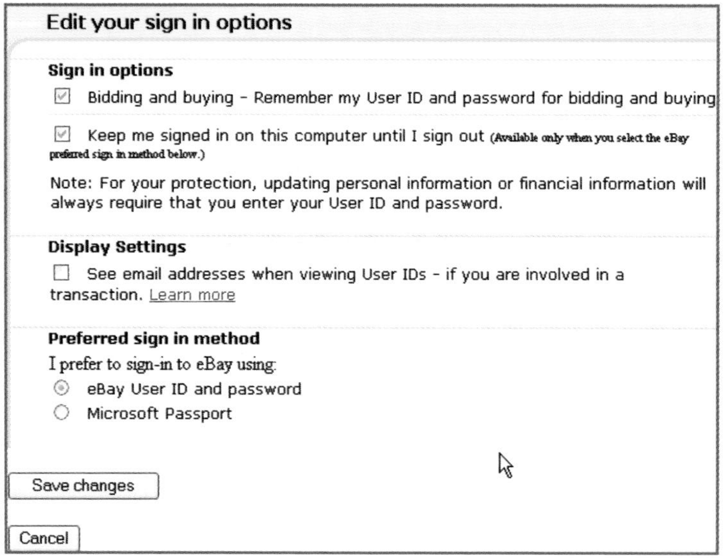

Edit your sign in options

Sign in options

☑ Bidding and buying – Remember my User ID and password for bidding and buying

☑ Keep me signed in on this computer until I sign out (Available only when you select the eBay preferred sign in method below.)

Note: For your protection, updating personal information or financial information will always require that you enter your User ID and password.

Display Settings

☐ See email addresses when viewing User IDs – if you are involved in a transaction. Learn more

Preferred sign in method

I prefer to sign-in to eBay using:

⦿ eBay User ID and password
◯ Microsoft Passport

Save changes

Cancel

Figure 1-16: Sign-in options are used to control when you are signed in and how and whether you will see another person's e-mail address.

Connect with the eBay Community

The eBay Community connects you to four main avenues of communication with other eBay users, as shown in Figure 1-17: **Talk** for discussion boards, chat rooms, and the Answer Center; **News** for General Announcements, System Announcements, and a newsletter, *The Chatter*; **Events**; and **People** for finding eBay Groups, reading about eBay Community Values, and learning about other members who have earned recognition.

Talk to Other eBay Users

To bring up the Talk features from the home page, click **Community** on the menu bar.

USE DISCUSSION BOARDS

Discussion boards are where you can tap into discussions about topics of interest. These may involve getting clarification or help on using eBay, or it may be about getting information on an item you want to buy or sell. A subject or topic of discussion is called a *thread*, and you *post* messages to a discussion board. To participate in discussion boards:

1. On the menu bar in the Talk segment, click **Discussion Boards**. The page shown in Figure 1-18 is displayed.

2. Scroll down to the General Discussion Boards, and select a subject, for example, The Front Porch. (Look for the joke thread for some good laughs.) Find a thread you like, and select it.

3. You'll have these buttons available to you for navigating through the messages:

   - **Search** allows you to search for a subject within a date range, identified with a user name or User ID.

Figure 1-17: The eBay Community offers several ways of connecting with other eBay users.

QUICKSTEPS

POSTING A MESSAGE

eBay provides features that you can use to spell check and preview your message before you post it. To post a message:

1. Log in by clicking **Board Login** or the **Login** button when you find a thread to which you want to post a message. Scroll down to the end of the thread, where a text box is displayed.

Reply To	What happened to eBay "Live Help"?

| Your Reply | |

☺ Check Spelling | Preview | Post Message

2. Type the message you want to post into the text box.

- Click **Check Spelling** to check your text for typos.

- Click **Preview** to see what your posted message will look like. You will see the posted message. Click **Edit** to make changes to it.

3. Click **Post Message** to place it on the bulletin board.

Figure 1-18: The eBay Talk Community is where you connect with others in a variety of ways, such as discussion boards, newsletters, workshops, and eBay groups.

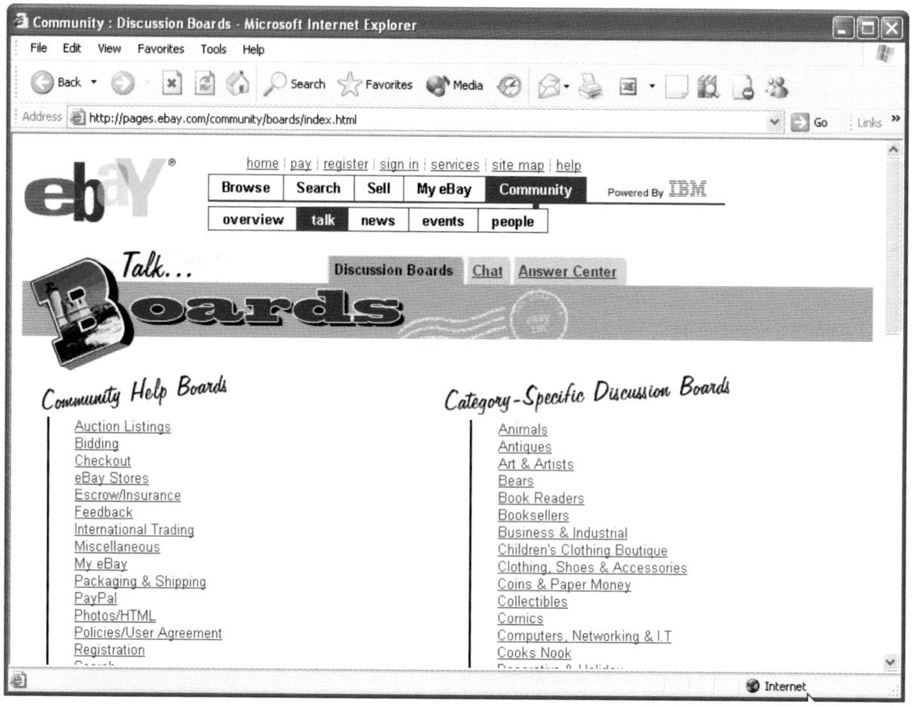

- **Previous and Next arrows** take you to the previous and next messages in the current thread.

- **Page numbers** take you to the specific message page, or you can type the page number in the Go To Page field and click **Go.**

Page 1 of 22

⇐ Previous **1** | 2 | 3 | 4 | 5 | 6 | 7 | 8 | 9 ... 22 Next ➡

Go to page
[   ] Go

- **Add Discussion** allows you to create a new thread or discussion board.

NOTE

Some subjects are forbidden, and you will be prohibited from participating in eBay discussion boards if you introduce them. These include comments about other eBay buyers or sellers, hate speech or vulgarity, attempts to sell or advertise a product or web site, attempts to "dis" another eBay participant or provide feedback on one, lewd or suggestive discussions, and so on. You can find a complete list of "Don'ts" from the Community Page by clicking **Discussion Boards | New To eBay Board** (scroll down, under General Discussion Boards) | **Board Usage Policies** (in the first paragraph).

TIP

Click the **Settings** icon to set View Preferences. If you don't see the Settings icon on the Answer Center link bar, you are not signed in for discussion board activity. Click **Board Log-In** on the Answer Center link bar.

Settings

4. To post a message, click **Login** to sign in to the discussion board—it is different from the eBay sign-in. You must log in before the text box for entering a message is displayed. (See the QuickSteps "Posting a Message" for information on how to do it.)

Login

CHAT ONLINE

Chats take place in real time. These messages are usually fast and short as people who are online at the moment participate in a conversation. To participate in a chat:

1. From the eBay Community page, click **Chat** in the Talk area.

2. Find a chat subject you are interested in, either from the General Chat Rooms list or the Category-Specific Chat Rooms list, and select it.

3. In the text box provided, type your message and click **Save My Message!** to post it.

Your message

```
Hi all,
I'm new to this particular Chat Room and am interested in
the discussion about pottery. Have you see any of the
Helga Goobis in the
```

Save my Message!   Clear form

Reload and show me Messages from the last 15 minutes ▾

---

4. Click **Clear Form** to erase the text typed in the text box.

5. Click **Reload**, click the **down arrow** next to the list box, and select how far back you want to see any postings. This option refreshes your chat thread.

> **TIP**
>
> You can click **View Answers** in an existing thread to see what others have had to say about a topic.

> **TIP**
>
> If you do not see an Answer link in your Answer Center question, you may not have a feedback rating of 10 or higher, which you must have in order to post an answer. Or, if the question has more than ten responses, it may be closed to additional answers.

USE THE ANSWER CENTER

The Answer Center provides a place where you can get answers to your questions from other eBay users.

1. From the eBay Community page, click **Answer Center** in the Talk segment. The page in Figure 1-19 is displayed.

2. Find a thread that seems to include the question you want to ask, and select it.

3. To answer another user's question, click **Answer** on the list of questions page,

   -Or-

   Scroll to the bottom of the current answers to the question, and click **Answer**.

4. Type your response, and click **Post Message**.

Figure 1-19: The Answer Center is where you can ask anything about eBay to the millions of eBay users and get up to ten answers immediately.

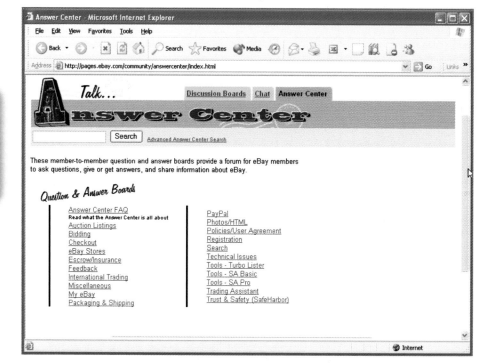

NOTE

To manage your Watch list, click the **Watches** icon on the Answer Center link bar.

FLAG QUESTIONS FOR WATCHING

To identify the questions you want eBay to watch and inform you by e-mail that a question has activity:

1. Find the question you want watched. For example, you may have a problem you are trying to solve immediately and you want to know as soon as information is available.

2. At the top of the question, click the **Watch This Question** link. The question is entered into your Watch list.

3. If you want to keep the question on your list, select when you want to be notified by e-mail: Never, Immediately, Daily, or Weekly.

4. Click **Save Watch** to keep it in your Watch list. Click **Delete** to remove it.

5. Click **Back** to return to the previous page.

ASK NEW QUESTIONS

To post a question to the Answer Center:

1. On the top of the list of questions, click the **Ask New Question** link.

2. Type the question you want to ask in concise terms in the Subject text box.

3. Type the full message describing the question, the reason for it, and the circumstances that are pertinent.

4. Click **Spell Check** to check for typos and misspellings.

5. Click **Preview** to review your question without posting it.

6. Click **Post Message** to post your question.

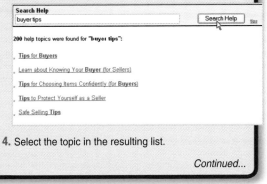

UICKSTEPS

GETTING EBAY HELP

eBay Help comes in several varieties. You can search for help topics alphabetically, type a question, or search by broad category, such as How Do I Sell An Item?

FIND ANSWERS BY TYPING THE TOPIC

1. Open the Help page by clicking **Help** on the top links bar from the eBay home page.

home | pay | register | sign in | services | site map | help

2. In the Search Help text box, type the topic for which you want to search.

3. Click **Search Help**.

4. Select the topic in the resulting list.

Continued...

GETTING EBAY HELP *(Continued)*

BROWSE TOPICS

You can browse topics alphabetically or by subject. Click **Help** from the home page, and either:

- Under eBay Help, click **A-Z Index**, for the alphabetic Help topics.

  –Or–

- Select one of the listed topics, either under Top Questions About Getting Started On eBay, or a linked topic beneath that Top Questions list.

eBay Help
Help Topics
A-Z Index
Contact Us

CONTACT EBAY

To contact eBay for help from the Help menu, you first must walk through a series of questions and topics to make sure that the answer is not already in the system. After you have gone through that, you can send an e-mail asking your question.

1. Click **Help** from the top links bar.
2. Under Help Topics, click **Contact Us**. A list of questions is displayed.
3. Select the topic that most closely meets your needs. The box below presents a second level of questions.
4. Click the second-level box for the topic most closely matching your needs. The third box displays more specific subjects, an example of which is shown in Figure 1-22.
5. Click the third-level box. Click **Continue**.
6. If the suggested topic does not help you, click **E-mail** under Contact Support.
7. An e-mail form is displayed. Type your question under Enter Your Question/Concern, and click **Send E-mail**. Allow 24 to 48 hours to receive an answer.

Follow eBay News and Events

Within the eBay community, you might be surprised at the depth of the news and events that eBay provides.

1. From the eBay Community page, in the News segment, click these links:

   - Click **General Announcements** for information on what is happening on the web site.

   - Click **System Announcements** to find out what changes are being made to the eBay system itself.

   - Click *The Chatter*, eBay's monthly newsletter, to read about what is going on in the eBay community, as shown in Figure 1-20.

Figure 1-20: The Chatter is a newsletter that keeps you up-to-date with eBay activities and people.

2. From the eBay Community page, in the Events segment, click these links:

   - Click **Calendar** to find out what is going on in eBay's expanding world.

   - Click **Workshops Event List** to see a list of all events, including workshops, eBay University classes, live events, and so on.

   - Click **Charity** to find out about the charity auctions, as shown in Figure 1-21.

USING CHARITY AUCTIONS

In November 2003, eBay signed on with MissionFish to
provide a charity/nonprofit auction arena. MissionFish,
a service of the Points of Light Foundation, operates
the charity auctions for eBay. The feature within
eBay is called eBay Giving Works. It helps nonprofit
organizations raise money for their charitable causes.
MissionFish does several tasks for eBay:

- It enables sellers to auction in-kind donations to
  raise funds.

- It verifies that the nonprofits receiving donations are
  real and valid entities.

- It collects the donations and distributes them for
  eBay.

- It handles online contribution tracking and tax
  receipts.

When you buy a product from eBay Giving Works,
a percentage of the money (from 10 percent to 100
percent, stated in the item description) goes to the
nonprofit organization that the seller is supporting.
Items associated with eBay Giving Works are identified
with an icon. You can tell what percentage goes to
the nonprofit recipient in the description.

The seller can be part of the nonprofit organization or
just be raising money for it as an individual—remember
that MissionFish actually distributes the money, so you
can be assured that the donation amount goes to the
nonprofit organization. Before they post an item for sale,
sellers must register with MissionFish, who then verifies
that the recipient of the donation is a valid nonprofit.
The nonprofit also has a web site you can check out
before you buy something from them. Click the **About
Me** page to see it.

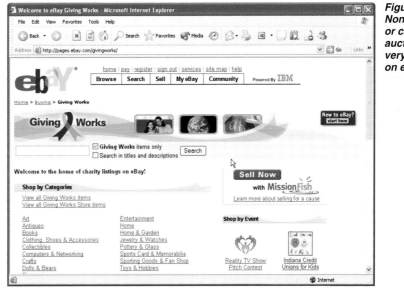

Figure 1-21:
Nonprofit
or charity
auctions are
very present
on eBay.

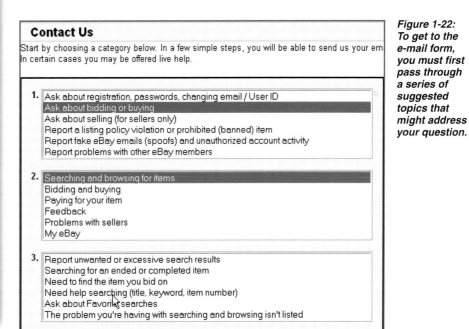

Figure 1-22:
To get to the
e-mail form,
you must first
pass through
a series of
suggested
topics that
might address
your question.

Read about People on eBay

The People segment of the Community page offers three interesting connections: eBay Groups, eBay Community Values, and Member Spotlight.

1. From the Community Page, click one of these links:

   - Click **eBay Groups** to connect with support groups, eBay sellers, new user groups, specialty item groups, and so on. You will be asked to "Join the Group" officially before you can read and contribute to a group.

   - Click **eBay Community Values** for a statement of the values that guide the eBay family, as seen in Figure 1-23.

   - Click **Member Spotlight** for an eBay success story.

2. Click **Home** to return to the home page.

Figure 1-23: The eBay Community Values page states the basic values that eBay incorporates into its culture.

How to...

Chapter 2
Researching on eBay (Buyers or Sellers)

Part of doing a good job in buying or selling an item on eBay is doing your homework. finding out everything you can about the item you want to buy or sell. This includes researching the actual item and comparing such things as price, components or parts available, condition (such as with coins or antiques), identification markings, and so on. You can also research the seller you are buying from. Does the seller have a history on eBay? Is the feedback mostly favorable toward the seller? Where is he or she located?

This chapter leads you through searching for and identifying the item you want to buy or sell, starting with how you can use eBay to help you find out about items.

QUICK**FACTS**

IDENTIFYING MY EBAY ICONS

My eBay uses icons to distinguish the type and status of listings. These icons are located on the right of the listing row. You can click the icon at the head of each column to sort the items by that icon.

- • Auction format
- • eBay Store inventory
- • Fixed-price item
- • Ad, such as for real estate
- • Checkout is complete
- • Item has been paid for
- • Item has been shipped
- • You have left feedback for this item
- • You have received feedback for this item
- • Item has been relisted

Use Tools Available in eBay

A handy way to see what is happening in your favorite categories is to establish Favorite lists in My eBay. You can also establish Favorite lists for your most common searches and your most regularly accessed sellers or stores. Other aids include the use of icons and the Search feature.

Find Your My eBay Favorites

You can set up your favorite categories, searches, and sellers in My eBay. This allows you to quickly find what you are looking for with ease.

1. From the menu bar on the top of the page, click **My eBay**.

Browse	Search	Sell	My eBay	Community
find items	find members		favorite searches	

2. Type your password, and click **Sign In**. The My eBay page is displayed.

3. On the My eBay Views sidebar, scroll down to the **All Favorites** link, and click it. The screen shown in Figure 2-1 is displayed. You will see all your favorites currently available.

Save Your Favorite Categories

When you save your favorite categories in My eBay, you can quickly see items currently for sale, items newly listed, auctions ending soon, and completed auctions in these categories. You can establish My Favorite Categories for up to four categories.

1. On the My eBay Views sidebar in My eBay, find All Favorites, and click **Categories**. If prompted, type your password and click **Sign In**.

2. The My Favorite Categories view is displayed. Click **Add New Category**. You will see the selection boxes for each of the four categories you can set up. Figure 2-2 shows an example of how the first category has been set up. Scroll down to see the four possibilities.

Add new Category

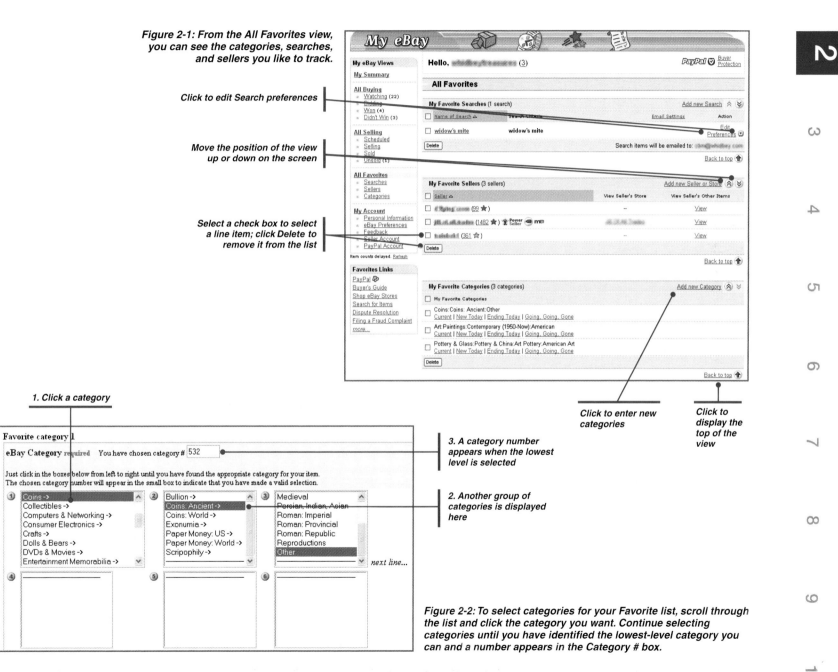

Figure 2-1: From the All Favorites view, you can see the categories, searches, and sellers you like to track.

Click to edit Search preferences

Move the position of the view up or down on the screen

Select a check box to select a line item; click Delete to remove it from the list

1. Click a category

3. A category number appears when the lowest level is selected

2. Another group of categories is displayed here

Click to enter new categories

Click to display the top of the view

Figure 2-2: To select categories for your Favorite list, scroll through the list and click the category you want. Continue selecting categories until you have identified the lowest-level category you can and a number appears in the Category # box.

Figure 2-3: Fill in the form, and click Search to save your favorite searches for quick access later.

| Basic Search | **Advanced Search** | By Seller | By Bidder | Stores |

Search keywords or item number (required)

[   ] [All of these words ∨] [Search] Learn more

Refine your search (optional)

Price range($) from	[ ] to [ ]	Words to exclude	[ ]
Category	All Categories ∨		
Expand search	☐ Title and description		
Item type	☐ Completed Items only		
	☐ Buy It Now Items only		
	☐ Gift Items only		
	☐ Quantity greater than 1		

Display format (optional)

View results
All items ∨

Sort by
Highest prices first ∨

Results per page
50 ∨

Location / International (optional)

◉ Items from eBay.com
All regions ∨

○ Items available to …
United States ∨

○ Items located in …
United States ∨

Currency [Any currency ∨]

Payment method (optional)

☐ Search for items that accept PayPal

[Search]

3. To set up a new category, click a category in the first box. The next level of items contained in the selected category is displayed. Continue to click the desired category until you have found the lowest-level item. The Category number will be displayed at the top of the dialog box. An example of category number 532 is displayed in Figure 2-2.

4. Repeat step 3 for up to three more categories.

5. Scroll down to the end of the page, and click **Submit** to add or change your favorite categories.

Save Your Favorite Searches

Saving your favorite searches in My eBay allows you to quickly see the results of up to 100 searches. You can receive e-mail notifying you of new actions for specific items.

1. From the menu bar on the top of the page, click **My eBay**.

2. In the My eBay Views sidebar, under All Favorites, click **Searches**. The My Favorite Searches view is displayed.

All Favorites
- Searches
- Sellers
- Categories

3. Click **Add New Search**. The form in Figure 2-3 is displayed.

4. First, enter the keyword or item number of the item for which the search is to be saved. This is the only required search entry.

5. Under Refine Your Search, complete any optional choices, as described in the sections "Use Basic Search Options" or "Use Advanced Search."

6. Click **Search** when you have the search parameters filled in.

7. When you see the search list and have refined it according to your preferences, click **Add To Favorites** in the upper-right area of the search list. A summary screen is displayed. Then:

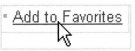

Add to Favorites

- Click **New Search** if this search is a new one.

- Click **Replace One Of These With My New Search** if you are replacing an existing search listed in the box. Then, click the name of the search to be replaced.

To have eBay notify you by e-mail when a new item is available in your search, click **Edit Preferences** in the My Favorite Searches view. On the Favorite Searches Preferences page, select **Email Me Daily Whenever There Are New Items**. Click the **For How Long** down arrow, and select the length of time the search is to be in effect. Click **Submit** to save the change.

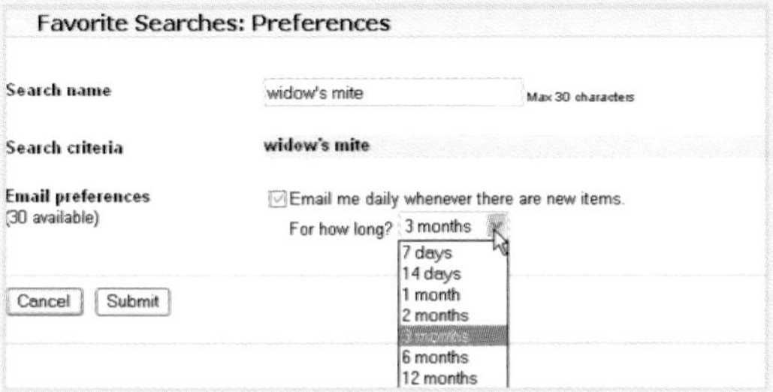

Favorite Searches: Preferences

Search name   widow's mite   Max 30 characters

Search criteria   **widow's mite**

Email preferences   ☑ Email me daily whenever there are new items.
(30 available)   For how long? 3 months

7 days
14 days
1 month
2 months
3 months
6 months
12 months

Cancel   Submit

To delete a favorite category, search, seller, or Store from your Favorite list, select the check box next to the name, and click **Delete**. To delete all items, select the check box in the column heading bar, and click **Delete**.

☑ **Old coins**   **widow's mite**

Delete

- Change the **Search Name** or **Search Criteria**, if you want.
- Click **Email Me Daily Whenever There Are New Items** if you want to track all activity in this search. Accept or change the **For How Long** duration by clicking the down arrow and selecting an option.

8. Click **Submit** to save the search.

9. On the Add To Favorite Searches page, click the link listed, or click **Search | Favorite Searches** to return to My Favorite Searches in My eBay.

Save Links to Favorite Sites

You can save up to 30 favorite sellers or eBay Stores.

1. From the menu bar at the top of the page, click **My eBay**.

2. On the My eBay Views sidebar, beneath All Favorites, click **Sellers**.

3. Click **Add New Seller Or Store**. The form in Figure 2-4 is displayed.

4. Type the seller's **User ID** or **Store Name**, and click **Save Favorite**.

Add a new favorite seller or favorite Store

Enter a seller's eBay User ID or Store Name below to add them to your Favorite Sellers / Favorite Stores list.

Seller's User ID: Store Name:

OR

Save Favorite

Note: You may save a maximum of 30 sellers / Stores to your list.

Figure 2-4: Add a new seller or Store to your Favorite list by typing the User ID or Store name and clicking Save Favorite.

QUICKFACTS

IDENTIFYING ICONS IN LISTINGS

eBay uses icons to identify certain characteristics of listed items. Some of the most common icons you will see in a listing include:

- The item is featured in the eBay Gallery, so you will see the photo in browsing and search results.

- *Buy It Now* • The item has a fixed price, so you can buy it directly from the seller without bidding in an auction.

- A picture is contained in the detailed listing.

- The item has been listed within the past 24 hours.

- The item would make a good gift for someone.

- The item is in the eBay Live Auctions.

- The item can be purchased using the Escrow.com Secure Pay feature.

- The seller accepts PayPal.

- The seller belongs to the PayPal Buyer Protection Program.

- This item is a real estate ad.

Use Basic Search Options

The Search feature can narrow your quest for information quickly. By defining a good search, you can get right to the item in question, although the search has some tricks to it. To perform a Basic Search:

1. On the menu bar, click **Search**. The page shown in Figure 2-5 is displayed.

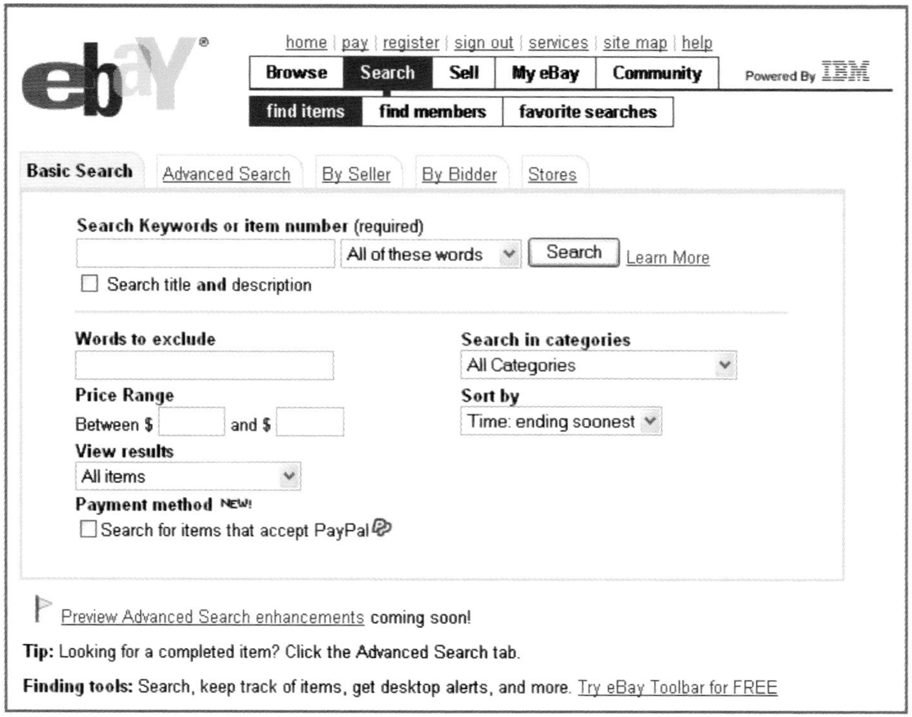

home | pay | register | sign out | services | site map | help

Browse **Search** **Sell** **My eBay** **Community** Powered By IBM

find items **find members** **favorite searches**

Basic Search Advanced Search By Seller By Bidder Stores

Search Keywords or item number (required)

[ ] All of these words ∨ [Search] Learn More

☐ Search title **and** description

Words to exclude **Search in categories**

[ ] All Categories ∨

Price Range **Sort by**

Between $ [ ] and $ [ ] Time: ending soonest ∨

View results

All items ∨

Payment method NEW!

☐ Search for items that accept PayPal

Preview Advanced Search enhancements coming soon!

Tip: Looking for a completed item? Click the Advanced Search tab.

Finding tools: Search, keep track of items, get desktop alerts, and more. Try eBay Toolbar for FREE

Figure 2-5: The Basic Search page is more powerful than you might imagine. You can use it to find items by price, location, or category, and sorted by price or auction time frame.

2. Identify the item you are searching for by typing a keyword or item number in the Search Keywords Or Item Number text box.

3. Refine your search accordingly:

   - Click the **All Of These Words** down arrow, and choose All Of These Words, Any Of These Words, or Exact Phrase.

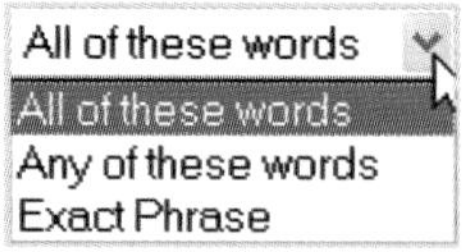

All of these words ∨
All of these words
Any of these words
Exact Phrase

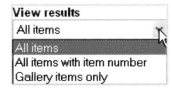

NOTE

Click **Preview Advanced Search Enhancements Coming Soon** to see changes that will be implemented to the Search feature. Changes to the Basic Search include a new sidebar identifying the search as pertaining to Items, Stores, and Members; the ability to quickly find favorite searches; and a Completed Items option for competitive pricing information.

TIP

Try to be precise about what you are searching for, naming the article, color, size, brand name, and so on. Keeping in mind that typos are not uncommon in the listings, use typical *misspellings* in addition to correct spellings for more results.

CAUTION

eBay includes common words, such as "and," "or," and "the," in its search, so it will only find items that have those exact words. For example, if you specify "mug or cup," it will find only "mug or cup" items, not any mugs *or* any cups, as you might expect.

- To search both the description and the title for your keyword(s), select the **Search Title And Description** check box.

- To identify items to be excluded from the search, type any **Words To Exclude**.

- To limit the price, type a **Price Range** in the range text boxes.

- To define which items are to be viewed, click the **View Results** down arrow, and select an option.

Bob, the buyer, is searching for antique hatpins from Bali.

View results

All items
All items
All items with item number
Gallery items only

- To search only for items that accept PayPal payments, select the **Payment Method** check box.

- To search by category, click the **Search In Categories** down arrow, and select a category.

- To sort the finished list, click the **Sort By** down arrow, and select a sort sequence.

Sort by

Time: ending soonest
Time: ending soonest
Time: newly listed
Price: lowest first
Price: highest first
Distance: nearest first

4. When the search criteria are as you want, click **Search**.

Use Advanced Search

Advanced Search allows you to widen your search parameters using several additional criteria.

1. From the top of a page, click **Search** on the menu bar. Click the **Advanced Search** tab. The page shown in Figure 2-6 is displayed.

Figure 2-6: The Advanced Search page allows you to further refine your search and consider international items.

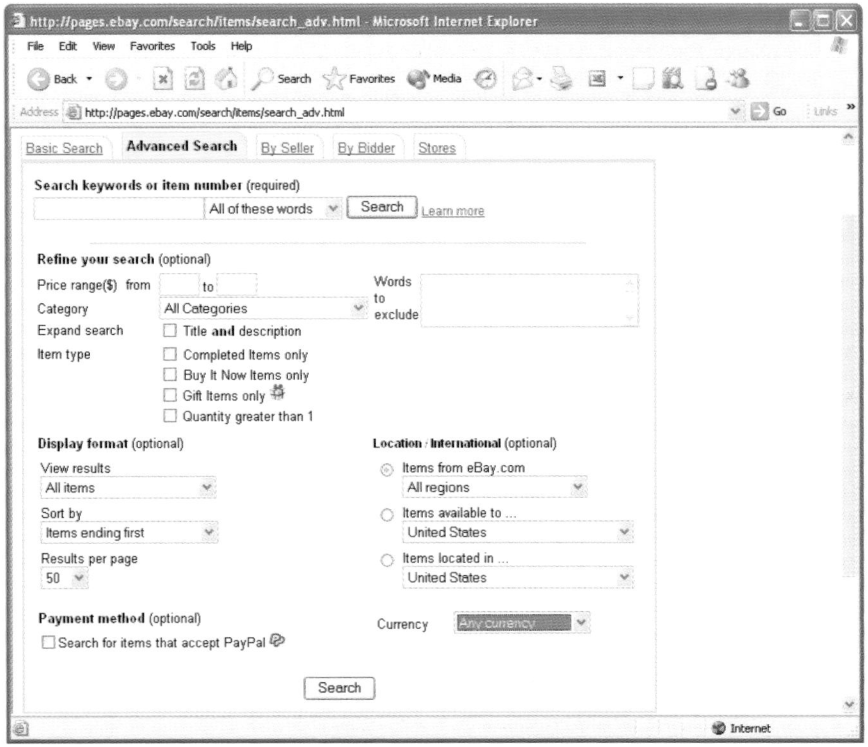

2. Type the required keyword or item number in the first text box. Click the **All Of These Words** down arrow, and select All Of These Words, Any Of These Words, or Exact Phrase.

3. To refine your search:

   ● In the Price Range text boxes, type the **From** and **To** prices.

   ● Click the **Category** down arrow, and select a category.

   ● To identify items to be excluded from the search, type any **Words To Exclude**.

   ● To search both the description and the title for your keyword(s), select the **Title And Description** check box.

   ● To identify a specific type of item to be included in the search, select the **Completed Items Only**, **Buy It Now Items Only**, **Gift Items Only**, or **Quantity Greater Than 1** check boxes.

4. To define the display format, enter any of the following information:

   ● Click the **View Results** down arrow, and choose between All Items, All Items With Item Number, or Gallery Items Only.

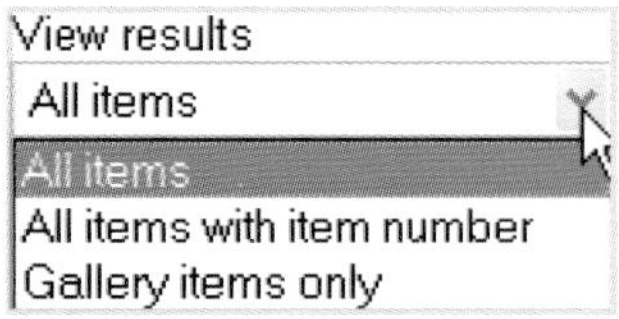

   ● To sort the results, click the **Sort By** down arrow, and choose from Items Ending First, Newly Listed Items First, Lowest Prices First, or Highest Prices First.

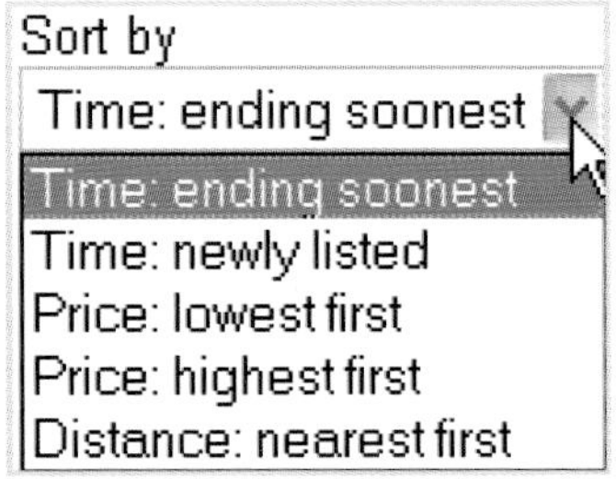

   ● To define the number of items listed on a page, click the **Results Per Page** down arrow, and choose 25, 50, or 100 results.

5. To identify the location more precisely, select one of the following options:

   ● To limit the search to Items From eBay.com, select the check box.

   ● To find items that will be shipped internationally, click the **Items Available To** down arrow, and choose a location.

   ● To find items located in specific countries, click the **Items Located In** down arrow, and choose an international location.

6. Click the **Currency** down arrow to choose an item that deals in a specific currency.

7. To look for PayPal transactions only, select the **Search For Items That Accept PayPal** check box.

8. When your search criteria are as you want them, click **Search**.

Figure 2-7: To find information about a specific seller, supply the User ID, and select the information you wish to see.

Search for a Seller's Items

To find items from a specific seller:

FIND AN INDIVIDUAL SELLER'S INFORMATION

To find a seller's feedback rating and items being sold:

1. From the menu bar, click **Search** and then click the **By Seller** tab. The page shown in Figure 2-7 is displayed.

2. Type a seller's **User ID** in the Single Seller text box.

3. Include these search criteria, if desired:

   ● If you are a seller to this user, click **Include Bidder Emails** to see e-mails sent by the seller.

Results per page	25
	All items on one page
	5
	10
	25
	50
	75
	100
	200

- To see the completed listings, click one of the **Include Completed Items**, choosing from among those items that sold in the Last Day, Last 2 Days, Last Week, Last 2 Weeks, or All Items that the seller has sold. Click **No** to ignore the seller's completed items.

- Select one of the **Sort By** options, choosing to sort the auctions by Newest First, Oldest First, Auctions Ended, or Current Price.

- Click the **Results Per Page** down arrow, and choose to see all results on a single page or a number of results per page.

4. Click **Search** at the top of the tab to see the results.

Sally, the seller, is researching items sold by her competitors. She has an edge!

FIND ITEMS FROM MULTIPLE SELLERS

To find items sold by a number of sellers, you can either search by items or by the sellers' User IDs.

1. From the menu bar, click **Search**. Click the **By Seller** tab. The page shown in Figure 2-7 is displayed. Scroll down below the yellow line, as shown in Figure 2-8.

2. In the Search Title text box, type one or more keywords identifying sellers, such as product name, size, color, and brand.

Figure 2-8: You can view items sold by multiple sellers, choosing keywords that identify items being sold.

Search title
Find items by keywords for multiple sellers

| some keyword | Search | Learn more |

☐ Search titles **and** descriptions

Multiple sellers 10 Sellers Maximum. Separate names by a comma.

```
SellerOne AnotherSeller
```

⊙ Find items from these sellers.
○ Find items excluding these sellers.

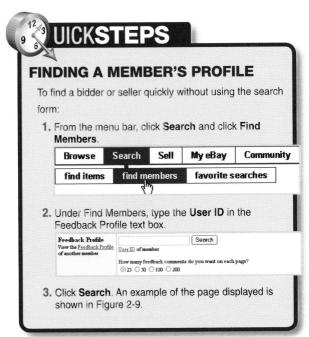

FINDING A MEMBER'S PROFILE

To find a bidder or seller quickly without using the search form:

1. From the menu bar, click **Search** and click **Find Members**.

Browse	Search	Sell	My eBay	Community
find items	find members	favorite searches		

2. Under Find Members, type the **User ID** in the Feedback Profile text box.

Feedback Profile
View the Feedback Profile of another member
User ID of member   [   ] [Search]

How many feedback comments do you want on each page?
⊙ 25 ○ 50 ○ 100 ○ 200

3. Click **Search**. An example of the page displayed is shown in Figure 2-9.

NOTE

To get personal contact information about another eBay member, you must be involved in a transaction with him or her. For example, you may be trying to find a winning bidder to send the item to him or her, or want to ask a seller a question about an item. Or, you may be trying to resolve a conflict. Sellers can get contact information for bidders in an active auction and for the winning bidder after the listing is closed. A bidder can get information about a seller during an auction, or after, if he or she is the winning bidder. See "Find Someone's Contact Information" for more information.

3. Select the **Search Titles And Descriptions** check box to include the description as well as the title in the search.

4. In the Multiple Sellers text box, type up to ten seller User IDs, separating each by a comma.

5. Choose between listing the items from the named sellers and excluding the items in the search.

6. Click **Search** when you are satisfied with your search criteria.

Figure 2-9: A member's Profile gives you the feedback rating and feedback comments.

Member Profile: ▇▇▇▇ (211 ☆)

Feedback Score:	211
Positive Feedback:	100%
Members who left a positive:	211
Members who left a negative:	0
All positive feedback received:	222

Learn about what these numbers mean.

Recent Ratings:

	Past Month	Past 6 Months	Past 12 Months
positive	0	1	2
neutral	0	0	0
negative	0	0	0

Bid Retractions (Past 6 months): 0

Member since: Jan-11-99
Location: United States
» ID History
» Items for Sale

[Contact Member]

All Feedback Received   From Buyers   From Sellers   Left for Others

222 feedback received by labvet80 (0 mutually withdrawn)   page 1 of 9

Comment	From	Date / Time	Item #
AAA+ FAST PAYER	Seller ▇▇▇1155 (550 ★)	Jan-28-04 17:58	▇▇▇
great buyer A+++++++++++	Seller ▇▇▇ (33 ☆)	Sep-02-03 09:17	▇▇▇
GREAT TRANSACTION! SUPER FAST PAYMENT, HIGHLY RECOMMENDED, THANKS! AAA+++++++++++	Seller ▇▇▇ (294 ☆)	Mar-22-03 07:48	▇▇▇
SMOOTH TRANSACTION, RECOMMEND, THANKS.	Seller ▇▇▇ (1395 ★)	Mar-07-03 16:16	▇▇▇
Fast payment Great communication! Thank you! A++++	Seller ▇▇▇ (210 ☆)	Feb-11-03 17:18	▇▇▇

Find a Bidder's Activity

To find items a bidder is interested in:

1. Click **Search** on the menu bar, and click the **By Bidder** tab.

2. In the Bidder's User ID text box, type the **User ID**.

Basic Search   Advanced Search   By Seller   **By Bidder**   Stores

Bidder's user ID	bidderid	[Search]

Enter bidder's user ID; you may look it up if you don't know it. Learn more.

Include completed items   ⊙ No ○ Yes

Even if not high bidder?   ⊙ Yes, even if not the high bidder   ○ No, only if high bidder

Results per page   [25 ▾]

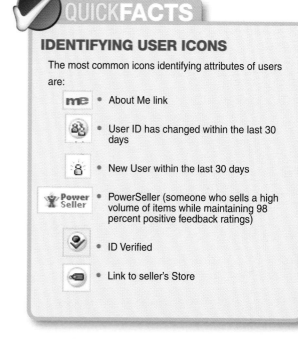

QUICKFACTS

IDENTIFYING USER ICONS

The most common icons identifying attributes of users are:

- **me** • About Me link

- • User ID has changed within the last 30 days

- • New User within the last 30 days

- **Power Seller** • PowerSeller (someone who sells a high volume of items while maintaining 98 percent positive feedback ratings)

- • ID Verified

- • Link to seller's Store

3. To Include Completed Items of the bidder, click **Yes**.

4. If you are only interested in looking at this bidder's high bids, click **No, Only If High Bidder**.

5. Click the **Results Per Page** down arrow, and choose the number of results you want displayed on a page.

6. Click **Search**. An example of what you may see is shown in Figure 2-10.

Figure 2-10: A bidder's activity shows details of the listed items the bidder is attempting to buy.

Current auctions bid on by ████████ (377 ☆)

For auction items, bold price means at least one bid has been received.

In some cases, ████████ (377 ☆) may no longer be the high bidder.

1 - 3 of 3 total. Click on the column headers to sort

Item	Start	End	Price	Title	High Bidder	Seller
████████	Jun-27-04	Jul-04-04 07:11:31	US $5.00	BEAUTIFUL ANTIQUE LOOK WOODEN FRAME	████████	████████
████████	Jun-28-04	Jul-05-04 19:43:11	US $2.00	White Stag Woman Capri Pants 2X	████████	████████
████████	Jun-26-04	Jul-06-04 12:37:39	US $51.00	Mongold Drop Spindle, hard to find	████████	████████

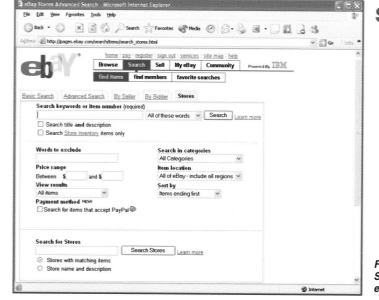

Search Stores for Items

Basic and Advanced Searches do not include eBay Store items (with a few exceptions, as noted in Chapter 10). To search for items by eBay Store:

1. From the menu bar, click **Search** and click the **Stores** tab. The page seen in Figure 2-11 is displayed.

2. Type the item keyword(s) or item number.

Figure 2-11: Searching for items in eBay Stores can show inventory that might not easily be found otherwise.

3. Click the **All Of These Words** down arrow, and choose whether to include all of the words, any of them, or exact phrases.

All of these words ▾	Search
All of these words	
Any of these words	
Exact Phrase	

4. Click the **Search Title And Description** check box to include both the title and description in a search.

5. By selecting the **Search Store Inventory Items Only** check box, you can restrict your search to items that may not be in listings but that are in eBay Store inventories. These items may be priced lower in order to move them. eBay Store sellers have store-only items (that may not appear in regular searches) and, possibly, regular auction items. Without selecting this option, you will get both types of listings.

6. Choose any of these search criteria:

- Type **Words To Exclude** to exclude items that may contain these words in the title or description.

- Type a **Price Range** to restrict the search to items that are priced in a certain range.

- Click the **View Results** down arrow, and select **All Items**, **All Items With Item Number**, or **Gallery Items Only**.

- Select the **Search For Items That Accept PayPal** check box if that's the way you prefer to pay.

- Click the **Search In Categories** down arrow, and select a category to search for.

- Click the **Item Location** down arrow, and select a location within which you want to restrict the search.

- Click the **Sort By** down arrow, and choose how you want the results sorted.

7. Click **Search** when the criteria are as you want them.

If you want a quick look at all Stores that carry certain items, use the **Search For Stores** text box at the bottom of the Store search form. You can search for all Stores that carry matching items (for example, Tibetan earrings) or just Stores that have the search words in their names or descriptions. The list will display fewer results using the name and description restrictions.

Search for Stores
Tibetan earrings   [Search Stores] Learn more
○ Stores with matching items
◉ Store name and description

Find Information about Others

You can find all sorts of information about other eBay members. In addition
to a member's user profile (see the QuickSteps "Finding a Member's Profile
Quickly"), you can see his or her history, his or her About Me page, and, in
special circumstances, contact information.

Find an About Me Page

To display an eBay member's About Me page:

1. From the menu bar, click **Search** and click **Find Members**.

Browse	Search	Sell	My eBay	Community
find items	find members		favorite searches	

2. In the About Me box (below the Feedback Profile), type the **User ID**, and click **Search**.
If the member has an About Me page, it will be displayed.

Find Someone's ID History

A user may have had more than one User ID. Many users previously used
an e-mail address for their User ID. This is no longer allowed, so changing
User IDs is not uncommon, nor is it something negative. Perhaps the user has
a new business or a different sense of what he or she wants to use as an ID.

However, a user might be hiding a negative rating by
trying to change User IDs. Be particularly careful if an ID
has changed recently. To find out what other User IDs have
been used by an eBay member:

1. From the menu bar, click **Search** and click **Find Members**.
2. In the User ID History box, type the **User ID**, and click **Search**.
The User ID History page is displayed.

eBay Member User ID History

The box below contains the User IDs that this member has used on eBay.

User ID	Effective Date	End Date
	Oct-23-03	Present
*****@pclv.net	Jan-11-99	Oct-23-03

eBay hides parts of User IDs with "*" to protect member privacy.

Find Someone's Contact Information

Finding someone's contact information can only be done if you have a current or newly ended transaction with that person.

1. From the menu bar, click **Search** and click **Find Members**.

2. In the Contact Info form, shown in Figure 2-12, type the **User ID**.

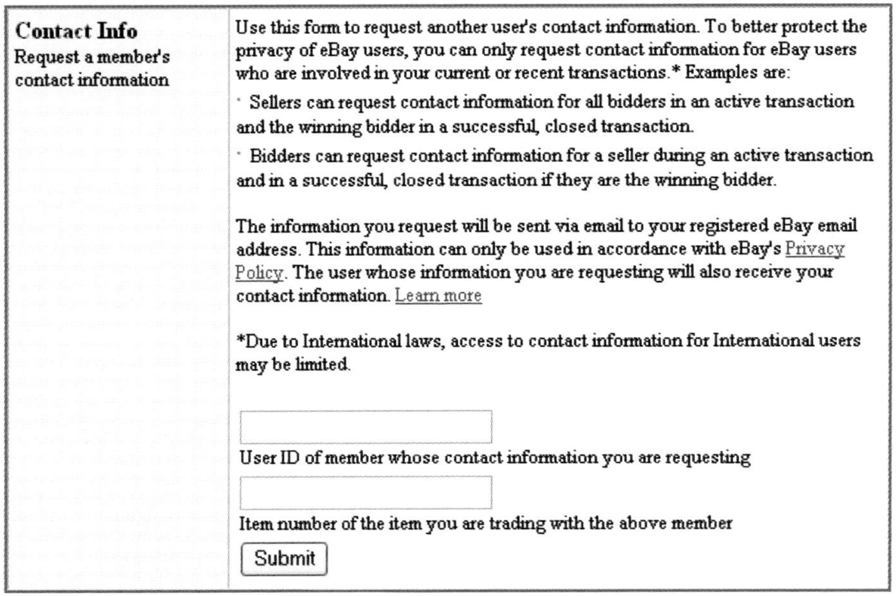

When you request information for another eBay user, you can only use the information to resolve problems or to complete a transaction that you have with this person. The information disclosed to you includes the contact information for both of you, and an e-mail is also sent to both of you. That is, the person for whom you are requesting information will receive an e-mail disclosing that you want his or her contact information and disclosing yours.

Contact Info
Request a member's contact information

Use this form to request another user's contact information. To better protect the privacy of eBay users, you can only request contact information for eBay users who are involved in your current or recent transactions.* Examples are:

· Sellers can request contact information for all bidders in an active transaction and the winning bidder in a successful, closed transaction.

· Bidders can request contact information for a seller during an active transaction and in a successful, closed transaction if they are the winning bidder.

The information you request will be sent via email to your registered eBay email address. This information can only be used in accordance with eBay's Privacy Policy. The user whose information you are requesting will also receive your contact information. Learn more

*Due to International laws, access to contact information for International users may be limited.

User ID of member whose contact information you are requesting

Item number of the item you are trading with the above member

Submit

Figure 2-12: The Contact Info form is only available if you are trying to obtain data about someone with whom you are doing business.

3. Type the **item number** that you are buying or selling.

4. Click **Submit**. If you are qualified, the contact information will be sent to your e-mail address.

TIP

A completed auction does not necessarily mean that an item has been sold. Many auctions, regardless of format, simply run out of time with no bids being placed.

NOTE

If you have just performed a search or have a list of items that you would like to refine, you may be able to find what you want without using the Search feature. The Search Options sidebar is displayed to the left of the list of items. You can refine the search for PayPal items, Completed items, Buy It Now items, Gift items, or items priced in a certain range. Select the options you want, and click **Show Items**.

Search Options

Show only:
- [ ] Items listed with PayPal
- [ ] Buy It Now items
- [ ] 🎁 Gift items
- [ ] Completed listings
- [ ] Items priced

[   ] to [   ]

Show Items

<u>Customize</u> options displayed above.

TIP

If you want to customize the Search Options sidebar, click **Customize Search Options**. The Customize Your Search page is displayed. You can add items to the sidebar by clicking an item in the Available Search Options list box, and clicking the right-pointing arrow. Remove items from the sidebar by clicking an item in the Options You Want Displayed list box, and then clicking the left-pointing arrow. Click **Save** to preserve the changes.

Research an Item

You may find yourself searching for special items, such as completed items, gift items, or Buy It Now items; or, perhaps, cars or real estate, where the item is more expensive and not necessarily an auction at all. There are unique ways to search for these items, as you'll find in this section.

Find Completed Items

To search for items on which the auctions have been completed so that you can compare prices:

1. From the home page, click **Search** on the menu bar.
2. Click the **Advanced Search** tab.
3. Type the keyword(s) of the item you want to find or the item number.
4. To restrict the search to a specific category, click the **Category** down arrow, and select a category within which the item may be found. Otherwise, leave **All Categories** selected to obtain a broader range of results.
5. Select **Completed Items Only**. Your screen may look something like Figure 2-13.
6. Click **Search**. A listing of all the items is displayed.

Figure 2-13: To find items on which auctions have been completed, use Advanced Search.

Basic Search	**Advanced Search**	By Seller	By Bidder	Stores

Search keywords or item number (required)

[diamond ring, white gold] [All of these words ▼] [Search] Learn more

Refine your search (optional)

Price range($) from	[ ] to [ ]		Words to exclude	[ ]
Category	Jewelry & Watches ▼			
Expand search	[ ] Title **and** description			
Item type	[✓] Completed Items only			
	[ ] Buy It Now Items only			
	[ ] Gift Items only 🎁			
	[ ] Quantity greater than 1			

Find Buy It Now or Gift Items

At times, you might be in a hurry to get an item or perhaps you are not interested in participating in auctions. In these cases, eBay has fixed-price items that you can buy without going through the auction process.

1. From the top menu bar, click **Search** and click the **Advanced Search** tab.
2. Enter the keyword(s) or item number for the item you want to buy.
3. To restrict the category, click the **Category** down arrow, and choose a category for the item. Otherwise, leave **All Categories** selected to obtain a broader range of results.
4. You can either:
   - Select **Buy It Now Items Only** to find something you can buy right now.

   –Or–

   - Select **Gift Items** to find an item for a gift.
5. Click **Search**. The results are displayed.

Find a Car or Other Vehicle

You can find automobiles, motorcycles, boats, or other vehicles on eBay just as easily as you can find a new shirt. Last year, over 300,000 cars were purchased on eBay. To find a vehicle:

1. From the home page, click **eBay Motors** in the Specialty Sites area. The eBay Motors home page is displayed.
2. Under **Categories**, select the make of vehicle for which you are searching. I am using Dodge as my example. The list of all vehicles under that make is displayed. There are 1,348 Dodges in our example, as shown in Figure 2-14.

Categories

Boats

Motorcycles
BMW | Harley-Davidson | Honda | Kawasaki | Suzuki | Yamaha | more

Parts & Accessories
ATV | Apparel | Aviation | Boats | Car & Truck | Collector Car & Truck | Manuals & Literature | Motorcycles | Other Vehicles | Tools | Wholesale Lots | Other

Passenger Vehicles
BMW | Cadillac | Chevy | Dodge | Ferrari | Ford | Mercedes Be | Shelby | Toyota | Triumph | VW | more

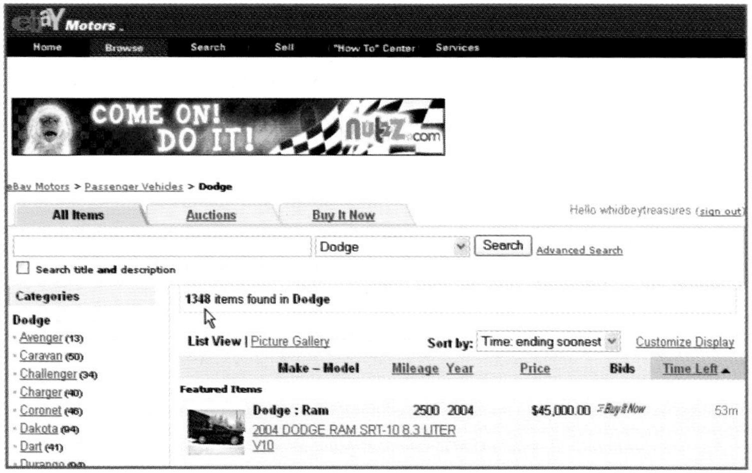

3. Select the model of Dodge under Categories. In our example, the model is Caravan. This narrows the search to 47 vehicles.

4. On the left of the screen, under Search Options, select the following search criteria:

Search Options

Show only:
- ☐ Items listed with PayPal
- ☐ Buy It Now items
- ☐ Completed listings
- ☐ Listings
  - Starting today ▾
- ☐ Items priced
  - ____ to ____

Show Items

<u>Customize</u> options displayed above.

- **Items Listed With PayPal**, for items using PayPal as the method of payment

- **Buy It Now Items**, for vehicles available right now

- **Completed Listings**, to see vehicles whose auctions are finished

- **Listings**, to select items Starting Today, Ending Today, or Ending Within 5 Hours

- **Items Priced**, to find vehicles in a specific price range

Figure 2-14: The first results show far too many cars, but you can quickly narrow your search and then sort by mileage, year, or price.

5. Click **Show Items**. The displayed list for our example is even smaller.

6. To sort the vehicles so that the ones you are most interested in are on top, select from the following:

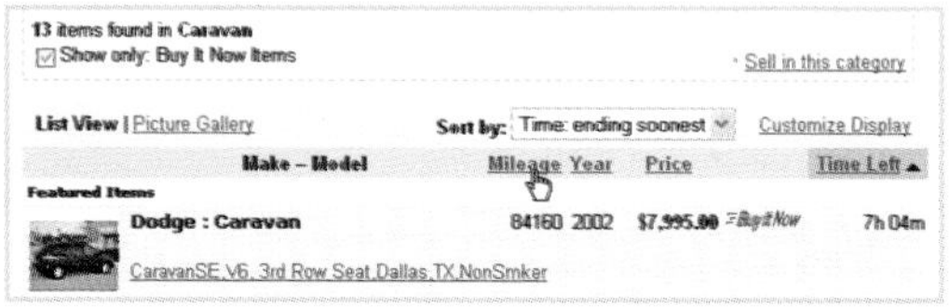

13 items found in Caravan
☑ Show only: Buy It Now Items   · Sell in this category

List View | Picture Gallery   Sort by: Time: ending soonest ▾   Customize Display

Make – Model   Mileage Year   Price   Time Left ▴

Featured Items

Dodge : Caravan   84160 2002 $7,995.00 *Buy It Now*   7h 04m
CaravanSE V6, 3rd Row Seat, Dallas, TX, NonSmker

- **Mileage**, to see vehicles with the lowest mileage

- **Year**, for the newest cars

- **Price**, for vehicles with the lowest price

- **Time Left** (default sort order), for the vehicle auctions ending soon

You will see an upward-pointing arrow next to the column name by which you are sorting the results if the sort is ascending. (In the previous illustration, the column we are sorting by is Time Left. For Buy It Now items, this column is called "Time Listed.") A descending sort shows a downward-pointing arrow, as in the Year column in the following illustration.

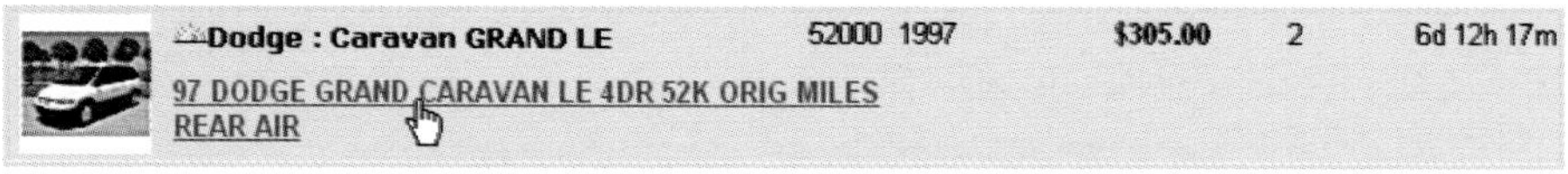

▾Dodge : Caravan GRAND LE   52000 1997 $305.00   2   6d 12h 17m
97 DODGE GRAND CARAVAN LE 4DR 52K ORIG MILES
REAR AIR

7. Click the link to see the listing for the vehicle you are interested in.

Research Property Ads or Timeshare Listings

Vacation home in Hawaii? Second home in the country? eBay provides real estate ads and listings for property, houses, and timeshares from all over. To research listings:

1. From the home page, under Categories, click **Real Estate**. A page similar to that shown in Figure 2-15 is displayed.

2. Under Categories, select the type of real estate for which you are searching. The listings for that type of property are displayed, as shown in Figure 2-16.

3. The tabs on the top of the page allow you to choose All Items, Auctions only, or Buy It Now only.

4. On the left side of the page is an item-specific search form, as shown in Figure 2-16. The search criteria vary, depending on the type of property you are looking at. Choose any criteria that apply to you, and click **Show Items**.

5. You can sort by **Price** and **Time Left** by clicking the column titles.

Figure 2-15: The Real Estate page introduces you to enticing property and timeshare listings.

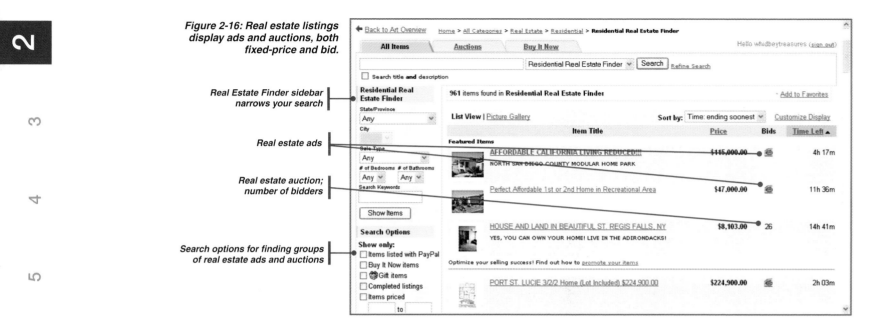

Figure 2-16: Real estate listings display ads and auctions, both fixed-price and bid.

Real Estate Finder sidebar narrows your search

Real estate ads

Real estate auction; number of bidders

Search options for finding groups of real estate ads and auctions

Understanding the Lingo

eBay has a vocabulary all its own. For example, if you read, "BTW, the CM diamond ring is TDF, and the SH is Free," you might be scratching your head, wondering what you are buying! Interpretation: "By the way, the customized diamond ring is to die for, and the shipping and handling is free." How can you let a potential buyer know what attributes your item has without being too wordy? Tables 2-1 through 2-4 contain some examples of common word usages for describing the conditions of an item, common auction terminology, shipping descriptions, and "chit chat" acronyms that communicate in a shorthand way.

A RUN of 1925 Peace dollars NGC MS 64 NEAR GEM!
THese puppies are NEAR GEM!!! $140 each in GEM!

TABLE 2-1: CONDITIONS
DESCRIBING AN ITEM

ACRONYM	WHAT IT STANDS FOR
AO	All Original
AUTO	Autographed
BU	Brilliant Uncirculated (coins)
CM	Customized
CU	Crisp Uncirculated
EC	Excellent Condition
EF	Extra Fine Condition
EX	Excellent Condition/Exceptional
FN	Fine Condition
FOR	Forgery
G/GD	Good Condition
Gently Used	(Item shows little wear)
GU/GW	Gently Used/ Gently Worn (clothing)
HIC/HIL	Hole In Cover/Hole In Label
LSW	Label Shows Wear
MCU	Might Clean Up
MIMB/MIMP/MIOP/MIP/MNB	Mint In Mint Box/Mint In Mint Package/Mint In Opened Package/Mint In Package/Mint No Box
Mint, MS	Mint Condition, Mint State
NBW	Never Been Worn
NC	No Cover
NGC	Numismatic Guarantee Company (coins)
NIB/NIP/ NIMSP	New In Box/New In Package/New In Manufacturer's Sealed Package
NM	Near Mint
NRFB/NRFSB	Never Removed From Box/Never Removed From Sealed Box
NW	Never Worn (clothing)
NWOT/NWT	New Without Tags/New With Tags
OB/OF	Original Box/Original Finish
OOP/OP	Out Of Package/Out Of Print
P/PC	Poor Condition (coins)/Poor Condition
PF/PR	Proof Coin/Poor Condition Proof
RARE	(This can be a subjective assessment)
SR	Slight Ring Wear
SW	Slight Wear
VF/VFU	Very Fine Condition
VG/VGC	Very Good Condition
VHTF	Very Hard To Find
VR	Very Rare (this can also be a subjective assessment)
WOB/WOC/WOF/WOR	Writing On Back/Writing On Cover/Writing On Front/Writing On Record

TABLE 2-2: AUCTION ACRONYMS

AKA	Also Known As
BIN	Buy It Now
FB	Feedback
FOR	Forgery
HTF	Hard To Find
NR/NORES	No Reserve
NARU	Not A Registered User
NPB	Non-Paying Buyer
SO	Sold Out

TABLE 2-3: SHIPPING ACRONYMS

ASAP	As Soon As Possible
DOA	Dead On Arrival (item is damaged when delivered)
FEDEX	Federal Express Shipping
FVF	Final Value Fee (a fee charged to the seller)
PP	Parcel Post
PPD	Post Paid
S/H, SH	Shipping And Handling
S/H/I, SHI	Shipping, Handling, and Insurance
Snail Mail	U.S. Post Office Delivery
UPS	United Parcel Service
USPS	United States Postal Service
V/M/D	Visa, MasterCard, Discover credit cards

TABLE 2-4: "CHIT CHAT" ACRONYMS

BTS	Back To School
HTF	Hard To Find
FAQ	Frequently Asked Questions
IMO/IMHO	In My Opinion/In My Humble Opinion
ITF	Impossible To Find
LMK	Let Me Know
RSVP	Respond As Soon As Possible
TIA	Thanks In Advance
TDF	To Die For
WYSIWYG	What You See Is What You Get

How to...

- *Reading the Item Description*

- Review a Seller's Feedback

- *Understanding Feedback*

- Look at a Seller's Other Products

- Ask the Seller Questions

- Review Other Bidders

- Contact Other Buyers

- Get in Preapproved Auctions

- Find the Official eBay Time

- Delay Your Bid

- *Understanding Auction Durations and Reserves*

- Be a Sniper

- View Bid History

- Bid on Multiple Items

- *Understanding Bid Increments*

- Use Proxy Bidding

- Find a Grading Service

- Use Authentication Services

- Install eBay's Toolbar

- Use eBay's Toolbar for Bidding

- Receive Wireless eBay Alerts

- Using Microsoft Alerts

Chapter 3
Buying Strategies

Your most important weapon in this bidding/buying game is information. Your buying strategies consist of arming yourself with information you need to know—about yourself and your own purchasing tendencies, and whether you are bidding or paying a fixed price. You need to know about the seller and his or her past history and feedback status. The competition you encounter during bidding is certainly a subject of concern, as is how your competitors typically bid on items. Of course, the product and how you judge its worthiness are important areas you want to investigate. First off, you want to protect yourself against buying an inappropriate or unsatisfactory product. (Protecting yourself against fraud or dishonesty is covered in Chapter 9.)

READING THE ITEM DESCRIPTION

One of the most obvious ways you can protect yourself is to read carefully the description of the item being auctioned. Do you understand what it is? (For example, is the item the dining room set with the chairs, or just the chairs? Pictures can deceive!) Is the description complete, or is important information missing? Are the pictures clear, or are they a little blurry in the important areas? What is the seller charging for handling and shipping? Will insurance be available? Do you have PayPal options? Are you restricted to only certain ways of paying for it? Will the seller ship internationally if you don't live in the seller's country? (An example of shipping and handling details is shown in Figure 3-1.) What is the return policy? If you don't like the item, what can you do about it? If it is broken or damaged when you receive it, what can you do?

Protect Yourself (Buyer Precautions)

Your first task is to protect yourself by learning all you can about what it is you want to bid on as well as the person selling it. A second task is to protect yourself against spending your hard-earned money on something you don't want. You can be buying the wrong item without realizing it, or because you get carried away in the auction momentum, valuing the game more than the thing you are buying. Either way, you'll end up feeling dissatisfied with your purchase.

Review a Seller's Feedback

One of the first things you will do is check out the seller's feedback rating. This tells you how the seller has transacted business in the past and if buyers have been satisfied with the seller's service and products.

1. When you find the item you want to bid on, click the seller's link.

Seller information

knightwest (898 ☆)

Feedback Score: 898
Positive Feedback: 100%
Member since Aug-14-99 in United States

Read feedback comments

Ask seller a question

View seller's other items

Buyer Protection Offered
PayPal ✅ See coverage and eligibility

Shipping and payment details

Shipping and handling: UPS Ground
(within United States)

Shipping insurance: Not offered

Will ship to United States only.

Seller's payment instructions & return policy:
Payment is due within 10 days of auction ending. If payment not received items may be relisted. Will accept PayPay, Money Order, Cashier's Check, or personal check. Will ship within 2-3 weekdays after receiving payment.

Calculate shipping 🖩

Enter your US ZIP Code:

[Calculate]

Learn more about how calculated shipping works.

Buyers outside US: If seller ships to your country, see item description or contact seller for details.

Figure 3-1: Shipping details are important to look at, as in the description of the item.

Payment methods accepted

• *PayPal*® (VISA ▭ ▭ ▭ ECHECK eBay)
• Personal check
• Money order/Cashiers check
Learn about payment methods.

eBay recommended services

Increase your PayPal sending limit. Get Verified today. ✅

TIP

Read the description carefully and *don't make any assumptions*. Don't assume something is included if it is not mentioned. If you have a question, ask the seller.

NOTE

Notice the colors of the feedback. Green indicates positive feedback; gray is neutral; and red indicates negative feedback.

CAUTION

Sellers have the option of keeping their feedback comments private. Be cautious about dealing with sellers using this practice. They have eliminated one of your most important ways to protect yourself.

TIP

You can get some understanding of how the seller cooperates and deals with buyers by reading the seller's comments to others. What is the tone of the communication? Helpful? Critical? Neutral? Click the **Left For Others** tab to see the seller's comments for others.

2. Scroll through the feedback ratings (an example of which is shown in Figure 3-2) to find out if they are consistent and positive.

3. Ask yourself:

- Does the seller deliver the expected item?

- Is the item delivered on time?

- Is the item in good shape when it arrives?

- Is the price as expected?

- If there are complaints, are they serious defects with the product or delivery or the result of ignorance on the part of the buyer?

- What is the overall tone of the comments?

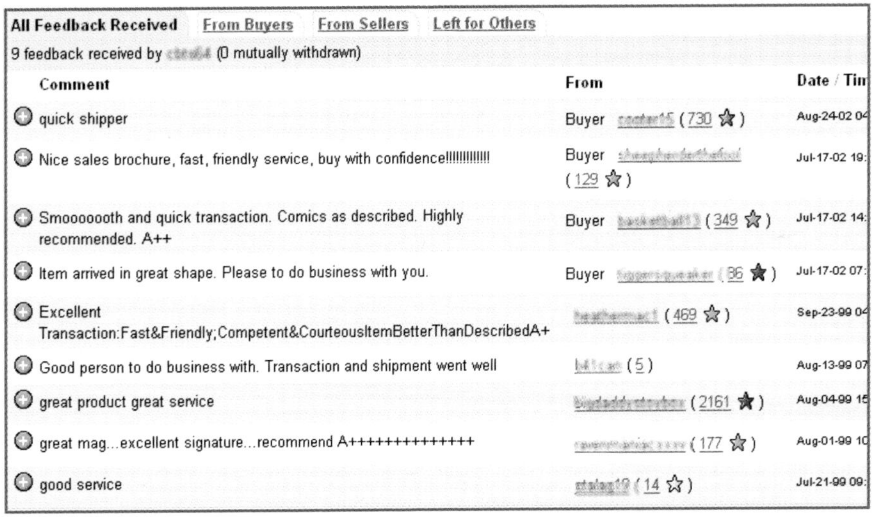

All Feedback Received	From Buyers	From Sellers	Left for Others		
9 feedback received by cbxxb4 (0 mutually withdrawn)					
Comment			**From**		**Date / Tim**
quick shipper			Buyer rooter15 (730 ☆)		Aug-24-02 04
Nice sales brochure, fast, friendly service, buy with confidence!!!!!!!!!!			Buyer sheephentedthefool (129 ☆)		Jul-17-02 19:
Smooooooth and quick transaction. Comics as described. Highly recommended. A++			Buyer basketball12 (349 ☆)		Jul-17-02 14:
Item arrived in great shape. Please to do business with you.			Buyer tuggers-queaker (86 ★)		Jul-17-02 07:
Excellent Transaction:Fast&Friendly;Competent&CourteousItemBetterThanDescribedA+			heathermac1 (469 ☆)		Sep-23-99 04
Good person to do business with. Transaction and shipment went well			b41cam (5)		Aug-13-99 07
great product great service			bigdaddystoybox (2161 ★)		Aug-04-99 15
great mag...excellent signature...recommend A+++++++++++++++			ravenmaniacxxxv (177 ☆)		Aug-01-99 10
good service			stalag19 (14 ☆)		Jul-21-99 09:

Figure 3-2: Feedback comments provide an important way to gauge the honesty and reliability of the seller.

UNDERSTANDING FEEDBACK

Feedback comments remain one of the most important tools you have to protect yourself. You can see three kinds of feedback comments: comments on an eBay user from sellers who have sold to this user, comments from buyers who have purchased an item from this user, and comments the user has given to others. Nevertheless, feedback ratings do have some drawbacks. For instance, new sellers do not have a history, so although you must take care in buying from them, you can also understand their lack of feedback— and they have to start somewhere! You can use other buyer feedback to get a sense of how sellers have handled eBay transactions in the past and how they followed through with the purchases.

A more important drawback to consider is that any buyer can enter misleading or even false and detrimental information about a seller if the transaction is slightly delayed or if the seller has not performed to some hypothetical standard or if the buyer is just having a bad day. If a seller's feedback ratings are mostly negative, then you can forget about dealing with this seller; but if the feedback comments are overwhelmingly positive and there are just one or two negative comments, then give the seller a break.

Another shortcoming of feedback ratings is that often a buyer or seller is hesitant to leave negative feedback because the recipient might retaliate and leave negative feedback on the other person's site. Keep the following guidelines in mind when providing feedback:

- Be fair and generous in your expectations of what the other person did. If the item arrived intact and pretty much on time, or if the item is as described, then it probably is not worth a negative comment even if you are somewhat disappointed.

Continued...

Look at a Seller's Other Products

You can see other items a seller has available by opening the **View Item** page and clicking **View Seller's Other Items** from the list of Seller Information links. A seller might have duplicate items available with fewer bidders, or one of these auctions might be ending sooner than the first one you looked at. You can also access the Seller's Other Items link from several My eBay views, such as Watching and Favorite Sellers.

Ask the Seller Questions

Find out all you can about the item you are considering buying before you make a bid. Ask the seller specific questions if the description does not provide the information you need. To ask a seller questions:

1. Browse or search for the item you want. Click the item to display the View Item page, such as you might see in Figure 3-3.

2. Click **Ask Seller A Question**.

3. Sign in with your User ID and password, if necessary.

4. The text box for entering your question is shown in Figure 3-4. Type your question and click **Send Message**. The seller, if he or she is interested in selling the item, will quickly respond to your question.

Seller information

onexpandamyallD-r5o (558 ⭐)

Feedback Score: 558
Positive Feedback: 100%
Member since Jan-30-00 in United States

Read feedback comments

Ask seller a question

View seller's other items

UNDERSTANDING FEEDBACK

- If the transaction is not going well, be sure to contact the seller and let him or her know you are dissatisfied. Give him or her a chance to improve the situation.

- If the transaction was clearly and seriously deficient, you can help others by commenting on your experiences. Chances are, yours will not be the only negative comment. (If the transaction is fraudulent, see Chapter 9 for more information.)

- If you get undeserved negative feedback, describe the conditions from your side and go on with life. If you deserved it, describe how you have changed your behavior so that the condition won't reoccur.

bad buyer, not recommended   Buyer ▮▮▮▮ (18 ☆)

Reply by ▮▮▮▮ I paid right away & 2 months later no product - finally refund after 25 emails

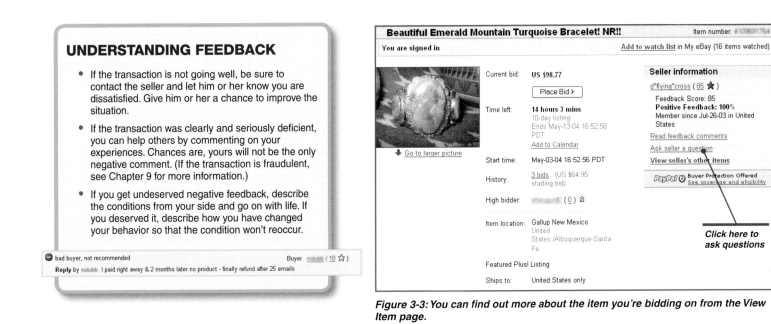

Figure 3-3: You can find out more about the item you're bidding on from the View Item page.

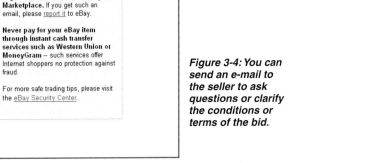

Figure 3-4: You can send an e-mail to the seller to ask questions or clarify the conditions or terms of the bid.

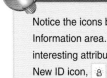
Look Up the Competition

If you seem to be running up against the same bidder and losing, or if you find that a competitor often bids on items you want, you can get additional information about him or her for that slight edge.

Review Other Bidders

When you are looking at the listing for an item, you also can investigate the other bidders.

1. Find the item on which you are bidding, such as you might find in Figure 3-5, by browsing or searching for an item. Click the title to display the View Item page.

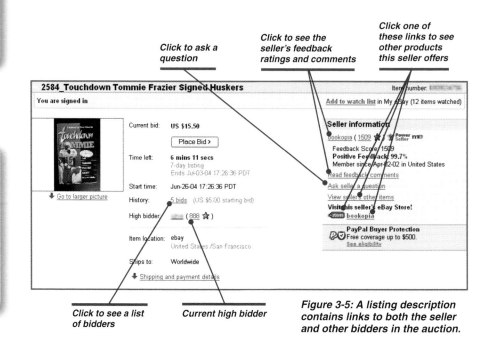

Figure 3-5: A listing description contains links to both the seller and other bidders in the auction.

CAUTION

Determine how much money you are willing to pay for an item and resolve not to spend more than that. Find out as much as you can about its value, decide what it is worth to you, and then let that be. Remember that the auction is a legally binding contract and you are required by law to pay for any item you bid on and win.

TIP

Notice things about a bidder, such as whether a high proxy keeps a high bidder in place and how close to the end of the auction the bidder gets involved. In free bidding, can you tell how much the bidder advances the bid each time? What types of items is the bidder after? Is the bidder a business or an individual?

NOTE

You may notice that a bidder has two bids, one right after the other. In this case, the bidder is probably not bidding against himself or herself. Rather, he or she increased the maximum bid after entering an initial bid. This causes two bids to be entered in the auction rather than one, even though they are from the same person and there is no higher bid amount. This is done when a person enters a higher bid, but the "highest bidder" is not changed, indicating that the current high bidder has a higher maximum proxy bid.

2. Click the **History** link to see a list of bidders. The Bid History page is displayed, as shown in Figure 3-6.

3. Click the bidder's **User ID link** to find out additional information.

Figure 3-6: On the Bid History page, you can see who is bidding on an item and how much time is left on the auction.

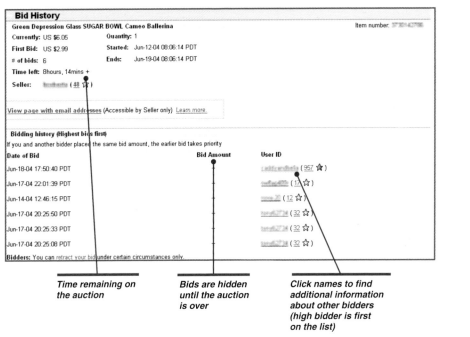

Time remaining on the auction

Bids are hidden until the auction is over

Click names to find additional information about other bidders (high bidder is first on the list)

NOTE

Chapter 2 describes how to get additional information on other eBay members—such as viewing their ID history, feedback comments, or About Me page.

Contact Other Bidders

You can contact another bidder, although you are not allowed to try to make a side deal with the bidder or to interfere with the honest give and take of the auction. You can contact a bidder for other reasons, however, especially after the auction is completed.

1. Click the bidder's **User ID** link to open the bidder's Profile page.

2. On the Member Profile page, click the **Contact Member** button.

Member Profile: (48 ☆)					
Feedback Score:	**48**	Recent Ratings:			Member since: Mar-02-02
Positive Feedback:	**100%**		Past Month	Past 6 Months	Past 12 Months	Location: United States
Members who left a positive:	48	☺ positive	14	24	26	→ ID History
Members who left a negative:	0	☺ neutral	0	0	0	→ Items for Sale
All positive feedback received:	51	☹ negative	0	0	0	
Learn about what these numbers mean		Bid Retractions (Past 6 months): 0				[Contact Member]

3. The Contact eBay Member page is displayed, as shown previously in Figure 3-4.

4. Type your message and click **Send Message**.

NOTE

If you are *blocked* from bidding, the seller has specifically placed you on a list of bidders to be excluded or blocked from bidding. In this case, you will not be able to participate in this seller's auctions. This can be for several reasons: you are an international buyer and this seller does not sell internationally; you do not fit the feedback rating profile that is required for this seller; you did not pay for previous winning bids or created other hassles for this seller; and so on. See Chapter 8 for additional information.

Get in Preapproved Auctions

You may find that you are not allowed to participate in an auction. In this case, you may see a message informing you that the item being bid on is only available to a restricted list of bidders. If you really want to bid on the item, send a message to the seller asking to be placed on the approved bidder list. (See Chapter 8 for additional information.)

Time Your Bid

Sometimes the way you will be most successful is by timing your bids. In cases where the item is highly desired by others, you may have to vigorously compete.

Find the Official eBay Time

The official eBay time is always Pacific Standard Time. To find it, click **Site Map** on the top links bar, and scroll down under Browse to **eBay Official Time**. The page shown in Figure 3-7 is displayed. The URL of the location is http://cgi3.ebay.com/aw-cgi/eBayISAPI.dll?TimeShow.

To find the time for a listing:

1. Open the **View Item** page by clicking the item title.

2. The Start Time and Time Left are usually displayed under the Current Bid price.

3. Be sure to note the time left, and track it closely. Add it to your Watch list if you want to quickly find it again (see Chapter 4).

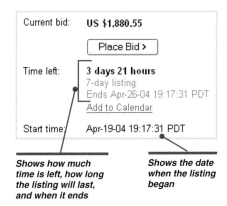

Shows how much time is left, how long the listing will last, and when it ends

Shows the date when the listing began

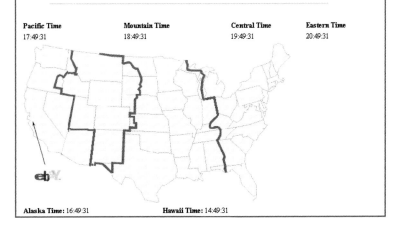

eBay Current Date and Time

Official eBay Time is the time at eBay headquarters in San Jose, California in the United States. If you find a reference to eBay Time, you can use this page to calculate the time in your area.

The official eBay Time is now:

Saturday, Jul 03, 2004 17:49:31 PDT

Pacific Time
17:49:31

Mountain Time
18:49:31

Central Time
19:49:31

Eastern Time
20:49:31

Alaska Time: 16:49:31   **Hawaii Time:** 14:49:31

Figure 3-7: Use the official time and date page to ensure that you are not out of sync in your timing on bidding in an auction.

UNDERSTANDING AUCTION DURATIONS AND RESERVES

UNDERSTAND AUCTION DURATIONS

Auctions or Buy It Now listings may be held for one, three, five, seven, or ten days. How long depends on the seller and what the item is. Some items, such as tickets or dated objects (such as chocolate Easter bunnies), may be placed for a short period of time, while higher-priced items may be on the market longer so bidders can compare prices and products. If you find an item you want to bid on, you must be aware of the time limitations and how long you have until the auction is over. The listing states how long the duration is and how far into it the auction is currently. Of course, for Buy It Now auction items, the auction ends if the first bid matches the Buy It Now amount. Otherwise, if the first bid is below the Buy It Now amount, the Buy It Now option disappears and the auction proceeds as usual.

Time left:	**11 hours 38 mins**
	10-day listing
	Ends Apr-23-04 11:11:00 PDT

UNDERSTAND AUCTION RESERVE PRICES

Reserve prices are minimum prices that sellers set for their items. The reserve price is not displayed for buyers, so you are bidding blindly as far as the reserve price is concerned. A reserve price assures the seller that he or she will get at least that amount for the item. If the reserve is not met by the end of the auction, the auction completes with no winner. If the reserve is met, then the highest bidder wins the item. In some cases, if the reserve is not met, the seller may notify the highest bidder and accept the bid even though it does not meet the reserve price (although you can't count on that).

| Current bid: | **US $229.49** (Reserve not met) |

Delay Your Bid

Many experienced eBay buyers hold their bids until the last minute to get the lowest price. The idea is that a bidding war will occur when buyers see activity on the bidding front. There is some truth to this, as bidders seem more interested in what others are bidding on; also, every time you enter a bid, someone else must bid higher to get the item. So you might be better off just watching the auction and jumping in at the last minute with your highest proxy bid.

Be a Sniper

You will know you've encountered a sniper when you are the high bidder and someone slips in a higher bid at the last second, squeezing you out of the winning bid. It is allowed by eBay, although it doesn't feel very good to be the victim of a sniper. You can do it, too, however, either doing it yourself or using specialized software.

Bob, the buyer, loves a good sniping opportunity.

USE PROXY BIDDING

Since eBay will automatically bump up your bid until your maximum is reached, you will always be the winner if you are willing to bid a high-enough maximum amount. Last-minute bidding can help you change your maximum amount if you are losing and need a higher maximum proxy amount. The following section describes how to do this.

USE TWO WINDOWS

To track the bidding process and to prepare your own maximum bid, you need two windows, as shown in Figure 3-8.

1. Find the item you want. Click the listing title so that the View Item page is displayed.

2. Press **CTRL+N** to split your browser window into two windows.

3. Select each window and drag the borders to resize them to fit the screen so that both windows are visible.

4. On one window, click the **History *n* bids** link, so you can see the current bid (labeled "Currently"), the bidders, and the current time. Click **Refresh** to keep the bid current, or press **F5** on your keyboard.

5. On the other window, click **Place Bid** to display the bid entry screen, Type your price and click **Continue**. The Submit Your Bid page is displayed. (You may have to fill in your User ID and password.) Delay pressing **Submit** until the time is just right, within the last 30 seconds. (You'll need to test how quickly your bid is processed on your computer and Internet service so you can time it just right.)

Figure 3-8: You can use two windows to keep an eye on the bidding and enter your own bid at the last second of the auction.

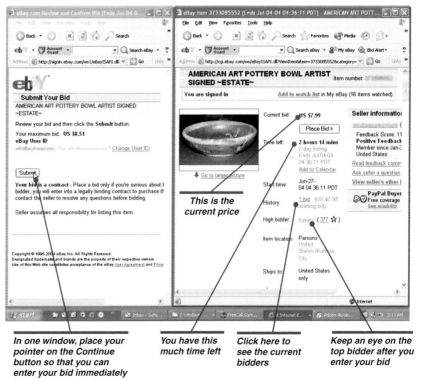

In one window, place your pointer on the Continue button so that you can enter your bid immediately

You have this much time left

Click here to see the current bidders

Keep an eye on the top bidder after you enter your bid

USE SNIPER SOFTWARE

If you do a search on "sniping," you will find a variety of sniping software, as seen in Figure 3-9. These packages, available by auction or fixed price, automatically watch your auctions, alert you when there is a change, place a time-delayed bid at the last second, and gather and display information for you so you can track your auctions easily and keep on top of them.

USE A BIDDING SERVICE

If you are uneasy performing sniping yourself or if you are going to be away from your computer during the auction, you can use a bidding service. These services will place a bid for you at a pre-established time that you set. You tell them when, how much, and your user information, and they will place the bid for you. Search on Google for "eBay Bidding Services."

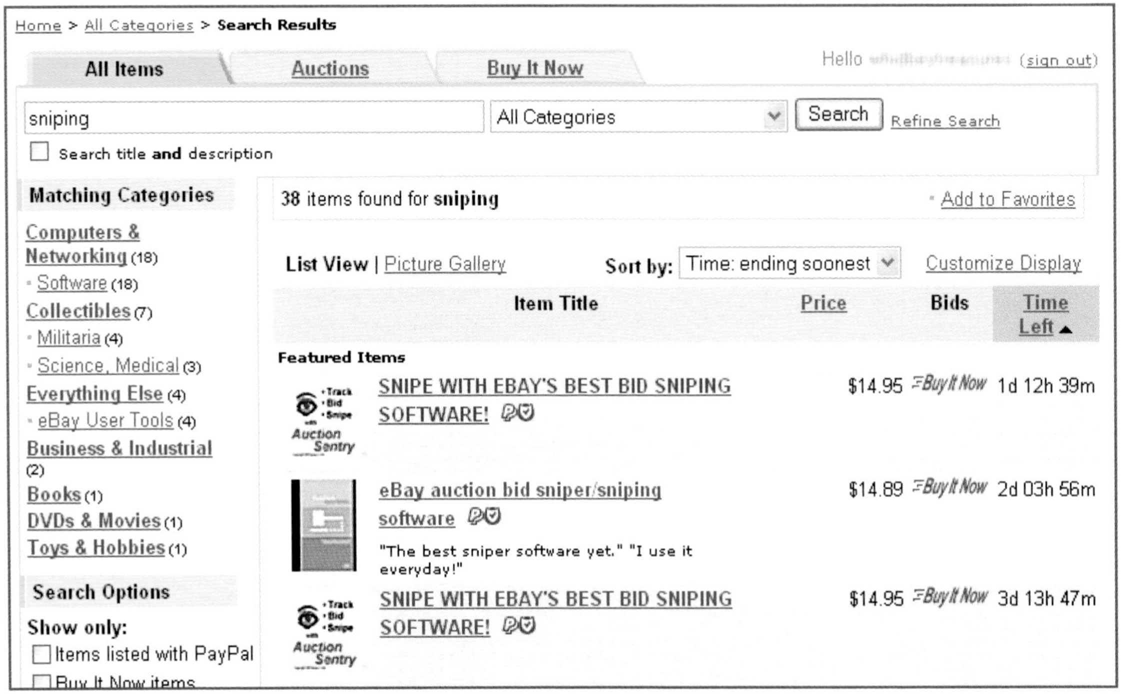

Figure 3-9: Sniping software is available for optimizing your bid timing and tracking your auctions.

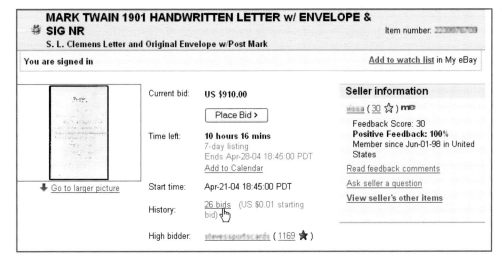

MARK TWAIN 1901 HANDWRITTEN LETTER w/ ENVELOPE & SIG NR

Item number: 　　　　　

S. L. Clemens Letter and Original Envelope w/Post Mark

You are signed in   Add to watch list in My eBay

Current bid: **US $910.00**

[Place Bid >]

Time left: **10 hours 16 mins**
                7-day listing
                Ends Apr-28-04 18:45:00 PDT
                Add to Calendar

↓ Go to larger picture

Start time: Apr-21-04 18:45:00 PDT

History: 26 bids   (US $0.01 starting bid)

High bidder: steves sportscards (1169 ★)

Seller information

xxxxa (30 ☆) me

Feedback Score: 30
Positive Feedback: 100%
Member since Jun-01-98 in United States

Read feedback comments

Ask seller a question

View seller's other items

Figure 3-10: To see current bidders, click the History link.

View Bid History

By looking at the bid history, you can see how many people are bidding, how much they are increasing each bid, who the bidders are, and their patterns.

To view the bid history:

1. Browse or search for an item, and, if necessary, open its View Item page by clicking its title. The top of the View Item form is displayed, as shown in Figure 3-10.

2. Click the **History** link. The Bid History page is displayed, consisting of two parts:

- A summary of information gives you the essential facts of the auction, including the beginning and current bids, the number of bidders, the quantity of items being sold, the starting and ending dates, the time left, and a link to the seller's information

Bid History

MARK TWAIN 1901 HANDWRITTEN LETTER w/ ENVELOPE & SIG NR   Item number: 2239976709

Currently: US $910.00   Quantity: 1

First Bid: US $0.01   Started: Apr-21-04 18:45:00 PDT

# of bids: 26   Ends: Apr-28-04 18:45:00 PDT

Time left: 10hours, 4mins +

Seller: xxxxa (30 ☆) me

- The itemized list of bidders, beginning with the highest bidder first

Bidding history (Highest bids first)

If you and another bidder placed the same bid amount, the earlier bid takes priority

Date of Bid	Bid Amount	User ID
Apr-26-04 20:33:17 PDT	--	steves sportscards (1169 ★)
Apr-26-04 14:08:30 PDT	--	joshh (32 ☆)
Apr-26-04 12:03:24 PDT	--	croydy (121 ☆)
Apr-25-04 04:44:05 PDT	--	silky9 (307 ☆)

3. Click the seller's or bidder's **User ID** links to find additional information. See "Review Other Bidders" in this chapter to dig deeper into the backgrounds of other eBay members.

Bid using Several Techniques

Common bidding techniques are bidding on multiple items and proxy bidding .

Bid on Multiple Items

You can bid on multiple items selling in a Dutch auction or on those selling for a fixed price.

Figure 3-11: A Dutch auction is one in which multiple items are sold at the same price, but the bids determine who gets how many items and for how much.

Winning Bidders List

ALABAMA COIN DEALERS COIN INVENTORY --DUTCH!!!   Item number:

Currently: US $1.00   Quantity: 2412
First Bid: US $1.00   Started: May-01-04 11:00:00 PDT
# of bids: 4 (may include multiple bids by same bidder)   Ends: May-02-04 11:00:00 PDT
Time left: 9hours, 13mins +
Seller: (2720 ⭐)

Quantity offered for sale

Multiple bids from one bidder help ensure that he or she gets the quantity desired

View page with email addresses and locations (Accessible by Seller only)
Learn more.

Dutch Auction High Bidders

View Bid History

Date of Bid	Item Price	Quantity	User ID	Payment
May-01-04 21:43:42 PDT	US $1.01	50	(701 ⭐)	Payment options available when auction ends.
May-01-04 12:44:40 PDT	US $1.00	100	(40 ⭐)	Payment options available when auction ends.
May-01-04 17:57:27 PDT	US $1.00	33	(56 ⭐)	Payment options available when auction ends.
May-01-04 23:25:21 PDT	US $1.00	20	(11 ⭐)	Payment options available when auction ends.

Quantity still available. Lowest successful bid is minimum bid amount.

Price per quantity now available

Quantity wanted by each bidder

BID ON MULTIPLE ITEMS (DUTCH AUCTION)

In a Dutch auction, multiple items are sold at the same price, but with a couple of differences. An example of a Dutch auction item is shown in Figure 3-11. See Chapter 4 for how to bid in a Dutch auction. With a Dutch auction:

- The seller lists the items, giving a minimum acceptable price.
- Bidders bid on the number of items they want and at what price.
- The winners pay the lowest acceptable price. That price is the lowest price made by a bidder, who is assured of getting at least one item; that is, his or her bid will zero out the total of the quantities available.
- The highest bidders will win first and get the quantities they want, even if the quantity is oversold.

For example, a seller offers 10 copper spoons at $10 each:

- Bidder A bids $10 for 3 spoons.
- Bidder B bids $10.50 for 5 spoons.
- Bidder C bids $12.00 for 8 spoons.
- Bidders B and C will both pay $10.50 for the spoons.
- Bidder B will only get 2 spoons.
- Bidder C will get all 8 spoons.
- Bidder A will get no spoons since Bidders B and C zeroed out the quantity available.

Sally, the seller, is preparing to sell her valued collection of dryer lint, collected over many years.

BID ON MULTIPLE ITEMS (FIXED PRICE)

In a fixed-price format, the seller sells all the items for a fixed price. Bidders enter the number of items they want at the given price. The copper spoons in the previous example would all sell for $10 each to bidders as long as the spoons last. When all the spoons are sold, the listing is over, whether the time has expired or not.

Use Authentication Services

Authentication services verify that the item is genuine. An example is the eBay Authenticator Pre-Certified Jewelry Program, available for verifying gems. The seller sends the stones you are interested in buying to a laboratory, such as International Gemological Information (IGI), which grades and appraises the stones, verifying that they are as advertised, and ships them directly to you, the buyer. These services are often already performed by sellers and are advertised in the listing descriptions.

Other services are available to you on-call. For instance, if you are interested in authenticating a book, you can pay a fee for an expert to examine the description of the item, review any photos, ask unanswered questions of the seller, and then issue an opinion to you within a period of time, such as 48 hours. To find a list of companies that offer these services:

1. Click **Services** on the top links bar.

2. Click **Options, Authentication & Grading** under Selling Services.

3. Scan the listings and look for authentication services.

These stones have been authenticated by a third party

68 items found in Authenticator Pre-Certified · Sell in this category

List View | Picture Gallery   Sort by: Time: ending soonest ∨   Customize Display

Item Title	Price	Bids	Time Left ▲
Featured Items			
AAA+ NATURAL LIGHT VIOLET SAPPHIRE 3.55cts ⌂☑ APJ VERIFIED IGI IDENTIFICATION REPORT	$42.00	3	5d 15h 45m
AAA+ TRANSPARENT PURPLE 6-RAY STAR SAPPHIRE 3.13cts ⌂☑ APJ VERIFIED by IGI WHAT A RING THIS WILL MAKE	$37.51	4	7d 14h 01m

Optimize your selling success! Find out how to promote your items

Use eBay Tools for Bidding Information

eBay offers the new eBay Toolbar, which you can use to get information from eBay; eBay Anywhere Wireless, which you can use to receive alerts on your PDA or cell phone; and Microsoft Alerts, which you can use to receive alerts on your computer.

Install eBay's Toolbar

The eBay Toolbar is free and is located on your Internet browser (Microsoft Internet Explorer 5 and 6 or Netscape Navigator versions 4.08 through 4.79). The eBay Toolbar provides a quick way for you to search eBay, watch your bids, receive alerts if you are outbid or the bid is over, and protect your account with the Account Guard feature (see Chapter 9 for more information on Account Guard). To install the eBay Toolbar:

(see Chapter 9 for more information on Account Guard)

1. Open the eBay home page, click **eBay Downloads** on the first bottom links bar, and, under Buying, click the **eBay Toolbar** link.

2. Under the Choose A Topic sidebar, for the eBay Toolbar, click **Download**.

3. Read the User License Agreement and Privacy Policy, and click **Agree**.

4. A Security Warning dialog box appears, asking if you want to download a program from eBay. Click **Yes**.

5. A screen is displayed, showing the eBay Toolbar loading. When it is finished, you are asked to enter your User ID and password. Do so and click **Continue**.

6. Click **Yes** when asked if you want eBay to remember your password when you are signed in. This automatically signs you in so you don't have to sign in when you want to use the eBay Toolbar. A successful sign-in message is displayed, as shown in Figure 3-13.

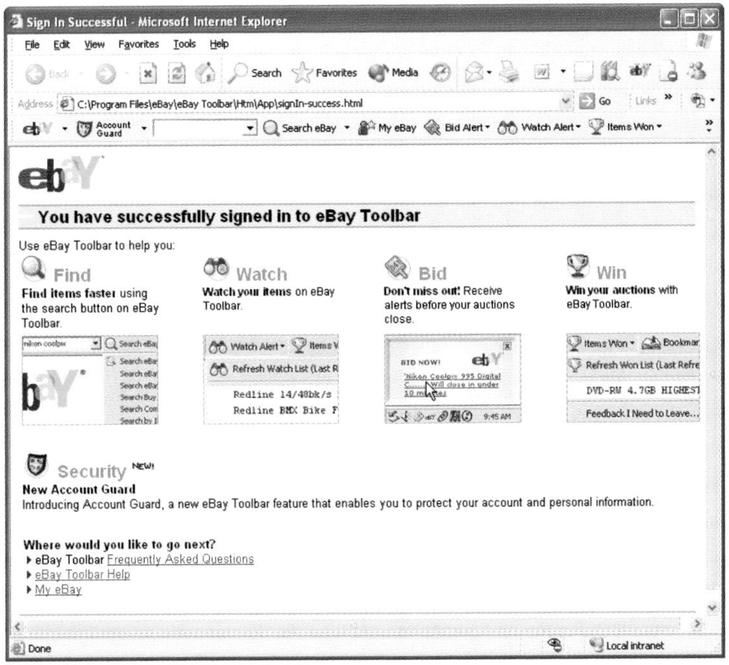

Figure 3-13: When you have successfully loaded the eBay Toolbar and signed in, you are given a quick overview of its features.

Use eBay's Toolbar for Bidding

When installed, eBay's Toolbar will be located on your Internet browser, as seen in Figure 3-14.

Receive Wireless eBay Alerts

You can receive eBay alerts on a wireless device, such as an Internet-enabled PDA or a cell phone. In other words, you never need to wonder what is happening with your eBay bids (or sale items). You can receive notices:

• When someone outbids you on an active listing

• When an auction ends and you learn whether you have won or not

• When someone leaves you feedback

• When a buyer pays for your item

• Of reminders for listing confirmations, bids made on your item, status reports for auctions you are participating in as buyer or seller, and items you are watching

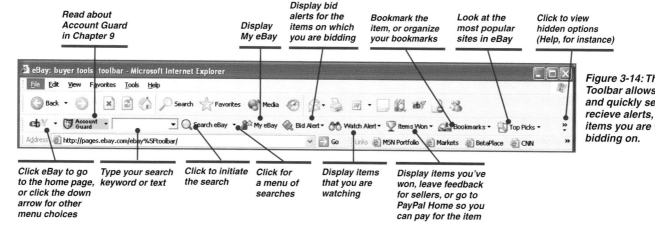

Figure 3-14: The eBay Toolbar allows you to easily and quickly search eBay, recieve alerts, and see the items you are watching and bidding on.

To instruct eBay to send messages to your wireless device:

1. Click **My eBay** from the menu bar or on the eBay Toolbar.

2. On the My eBay View sidebar, under My Account, click **eBay Preferences**.

3. Click **View/Change** under Notification Preferences.

My Account
- Personal Information
- eBay Preferences
- Feedback
- Seller Account
- PayPal Account

eBay Preferences

Notification preferences
Turn on/off the emails that you receive from eBay — view/change

Display "My Recently Viewed Items": Yes — change

4. Sign in again to eBay since you are changing personal information.

5. Under Notification Methods, click **Add Or Change Notification Services**. You will have to sign in again. (Throughout this process, you may have to sign in several times.) The Change Your Notification Preferences page is displayed, as shown in Figure 3-15.

NOTE

There are third-party software applications created by members of the eBay Developers Program that are specifically for wireless devices interacting with eBay. They provide even more capabilities. To find out more, click **Site Map** on the top links bar, click **Services | Buyer Tools**, and click the link for **eBay Anywhere Wireless**. Scroll to the bottom of the page to see eBay Developers.

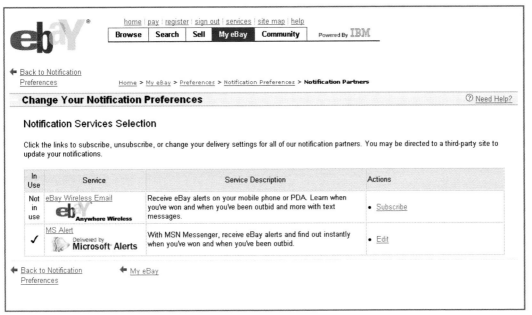

Figure 3-15: You can establish eBay notification settings that will send messages to your Internet-enabled wireless device.

USING MICROSOFT ALERTS

Microsoft Alerts deliver eBay messages to your desktop. If you have a Microsoft Passport, you can receive these messages automatically. If you don't, you can still receive eBay Alerts; you just need to create an eBay Alert Account first. With eBay Alerts, you will receive notices when you are outbid during an auction so that you have a chance to bid higher, and at the end of auctions so that you immediately know whether you've won or not. To sign up for eBay Alerts:

1. Follow the steps in "Receive eBay Wireless Alerts," and click **MS Alert** instead of the wireless link.

2. On the eBay Alerts page, click **Alerts Sign Up**.

3. If you have a Microsoft Passport, sign in and click **Finish Signing Up For Microsoft Alerts**. If not, you are first diverted to a Microsoft site, where you create an eBay Alert Account, and then you are returned to eBay.

4. When you have finished, your eBay notifications will be changed.

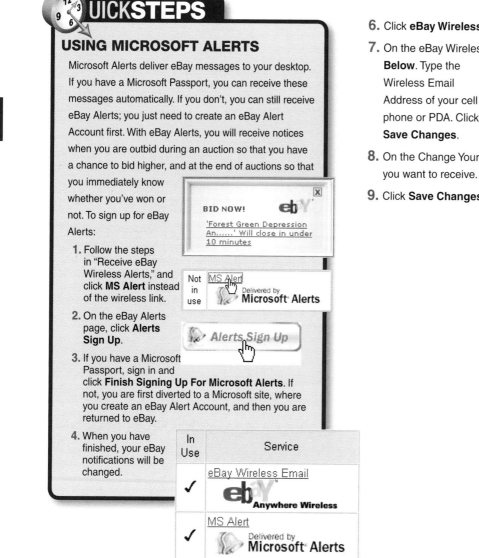

6. Click **eBay Wireless Email**.

7. On the eBay Wireless Email page, click **Send Wireless Email Alerts To The Address Below**. Type the Wireless Email Address of your cell phone or PDA. Click **Save Changes**.

8. On the Change Your Notification Preferences page, scroll down and select the notices you want to receive.

9. Click **Save Changes**.

Chapter 4

Making a Purchase

This chapter leads you through the process of actually bidding on an item in eBay, be it a fixed-price item, a Buy It Now item, a straightforward auction item, or a live-auction item. You will also see how to track bids, maintaining awareness of them in My eBay until you are ready to bid. You will see how to register for PayPal and to pay for your purchases in a variety of ways. Your transaction is not complete, however, until you receive your package, assess it, and give feedback to the seller. This chapter focuses on those things as well.

Bid on a Purchase

You have found the item you want to buy, have researched its condition and price, have asked the seller questions, and have satisfied yourself that you are now ready to bid. You may want to track the item for a while until the time is right to bid, and then you may bid by proxy, on a Dutch auction (multiple items auctioned), on Buy It Now auction items, or on a fixed-price purchase. First, however, you'll want to double-check that the item is what you want.

Review the Item Listing

When you are preparing to bid, you want to find the item description.

Figure 4-1: Carefully examine the listing description for as much information about the item as you can get.

Description

This auction is for a brand new, beautiful Emerald Mountain turquoise and sterling silver cuff! Handcrafted in Gallup, New Mexico, the genuine turquoise stones on this bracelet have a high polish and are without any chips or cracks. The inside circumference measures 5 inches with a gap of 1 inch for a total wrist measurement of 6 inches. The center stone measures 1 1/2 inches x 1 inch and the side stones measure just about 1 inch x 1/2 inch. This is truly a gorgeous bracelet. If you have any questions about this piece, feel free to send an e-mail. Happy Trails! :)

Click on a picture to enlarge

1. Using whatever means fits your search, find the item.

   - You can search through the categories, as explained in Chapter 1.
   - You can use the Search feature, as discussed in Chapter 2.
   - A friend can alert you to the item.
   - You can find it by watching similar items.

2. Look over the description, and verify that it is what you want. A sample listing description is shown in Figure 4-1.

3. Examine the price, the shipping and handling information, and the insurance information. Decide how you will pay for it. A sample of shipping and payment details is shown in Figure 4-2.

4. When you are ready to bid, click **Place Bid** or **Buy It Now**, depending on the listing.

Figure 4-2: Pay careful attention to the shipping and handling information, making sure it is clear and complete.

Shipping and payment details

Shipping and handling: US Postal Service Priority Mail: US $6.00
(within United States)

🏷 FREE shipping **for each additional item you buy!**
(Shipping Discounts are offered directly from the seller.)

Shipping insurance: Included in shipping and handling cost

Will ship to United States only.

Seller's payment instructions & return policy:
I will accept PayPal, money order or cashiers check. S&H $6.00 includes insurance as well. Sorry, no sales in the state of New Mexico. Thank you!

Payment methods accepted

💳 This seller, ~~elbong~~, **prefers PayPal.**

• **PayPal** (VISA 💳 💳 💳 ECHECK 🅑)
• Money order/Cashiers check
Learn about payment methods.

eBay recommended services
Increase the security in the eBay and PayPal community by becoming a verified buyer. Get Verified today. 🅥

4. When you are ready to bid, click **Place Bid** or **Buy It Now**, depending on the listing.

Starting bid: **US $31.00**

Place Bid >

≡ *Buy It Now* Price: **US $23.99** (immediate payment required)

Buy It Now >

Watch Interesting Items with My eBay and the eBay Toolbar

When you are hot on the trail of an interesting item, you might want to watch it for a while. You might also want to monitor items on which you have placed a bid as the auction end grows near. You can track activity using the eBay Toolbar or My eBay. To use the eBay Toolbar, you first need to set your eBay Toolbar preferences.

SET EBAY TOOLBAR PREFERENCES

1. On the eBay Toolbar, click the **eBay** down arrow to open the menu. (You have to be signed in.)

2. Click **eBay Toolbar Preferences**. The page shown in Figure 4-3 is displayed.

3. If not already selected, click the **General Preferences** tab.

   - Set the **Bid Alert** to receive a notification before the auction ends on an item on which you have placed a bid.

   - Select **Audio Notification** if you want sound indicators.

   - Select **Desktop Notification** to see a desktop message. Indicate whether the message will be dismissed by a right-click or will disappear after a period of time.

   - Set the **Watch Alert** time, and select the modes of notification, as you did with Bid Alert.

   - Select to see **eBay Official Time**, noted in military format, or **My Local Time**, noted in 12-hour blocks.

   - Set the **Search** options to search by title, title and description, or item number. Type the number of items to be included in the Recent Searches list. Select whether to Show Categories in the Search eBay menu.

   - Use **Bookmarks** to edit or organize your favorite sites as desired.

4. Click **Save Changes** to keep your settings.

Figure 4-3: The eBay Toolbar Preferences page is where you set the timing and mode of Bid Alerts, Watch Alerts, the time format, Search options, and Bookmark organization.

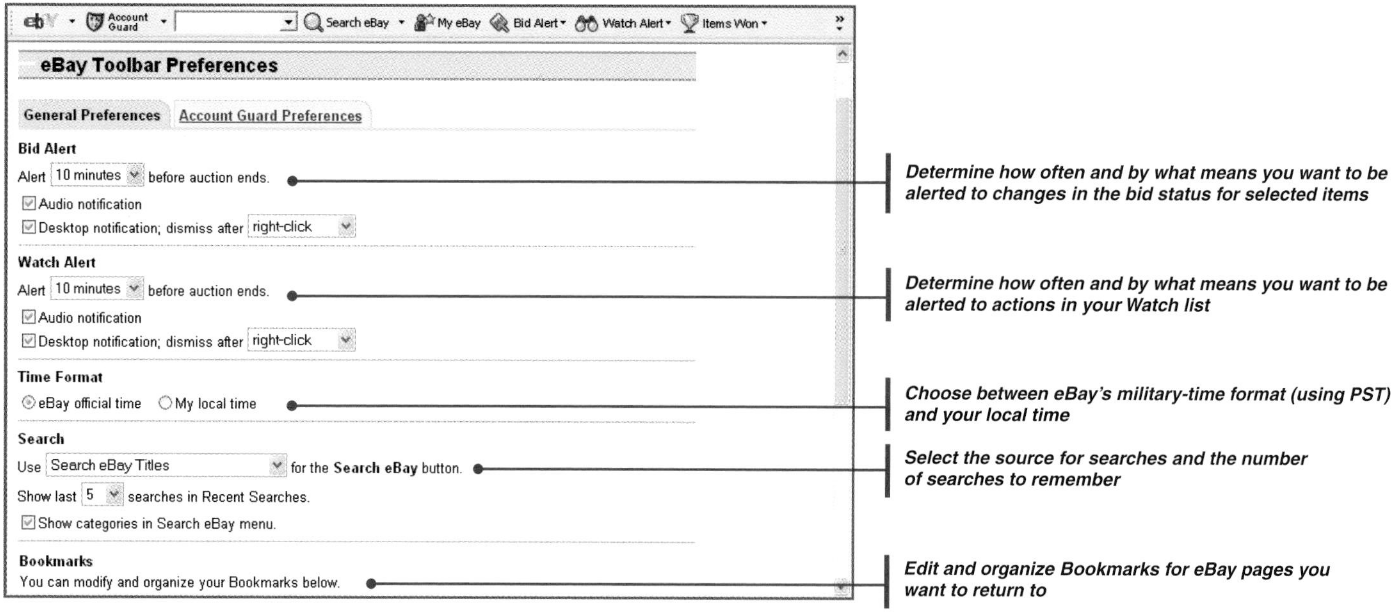

eBay ▼ | Account Guard ▼ | [   ] ▼ | 🔍 Search eBay ▼ | 🏠 My eBay 🔍 Bid Alert ▼ 🔭 Watch Alert ▼ 🏆 Items Won ▼ | »

eBay Toolbar Preferences

General Preferences   Account Guard Preferences

Bid Alert

Alert [10 minutes ▼] before auction ends. ●───────────────────────── *Determine how often and by what means you want to be alerted to changes in the bid status for selected items*
☑ Audio notification
☑ Desktop notification; dismiss after [right-click ▼]

Watch Alert

Alert [10 minutes ▼] before auction ends. ●───────────────────────── *Determine how often and by what means you want to be alerted to actions in your Watch list*
☑ Audio notification
☑ Desktop notification; dismiss after [right-click ▼]

Time Format

◉ eBay official time   ○ My local time ●───────────────────────── *Choose between eBay's military-time format (using PST) and your local time*

Search

Use [Search eBay Titles ▼] for the **Search eBay** button. ●──── *Select the source for searches and the number of searches to remember*
Show last [5 ▼] searches in Recent Searches.
☑ Show categories in Search eBay menu.

Bookmarks

You can modify and organize your Bookmarks below. ●───────── *Edit and organize Bookmarks for eBay pages you want to return to*

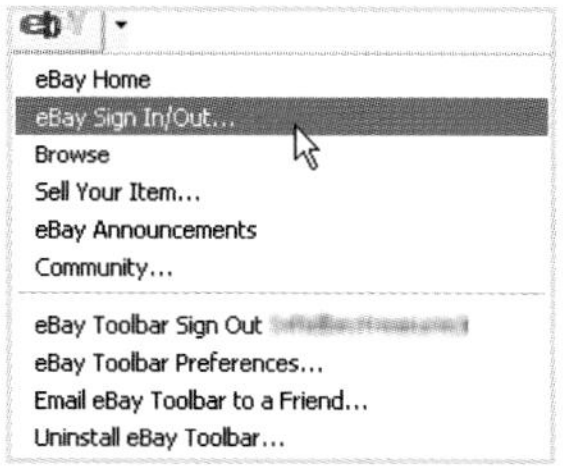

---

eBay ▼ | ▼
eBay Home
eBay Sign In/Out...
Browse
Sell Your Item...
eBay Announcements
Community...

eBay Toolbar Sign Out
eBay Toolbar Preferences...
Email eBay Toolbar to a Friend...
Uninstall eBay Toolbar...

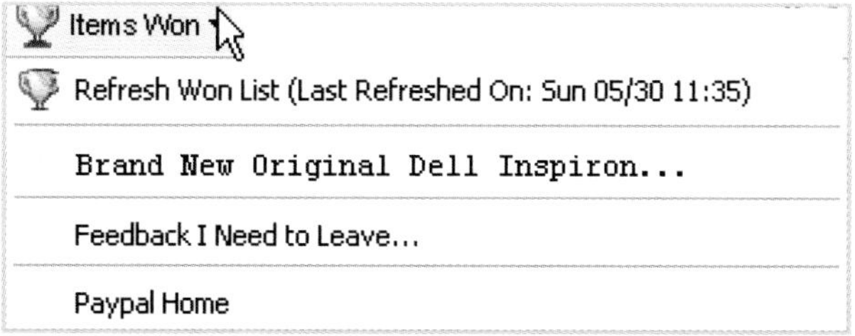

🏆 Items Won 👆

🏆 Refresh Won List (Last Refreshed On: Sun 05/30 11:35)

Brand New Original Dell Inspiron...

Feedback I Need to Leave...

Paypal Home

USE THE EBAY TOOLBAR TO TRACK ACTIVITY

1. Install the eBay Toolbar, as described in Chapter 3.

2. Sign in by clicking **eBay**, and then clicking **eBay Sign In/Out**. Enter your **User ID** and **password**.

3. Select the following to immediately see your eBay activity:

- Click **My eBay** to display your My eBay default page.   🏠 My eBay

- Click **Bid Alert** to see the list of bids you have made that are currently active.   🔍 Bid Alert ▼

- Click **Watch Alert** to see the list of items on your Watch list.   🔭 Watch Alert ▼

- Click **Items Won** to see what you've successfully bid on.

USE MY EBAY TO TRACK ACTIVITY

1. Click **My eBay** from the eBay Toolbar or from the menu bar.

2. Under the My eBay Views sidebar, click **All Buying** to see a page of all your buying activities: Watching, Bidding, Won, or Didn't Win. You can scroll down the page to see individual views. (See Chapter 1 for information on setting preferences and changing the display in My eBay.) You can also click **Watching**, **Bidding**, **Won**, or **Didn't Win** to see the individual views.

My eBay Views

My Summary

All Buying
- Watching (12)
- Bidding
- Won (4)
- Didn't Win (1)

Make a Proxy Bid

The basic bid type in eBay is a proxy bid. You tell eBay the maximum amount you are willing to bid for an item, and eBay applies the bid for you in increments against other bidders until your maximum is reached.

1. On the Item Description page, click **Place Bid**, as shown in Figure 4-4.

2. On the Place A Bid page, type the maximum bid amount, and click **Continue**. Note that eBay tells you what the current bid amount is at so you will know what your bid must be higher than in order to win.

3. Enter a bid amount.

4. A summary of your bid is displayed, as shown in Figure 4-5. If you accept it, click **Submit**. A confirmation message is displayed that you are now the high bidder.

Figure 4-4: On the Item Description page, click Place Bid to put your bid in for the item.

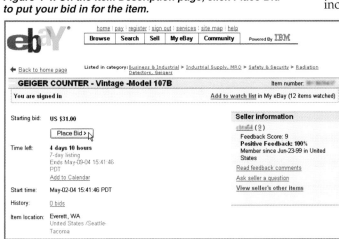

Place a Bid

GEIGER COUNTER - Vintage -Model 107B

Current bid: US $31.00

Your maximum bid: _____ (Enter US $31.00 or more)

Continue >

eBay automatically bids on your behalf up to your maximum bid. Learn about bidding.

GEIGER COUNTER - Vintage -Model 107B	Item number: 3913609417
You are signed in	This item is being tracked in My eBay (12 items watched)

✓ **You are the current high bidder**

Important: Another user may still outbid you, so check this item again before it ends. eBay will send you an email if you're outbid.

Current bid: US $31.00

How do you check the status of this item? Use My eBay, a convenient feature that keeps track of all your buying activities.

How does bidding work? eBay automatically bids on your behalf up to your maximum bid. If the item ends for less than your maximum, that's all you'll have to pay. See example.

Increase your PayPal sending limit. Get Verified today.

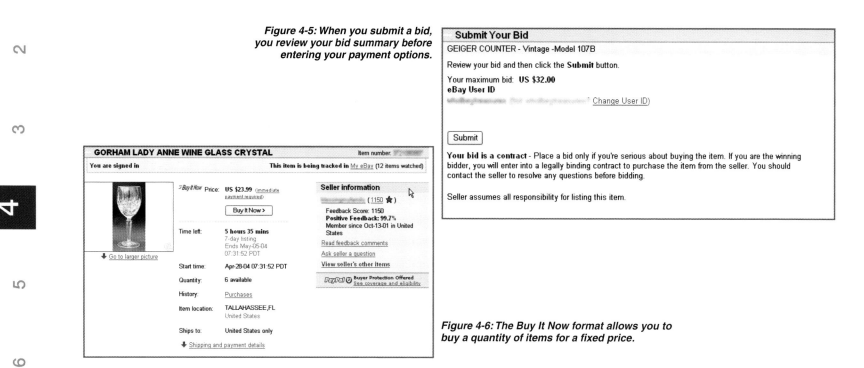

Figure 4-5: When you submit a bid, you review your bid summary before entering your payment options.

Submit Your Bid

GEIGER COUNTER - Vintage -Model 107B

Review your bid and then click the **Submit** button.

Your maximum bid: US $32.00
eBay User ID

~~........................~~ Change User ID)

Submit

Your bid is a contract - Place a bid only if you're serious about buying the item. If you are the winning bidder, you will enter into a legally binding contract to purchase the item from the seller. You should contact the seller to resolve any questions before bidding.

Seller assumes all responsibility for listing this item.

GORHAM LADY ANNE WINE GLASS CRYSTAL   Item number:

You are signed in   This item is being tracked in My eBay (12 items watched)

Buy It Now Price: **US $23.99** (immediate payment required)

Buy It Now >

Time left: **5 hours 35 mins**
             7-day listing
             Ends May-05-04
             07:31:52 PDT

Start time: Apr-28-04 07:31:52 PDT

Quantity: 6 available

History: Purchases

Item location: TALLAHASSEE,FL
             United States

Ships to: United States only

↓ Go to larger picture

↓ Shipping and payment details

Seller information

~~............~~ (1150 ★)

Feedback Score: 1150
Positive Feedback: 99.7%
Member since Oct-13-01 in United States

Read feedback comments

Ask seller a question

View seller's other items

PayPal **Buyer Protection Offered**
See coverage and eligibility

Figure 4-6: The Buy It Now format allows you to buy a quantity of items for a fixed price.

Bid on Multiple Items (Buy It Now)

The item shown in Figure 4-6 is an example of a Buy It Now auction for multiple items. After you have asked questions and received answers to all your questions, and you still want to bid:

1. Click the **Buy It Now** button on the Item Description page. The Buy It Now form is displayed.

2. Type the quantity of items you want, and press **Continue**.

3. A summary of your bid is displayed. If you are satisfied with the amount, click **Submit**.

4. Complete payment as directed.

ebY

Submit Your Purchase

GORHAM LADY ANNE WINE GLASS CRYSTAL

Review the price and then click the **Submit** button.

Buy It Now price: **US $23.99**
Quantity: x 6
Sub-Total: **US $143.94**
US Postal Service Priority Mail:US $0.00
Shipping insurance: US $1.30

eBay User ID

~~...............~~ ? Change User ID)

Password

••••••

Forgot your password?

Submit

ebY

Buy It Now

GORHAM LADY ANNE WINE GLASS CRYSTAL

Buy It Now price: **US $23.99**

Quantity: x 6

Continue >

Purchase this item now without bidding.
Learn about Buy It Now.

TIP

The Buy It Now price does not include the shipping and handling costs. If they are not spelled out in the payment details, you may need to contact the seller to find out the true cost of the item. If the item is a Pay Now item, requiring immediate payment, you will see the charges in the listing description.

NOTE

In order to purchase a Buy It Now item, you must have feedback equal to or greater than 0 or have a credit/debit card on file or be ID Verified.

Bid to "Buy It Now"

There are two types of Buy It Now listings: fixed-priced format and auction format.

BUY IT NOW (FIXED-PRICE FORMAT)

With the Buy It Now fixed-price format, an item is sold at a fixed price. The reserve price and the Buy It Now price are the same. There is no auction. This is similar to buying an item in a regular store or its online web site. The advantage is that you know how much you will pay and you know you can buy the item right now.

1. When you find the item you want in the listings, click it to look at the item description.

> ⚞ Brand New Original Dell Inspiron 4150/8200 Battery $59.00 ⊨*Buy It Now*   2d 12h 47m
>
> Optimize your selling success! Find out how to promote your items

2. Review the item description, investigate the seller, and do all the other tasks to assure yourself that this is a good deal.

3. Click the **Buy It Now** button.

Figure 4-7: Verify the Buy It Now price and shipping and handing information, and click Submit.

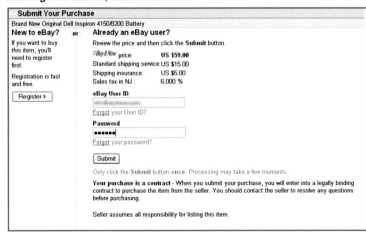

4. If the seller has more than one of this item to sell, you may be asked to enter a quantity. Do so and click **Continue**.

5. The Submit Your Purchase page is displayed, as shown in Figure 4-7. Verify the item purchase price and shipping and handling amounts. If you are satisfied, click **Submit**. (If you are already signed in, you will not see the Register page.)

Bob, the buyer, figures out what the shipping and handling charges will be before bidding. He doesn't want any last-minute surprises.

6. The Buy It Now Confirmation page is displayed. Click **Pay Now**.

7. The Review Your Purchase page is displayed. Verify that your shipping address is correct and that the payment details are what you expected.

8. Under Select A Payment Method, click the method that you want to use (your options may differ depending on the seller).

Select a payment method (seller accepts the following)

For fast, secure online payment with your credit card or bank account, use PayPal - it's **free**.

- ⊙ *PayPal*® (VISA 🃏 🃏 🃏 ECHECK eBay)
  PayPal Buyer Protection offered. See coverage and eligibility.
- ○ Money order/Cashiers check
- ○ Other online payment services

Continue >

- Click **PayPal** to use the default and recommended method. The transaction will flow smoothly, and you don't have to do much more.

- Click **Money Order/Cashier's Check** to send a cashier's check or money order. You will see an e-mail text box so that you can notify the seller of your intent. The seller will, in turn, e-mail his address to you.

- Click **Other Online Payment Services** to use a credit or debit card. The first time you do this, you will be encouraged to use PayPal if the seller has chosen that as his preferred method of receiving payments. If you reject this method, you will see an e-mail form that you can use to inform the seller how you intend to pay.

From:
To:
Subject: I will be sending payment of $79.00 shortly for item#

Dear ,

I will be sending payment of **$79.00** via **other online payment services** shortly.

You can enter an additional message to the seller of up to 500 characters, or leave this box blank

Item #	Item Title	Qty	Price	Subtotal
	Brand New Original Dell Inspiron 4150/8200 Battery	1	$59.00	$59.00

9. If you have chosen PayPal, click **Continue**.

10. The Payment Details page is displayed. Under PayPal Login, type your PayPal password, and click **Continue**.

11. The Confirm Your Payment page is displayed, summarizing the transaction. Click **Pay** to disburse payment to the seller.

NOTE

You cannot retract a Buy It Now purchase.

Confirm Your Payment   Secure Transaction 🔒

Review the payment details below and click **Pay** to complete your secure payment.

Item #	Item Title	Qty	Price	Subtotal
	Brand New Original Dell Inspiron 4150/8200 Battery	1	$59.00 USD	$59.00 USD

Shipping & Handling via Standard Delivery : $15.00 USD

Shipping Insurance (required): $5.00 USD

Total: $79.00 USD

12. The You Made A Payment page is displayed. Click **My eBay Account** or **My PayPal Account**.

BUY IT NOW (AUCTION FORMAT)

With the Buy It Now auction format, as shown in Figure 4-8, there is a beginning Buy It Now amount, and you can buy the item for that amount without going through an auction. Once a bid is placed that is less than the Buy It Now price, however, the option to buy it for that fixed amount goes away. The item is now sold at the highest bid price, which can be less than or more than the original Buy It Now price.

Figure 4-8: A Buy It Now listing displays a price at which you can buy the item without further bidding.

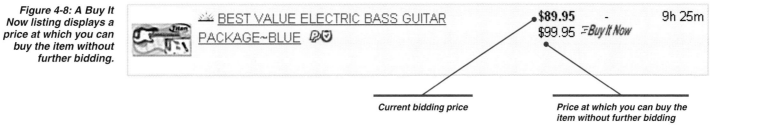

Current bidding price

Price at which you can buy the item without further bidding

4

1. Click the item link to display the listing. A page similar to that shown in Figure 4-9 is displayed.

Figure 4-9: You can choose between bidding or Buy It Now to purchase a Buy It Now auction-format item.

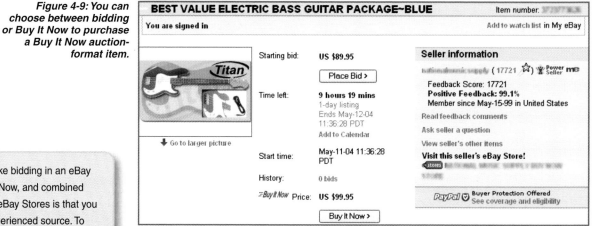

> **NOTE**
>
> Bidding in an eBay Store is just like bidding in an eBay site. Stores offer auctions, Buy It Now, and combined formats. The advantage of using eBay Stores is that you are dealing with a known and experienced source. To bring up the eBay Stores page, click **eBay Stores** in the Specialty Sites sidebar on the eBay home page.

2. Click **Buy It Now** to buy the item immediately, or click **Place Bid** to bid on the item.

3. The steps that follow will depend on your choice. Refer to "Buy It Now (Fixed-Price Format)" to see the steps to complete the purchase.

Participate in Live Auctions

Selected auction houses are making their live auctions available on eBay. These auctions are scheduled at particular times, and you can join in, either as a spectator or as a bidder on lots (in a live auction, a *lot* is the same as an item). To bid in a live auction:

FIND LIVE AUCTIONS

> **NOTE**
>
> To bid in a live auction, you must be a registered eBay user and signed up to participate in the auction. When you sign up, you have to enter your User ID, password, and some form of identification. It can be a credit card or an alternate ID from Equifax. (See "Sign Up to Bid in a Live Auction.") If you are already ID Verified, you do not have to do this last step. If you just want to view the auction, you do not have to be registered or signed up.

1. From the home page, scroll down the **Categories** sidebar until you see Live Auctions, close to the bottom.

Business Marketplace
Giving Works (Charity)
Live Auctions
Professional Services
Wholesale

Figure 4-10: With eBay live auctions, you can bid in real-time auctions conducted around the world.

TIP

If you need to register as an eBay user first, click **Registration** on the menu bar. If you want to bid, sign in to eBay. (See "Sign Up to Bid in a Live Auction.")

2. Click **Live Auctions** to see the eBay Live Auctions home page, as shown in Figure 4-10.

- Click **Start Here** to learn how to navigate live auctions.

- Under Categories, click the link to see auctions containing items in the category you want.

- Under Special Events or Upcoming Auctions, click a link to see catalogs for these types of auctions.

- On the Live Auction Catalogs page, click **View All Lots In This Catalog**. Browse through the lots until you find one you want to bid on or view.

View all lots in this catalog

TO VIEW A LIVE AUCTION

On the eBay Live Auction home page:

1. Click **View Live** on the live auction you want to view.

2. On the What You Need To View A Live Auction page, verify that your computer system is compatible with the minimum system configuration.

3. Click **View Live Now**. A window opens, displaying the auctioned item, as shown in Figure 4-11.

4. If you want to bid, sign in to the auction house by clicking **Sign Up To Bid Now**, as shown in Figure 4-11. (See "Sign Up to Bid in a Live Auction.")

Catalog:	Fine Brand Name Watches & Jewelry NO RESERVE
Auction Date:	May-12-04 15:30:00 PDT
Seller:	J Antique Jewelry

View Live Now

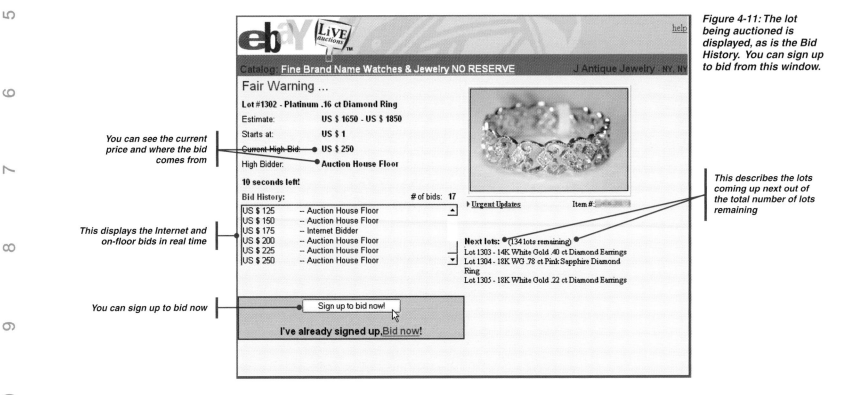

Figure 4-11: The lot being auctioned is displayed, as is the Bid History. You can sign up to bid from this window.

PLACE AN ABSENTEE BID

Before a live auction is opened, you can enter an absentee bid. eBay will gather all the absentee bids, and when the bidding starts, the highest absentee bid will be used like a proxy bid against the live bidders.

1. From the eBay Live Auctions home page, find the catalog containing the lot you want. Click the name of the catalog link.

You can place an absentee bid on lots contained within the catalogs

UPCOMING AUCTIONS   *all auctions...*

Robert White Estate & Senator Daniel Moynihan
Collectibles & Memorabilia
Hantman's Auctioneers & Appraisers
May-16-04 06:00:00 PDT

SIGN UP
FOR THIS AUCTION

MCKEE COINS, INC. SPRING COIN & COLLECTIBLES
Coins
McKee Coins, Inc.
May-16-04 07:00:00 PDT

SIGN UP
FOR THIS AUCTION

These are auctions not yet opened

During an auction, you may see a "Fair Warning" label as a lot approaches its closing. This reminds you that you must bid soon if you want the lot.

2. On the catalog pages, find the lots you want to bid on, and click the name of the lots. You may first have to go through categories or subcategories to find the items.

3. When you find an item, click its name. The description page is displayed, an example of which is shown in Figure 4-12.

1173: Japanese Imari Porcelain Charger   US $250.00-US $350.00   US $125.00   May-16 06:00

4. To place an absentee bid on the item, click **Place Absentee Bid**.

5. In the Place Absentee Bid area, type your maximum amount in the text box. It must be greater than the starting bid above it. Click **Continue**.

Place Absentee Bid
1173: Japanese Imari Porcelain Charger

Starting bid: US $125.00
Your maximum bid: [   ]
                     Continue >

eBay automatically bids on your behalf **up to** your maximum bid.
Learn about Absentee bidding.

6. Follow the instructions as eBay leads you through the process of completing the bid.

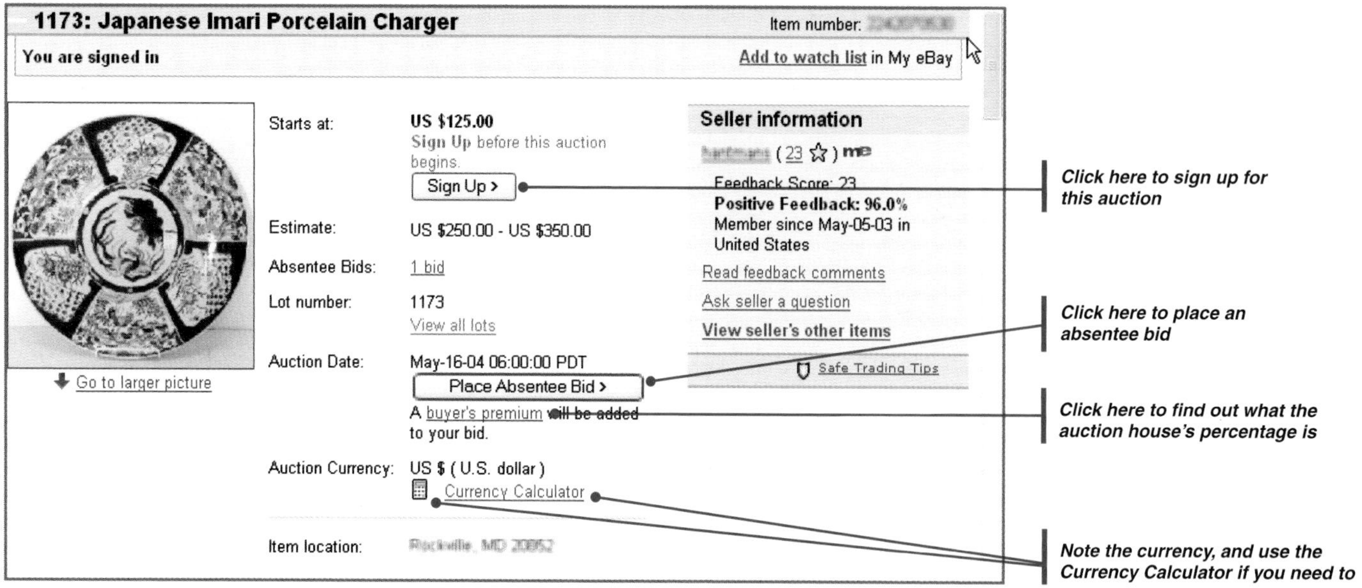

1173: Japanese Imari Porcelain Charger

Item number: ████████

You are signed in   Add to watch list in My eBay

Starts at: **US $125.00**
                  Sign Up before this auction
                  begins.
                  [Sign Up >]

Estimate: US $250.00 - US $350.00

Absentee Bids: 1 bid

Lot number: 1173
                  View all lots

Auction Date: May-16-04 06:00:00 PDT
                  [Place Absentee Bid >]
                  A buyer's premium will be added
                  to your bid.

Auction Currency: US $ (U.S. dollar)
                  📧 Currency Calculator

Item location: Rockville, MD 20852

Seller information

████████ (23 ☆) me

Feedback Score: 23
Positive Feedback: 96.0%
Member since May-05-03 in
United States

Read feedback comments

Ask seller a question

View seller's other items

🛡 Safe Trading Tips

Click here to sign up for this auction

Click here to place an absentee bid

Click here to find out what the auction house's percentage is

Note the currency, and use the Currency Calculator if you need to

Figure 4-12: You can sign up for a live auction on the lot description form or cast an absentee bid.

Figure 4-13: When you successfully sign in to a live auction, you will see a Sign Up Confirmation page.

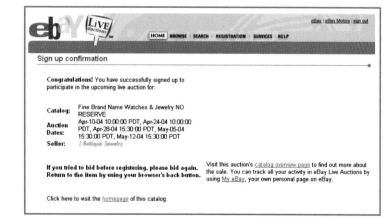

SIGN UP TO BID IN A LIVE AUCTION

1. From the eBay Live Auctions home page, click **Bid Now**, or from the Live View window, click **Sign Up To Bid Now**.

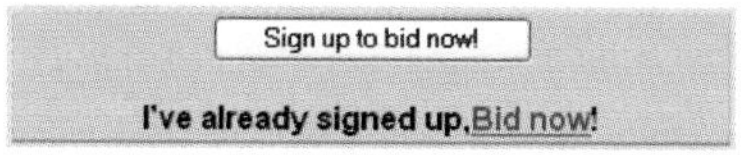

[Sign up to bid now!]
I've already signed up, Bid now!

2. You are asked to enter your password. Click **Sign In** again. (If you just click **Bid Now**, you will see the Sign In To Bid Now page first.)

3. You must review the seller's terms and conditions. Note the premium to be paid and any other charges. Select **I Have Read The Terms And Conditions Of Sale Above And Accept Them**. Click **Continue**.

4. On the Review Of The Terms And Conditions page, click **I Have Read The User Agreement And Accept All Of Its Terms And Conditions**. Click **Submit**. (At this point, you may encounter a Seller Authorization Required page, which some sellers require. In this case, you need to contact the seller for permission to participate in this auction.)

5. The Sign Up Confirmation page is displayed, as shown in Figure 4-13. Return to the current auction either by clicking **Back** on your browser or by returning to the eBay Live Auctions home page and clicking **Bid Now**.

You may see that you are the high bidder with your bid placed in the Bid History. If not, it will be because someone else bid first and faster with an equal or larger bid.

QUICK**FACTS**

LEARNING ABOUT LIVE AUCTIONS

Bidding in a live auction involves learning some new terminology and techniques. You are no longer bidding against other online bidders over a period of days, but are bidding online on a real-time auction, conducted on the floor of an actual auction house.

- A *catalog* listing the items is made available. Catalogs often follow a theme of the items contained—such as Asian Art, Jewelry and Timepieces, Memorabilia, or Wine—so that you can limit yourself to those live auctions dealing with the items you want.

- You *browse* the catalog looking for interesting items, called *lots*. A lot may consist of one or more items that are sold together in a group. Bids are for the whole lot.

Continued...

BID IN A LIVE AUCTION

1. After you have signed in to participate in a live auction, click the **Bid Now** button. The current bid window opens, an example of which is shown in Figure 4-14. You can see that the next bid amount is already calculated.

2. If the amount of the bid is acceptable, click the **Bid Now** *currency and price* to place a bid against other Internet bidders as well as those on the auction house floor. The bid is immediately placed.

3. When you are finished with the live auction, click **eBay** on the top links bar to return to the regular eBay site.

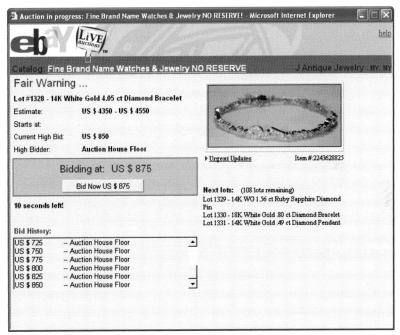

Figure 4-14: The Bid Now US $ area tells you how much the next bid will be.

Retract a Bid

Under some conditions you can retract a bid. There are both timing conditions and reasons why the bid is being retracted that need to be considered. See the QuickFacts "Retracting a Bid." To retract a bid:

1. In the View Item page, click the **History bid *n*** link, and scroll down to Bidders: You Can Retract Your Bid Under Certain Circumstances Only.

> **Bidders:** You can retract your bid under certain circumstances only.
> **Sellers:** See how to cancel bids if you need to.

2. Click **Retract Your Bid**.

3. Enter your eBay User ID and password, and click **Sign In**. The Bid Retractions page is displayed. It explains the reasons and seriousness of retracting a bid.

4. Scroll down the Bid Retraction page, and type the **Item Number Of Auction In Question**.

5. Choose **Your Explanation Of The Retraction** from the menu.

> Your explanation of the retraction:
> Choose one
> Choose one
> Entered wrong bid amount
> Seller changed the description of the item
> Cannot contact the seller
> Retract bid

6. Click **Retract Bid**.

Talk to the Seller

After you have purchased an item, you may or may not need to talk to the seller. The seller will know you are the winner and will have your address information. If you don't receive your items or you have a question about the delivery, however, you may need to contact the seller.

> **Seller information**
> *ChrcCcrrc* (85 ★)
> Feedback Score: 85
> **Positive Feedback: 100%**
> Member since Jul-26-03 in United States
> Read feedback comments
> Ask seller a question
> View seller's other items
> **PayPal** ✓ **Buyer Protection Offered** See coverage and eligibility

1. In the Seller Information box in the View Item page, click **Ask Seller A Question**. You can also click the seller's **User ID** link or click **Contact Member** in the Member Profile.

QUICKFACTS

RETRACTING A BID

Retracting a bid is considered an exception. It is generally not permitted.

CONSEQUENCES OF RETRACTING A BID

Retracting bids is a serious matter, and eBay may investigate in some cases where you have several retractions within the last six months, where bids are continuously retracted during the last 24 hours (could be *bid shilling*, which is trying to raise the bid amount), or where a seller has complained. If you are found guilty of misusing the retraction feature, you can be suspended and the number of bid retractions over the past six months will be displayed with your feedback.

TIMING CONSIDERATIONS

- You can retract a bid if there are more than 12 hours until the auction ends. In this case, all bids for the listing are retracted.

- You cannot retract a bid if there are fewer than 12 hours left in the auction unless the seller agrees (see Chapter 8 for more information).

- Within the last 12 hours until the auction ends and within one hour of placing your bid, you can retract a bid, and only that bid will be retracted. If you have other bids in the auction during those last 12 hours, they will remain.

REASONING CONSIDERATIONS

You can cancel a bid for these reasons:

- The description of the listing has changed so that it no longer is what you want. It must be a substantial change.

- You have entered an incorrect bid amount. In this case, you must first retract the bid, giving this as a reason, and then enter the correct bid amount at once.

- You have a question about the item, but you cannot contact the seller by e-mail or telephone. This is not about the seller not answering the e-mail or phone, but that the e-mail is returned as undeliverable or the phone number is incorrect.

2. The Ask The Seller A Question text box is displayed. Type your question and click **Send Message**.

Pay for Your Purchase

When you win a bid, you are sent a congratulatory e-mail/invoice confirming what you have purchased, as shown in Figure 4-15. You must first determine how you will pay for the item. How you pay depends upon what the seller allows. He or she may accept cashier's or personal checks, credit cards, money orders, or PayPal. You will have to arrange your payment according to what he or she accepts and how you want to pay. eBay may help facilitate payment, or you may handle it directly with the seller.

Figure 4-15: A congratulatory e-mail not only reminds you to pay for your new purchase, but also provides you with the options for paying it.

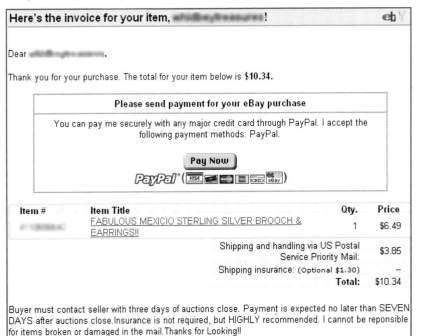

Pay with PayPal

eBay uses PayPal as an intermediary between the buyer and the seller. You provide your bank account or credit card information to PayPal within eBay, and it pays for your purchases per your directions and deposits any refunds into your account. The seller will never know any of your banking or credit account information. Using PayPal to pay for your purchases is the recommended way to go: the seller is paid instantaneously, and you will get your item sooner. Also, PayPal offers a Buyer Protection feature that insures up to $500 of your eBay purchases.

1. On the e-mail, click **Pay Now** to link to the payment procedure.

    –Or–

    On the View Item page, click **Pay Now**, as shown in Figure 4-16.

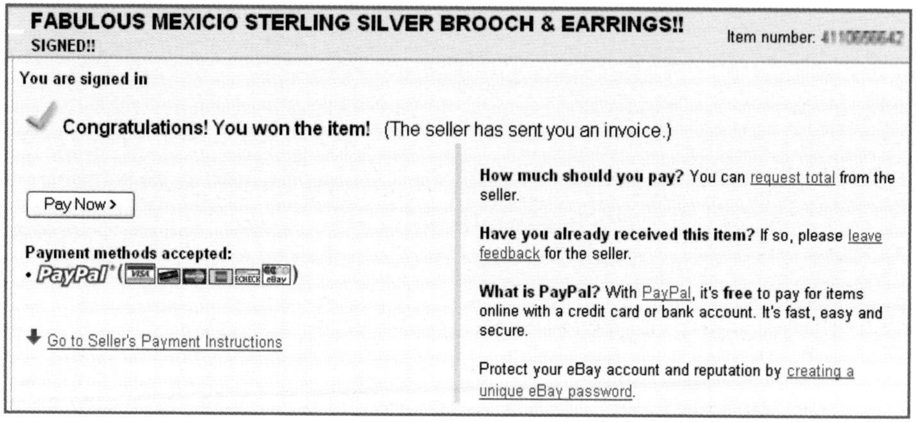

NOTE

The seller may accept some payments that are not automatically displayed on the eBay-generated form, so be sure to look at the seller's payment description to see if there are payment methods not automatically shown.

TIP

See Chapter 3 for additional information on how you can find information about sellers or contact them.

NOTE

There are some limitations to the PayPal Buyer Protection program. For instance, the program only covers tangible goods paid for using PayPal within 30 days of the auction close; it covers items not received or not the same as the description advertised; and you can only file two claims per year.

FABULOUS MEXICIO STERLING SILVER BROOCH & EARRINGS!!
SIGNED!!

Item number: 411099642

You are signed in

✓ **Congratulations! You won the item!** (The seller has sent you an invoice.)

Pay Now >

Payment methods accepted:
• PayPal° (VISA))

⬇ Go to Seller's Payment Instructions

How much should you pay? You can request total from the seller.

Have you already received this item? If so, please leave feedback for the seller.

What is PayPal? With PayPal, it's **free** to pay for items online with a credit card or bank account. It's fast, easy and secure.

Protect your eBay account and reputation by creating a unique eBay password.

Figure 4-16: When you win a bid, the View Item page recognizes you as the winner and displays the pertinent information. Click Pay Now to begin payment proceedings.

1
2
3
4
5
6
7
8
9
10

If you do not have adequate information about shipping and handling costs, click **Request Total From The Seller** on the View Item page.

2. The Review Your Purchase page is displayed, confirming where the item should be sent and how much you must pay.

   ● First you will see where item is to be shipped. If this is incorrect, click **Change Shipping Address**.

   ● Under Review Payment Details, you will see how your seller accepts payment. Enter the shipping and handling charges if they are not automatically filled in. (Click **Request Total From Seller** if the View Item page does not provide this information.)

   ● You may be given the option of adding insurance (it may be required). To do so, in the Seller Discounts Or Charges column, click **Add** and then click **Recalculate** to refigure the total amount you owe.

   ● If you are using an eBay gift certificate or coupon, select the relevant check box.

   ● Beneath Select A Payment Method, click the mode of payment offered by the seller that you want to use. PayPal is usually the default mode of payment.

Shipping and payment details

Shipping and handling: Other (see description): US $6.95
(within United States)

Shipping insurance: US $1.30 (Optional)

Will ship worldwide.

Seller's payment instructions & return policy:
I ACCEPT PAYPAL, CHECKS AND MONEY ORDERS .. PLEASE EMAIL ME YOUR METHOD OF
PAYMENT AND YOUR SHIPPING ADDRESS UPON WINNING .. THANK YOU,

Payment methods accepted

This seller, _____ prefers PayPal.

● PayPal (VISA ▭▭▭▭)
● Personal check
● Money order/Cashiers check
● See item description for payment methods accepted
Learn about payment methods.

eBay recommended services
Increase the security in the eBay and PayPal community by becoming a verified buyer. Get Verified today.

---

3. Click **Continue** when you are satisfied.

4. At this point, the Payment Details page should reflect your understanding of what the payment will be. If you have a PayPal account, type your PayPal password in the PayPal Login area, and click **Continue**.

Figure 4-17: When you have successfully paid for your purchase(s) through PayPal, you will see a confirmation notice verifying that you have paid and the amount.

5. The Confirm Your Payment page is displayed, as shown in Figure 4-17. Verify that the information is accurate.

6. You can type a short note to the seller if you choose, and then click **Pay**. The You Made A Payment page is displayed, confirming that you have successfully paid the seller.

PayPal
an eBay company

Confirm Your Payment   Secure Transaction 🔒

Review the payment details below and click **Pay** to complete your secure payment.

Item #	Item Title	Qty	Price	Subtotal
#_____	FABULOUS MEXICIO STERLING SILVER BROOCH & EARRINGS!!	1	$6.49 USD	$6.49 USD

Shipping & Handling via USPS Priority Mail :	$3.85 USD
Shipping Insurance (optional):	--
Total:	$10.34 USD

Source of Funds
   PayPal Balance: $10.34 USD

Message to Seller (Optional)

Looking forward to seeing the brooch and
earrings.

[Pay] [Cancel]

7. Click **My eBay Account** to return to your bidding information, or click **My PayPal Account** to see details of your account information.

[My eBay Account]   [My PayPal Account]

TIP

Figure 4-17 shows that the source of funds is a PayPal Balance. PayPal acts as a balancing mechanism: when you get a refund, the excess dollars will be held in your PayPal account to pay for future purchases. The source of funds could also be from a credit card.

NOTE

Premier and Business Accounts are useful for larger sellers and sellers accepting recurring payments, such as subscription services. They allow you to accept unlimited credit card payments. These accounts have special privileges, such as getting immediate access to PayPal funds from ATMs or PayPal credit cards and making payments to several people at once. There is a fee for receiving funds into the account. Personal Accounts are for individuals. They are free and include standard benefits for sending and receiving money, but they cannot accept credit card payments and do not have the special benefits that Premier and Business Accounts have.

TIP

You may be able to enter your ZIP code into a Calculate Shipping tool so that you will know how much to pay for shipping.

Sign Up for PayPal

On the Payment Details page, when you are reviewing the amount you owe on the item, you can sign up for PayPal.

1. On the Payment Details page, click **If You Do Not Currently Have A PayPal Account, Click Here**.

   –Or–

   Go down below My Account in the eBay Views, and click **PayPal Account**. Click the link to set up an account. The Sign Up For A PayPal Account page is displayed.

2. Choose whether you want a Personal Account or a Business Account, and click the **down arrow** to choose a country. Click **Continue**.

3. In the Account Sign Up, Personal Account page:

   - Type your personal name and address information.

   - Scroll down and fill in your e-mail address and password.

   - In the Security Questions area, answer the questions that enable you to prove your identity.

   Security Questions - If you forget your password, we will use the answers you provide to the security questions to verify your identity. Please select 2 different questions.

   Security Question 1: —Choose a Question—
   —Choose a Question—
   Answer 1: Mother's maiden name
   Last 4 digits of driver's license numbe
   Security Question 2: Last 4 digits of social security number
   Answer 2: City of birth

   - To have this account be a Premier Account, click **Yes**. This is useful for sellers. See Chapter 5 for more information.

   - Scroll down more and you will see a User Agreement and Privacy Policy, which you must agree to before you can continue. Click **Yes** to the question, Do You Agree To The User Agreement And Privacy Policy, And Terms Incorporated Therein? Click **Yes** to the second question, Do You Understand Your Rights With Regard To The Arbitration Of Claims As Outlined In The Legal Disputes Section Of The User Agreement?

   - A final security measure requires that you type the characters in the yellow checked box.

Figure 4-18: You are given clear instructions at the end of your PayPal sign-in for how to complete your registration.

Account Sign Up
Personal Account

✓ Enter Your Information
2 Confirm Your Email Address

Thanks, you're almost done!
To complete your registration, please confirm your email address.

How to Confirm Your Email Address

✉ **Step 1: Go to Your Email**
We sent you an email to:
carolebmatthews@yahoo.com

Step 2: Click On The Link
Click on the link in the email. You will be returned to PayPal. Click here if a link does not appear in the email.

Step 3: Enter Your Password
You will be asked to enter your password. You will need your password every time you use PayPal. If you need to, please write it down and keep it somewhere safe.

If you want to confirm your email address at a later time, click **Continue**.

Continue

4. Click **Sign In**. The Account Sign Up page is displayed, showing you how to confirm your e-mail address, as shown in Figure 4-18.

5. Go to your e-mail account, and in the new e-mail that eBay has just sent you, click **Click Here To Activate Your Account**.

6. Type your password and click **Confirm**.

7. You can at this point choose to link a bank account to eBay. To do this, click **Continue**. (As a buyer, this is unimportant unless you want to pay for your items by directly deducting payments from your checking account. You would be a *Verified* eBay user, which is another way of assuring others on eBay that you are a valid person with whom to do business.) Otherwise, click **Skip**.

Enter Password   Secure Transaction 🔒
Please enter your PayPal password to confirm your email address.

Password: ●●●●●●●●   Forget your password?
NEW! For your security

Confirm

8. The U.S. Personal Account Overview page is displayed. You have officially signed up with PayPal.

9. Click **Log Out** to leave the PayPal arena.

Give Feedback

The final part of the transaction is to give feedback. Giving and receiving feedback is part of the currency you exchange with the seller. In theory, when you pay, the seller leaves feedback for you, and when you receive the item, you give feedback to the seller. In practice, however, it is a bit different. Typically, the seller waits to give feedback until he or she is paid or until he or she receives your feedback (at which point he or she knows you accept the item). To provide feedback:

Sally, the seller, gives positive feedback to buyers who are quick to pay.

1. In My eBay, click **All Buying** on the My eBay Views sidebar.

2. Click **Won**. (From the eBay Toolbar, click **Items Won**.) A page similar to that shown in Figure 4-19 is displayed.

3. Click the **Leave Feedback** link. The Feedback Forum page is displayed.

USING OTHER PAYMENT MEANS

PAY BY CHECK OR MONEY ORDER

First, verify that the seller accepts payments by check or money order. (In this case, you pay the seller directly, not eBay.) If the seller accepts such payments, you can select this option when paying, and you will be given an e-mail form to notify the seller that you intend to pay by check and when. Be aware that your purchase probably will not be mailed to you until your check has been received, deposited, and cleared. Include a copy of the invoice with your payment to the seller to ensure that he or she will credit the appropriate item as being paid. Write the item number on the check.

PAY BY CREDIT CARD

Using a credit card, either through eBay's PayPal or through the seller's charge program, is fairly safe, as most credit cards, such as Visa or MasterCard, have programs for protecting buyers from fraudulent use.

USE ESCROW

When you are buying a higher-priced item, say over $500, you can pay for it using www.escrow.com, an escrow service. In this case, the escrow service receives the buyer's money, holding on to it until the buyer receives the item. If everything is acceptable with the buyer, he or she approves distributing the money to the seller. There is a problem, however, with fraudulent escrow services, which is why eBay asks that you use their approved escrow service only, www.escrow.com.

4. Click the **Rating** that you want to give this seller.

5. Type a **Comment** that tells how you feel about the transaction.

6. Click **Leave Feedback**.

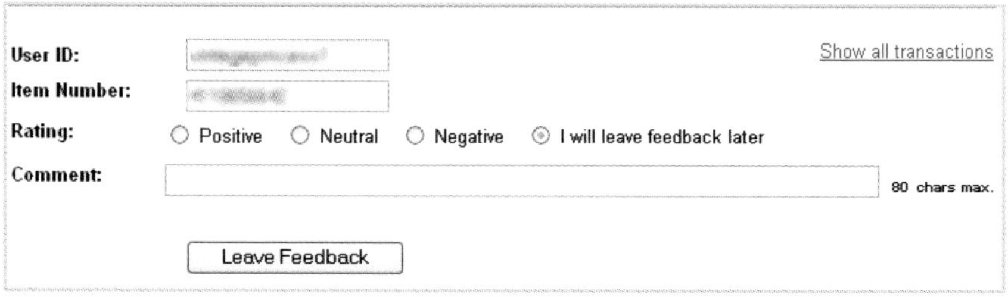

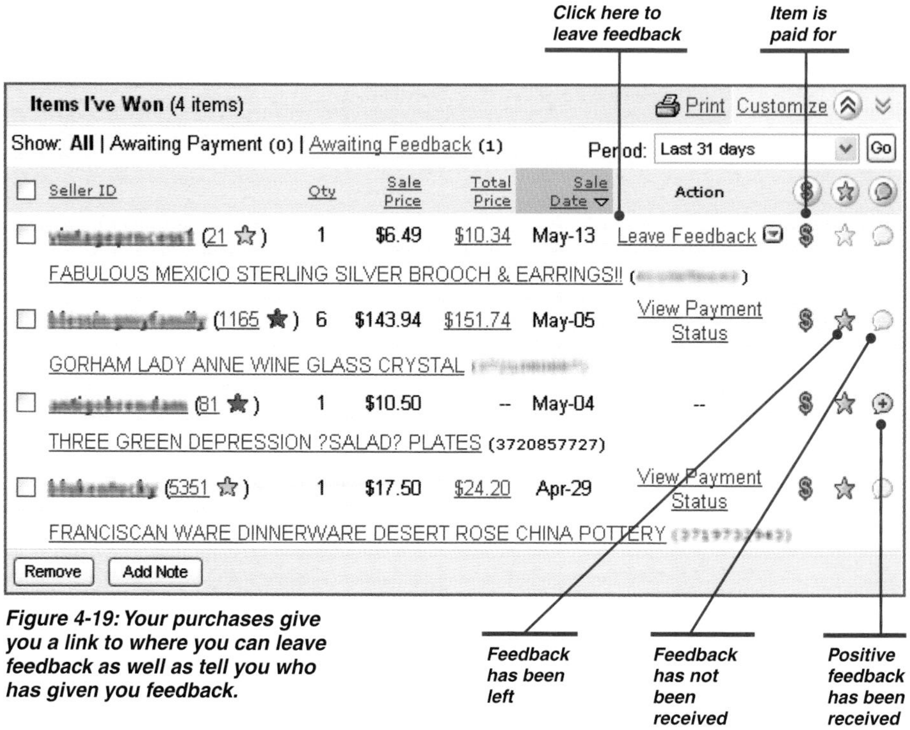

Figure 4-19: Your purchases give you a link to where you can leave feedback as well as tell you who has given you feedback.

Chapter 5
Listing an Item to Sell

In this chapter you will learn how easy it is to perform a sale on eBay. The eBay selling (or *Sell Your Item*) form is divided into five sections that walk you through the process, from choosing a category where your item will be cataloged to creating a title and a description of the item to adding pictures, providing payment and shipping details, and ending with an opportunity to review your finished listing and make any last-minute changes.

The sections in this chapter walk you through the eBay selling form and dissect the actions involved. Details on selling strategies and selling on eBay are covered throughout this chapter, as well as in Chapters 6, 7, and 8. Advanced techniques used to produce more robust listings are described in Chapter 6, and selling in volume or as a business on eBay is covered in Chapter 10.

Prepare to Sell

In order to sell on eBay, you need a seller's account, items to sell, basic computer and camera equipment, services (such as DSL), and an understanding of what you're getting yourself into. This section will get you going.

Get a Seller's Account

In addition to *registering* on eBay (see Chapter 1), to sell on eBay, you have to obtain a separate seller's account that:

- Verifies your registration information
- Identifies who you are through one of your financial accounts
- Determines how you will pay eBay for the various selling fees you will incur

Before you start the online process, gather the credit or debit card and checking account numbers you want to associate with your seller's account. (If you don't have or don't want to use these accounts with eBay, you can use ID Verify. See Chapter 1 for more information on ID Verify.)

1. Click **Sell** on the menu bar at the top of any eBay page.

2. On the Sell Your Item - Sign In page, under New To Selling?, click **Seller's Account**.

3. On the Create A Seller's Account page, type your eBay **User ID** and **password**. Click **Secure Sign In**. (An AutoComplete dialog box might appear that offers to remember the password associated with your User ID so you don't have to re-enter it in the future. A handy feature, although if you choose **Yes**, you are degrading your account security if other persons use your computer.)

> **Already an eBay user?**
>
> **New to selling?** Make sure you do the following:
> - Learn how to sell
> - Create a seller's account
> - Review the seller's checklist
> - Learn about selling fees
>
> **Enter your User ID and password to start selling.**

> **TIP**
>
> Seller Central is your best one-stop location in eBay for links to all things pertaining to selling. Click **Site Map** on the links bar at the top of any eBay page, and, under Sell, click **Seller Central**.

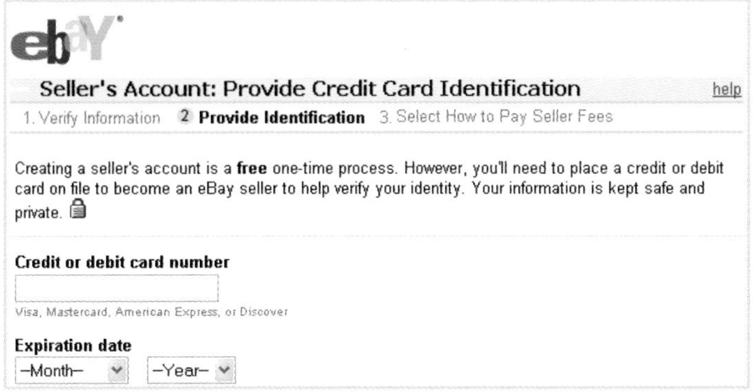

Seller's Account: Provide Credit Card Identification

1. Verify Information 2 **Provide Identification** 3. Select How to Pay Seller Fees *help*

Creating a seller's account is a **free** one-time process. However, you'll need to place a credit or debit card on file to become an eBay seller to help verify your identity. Your information is kept safe and private.

Credit or debit card number

Visa, Mastercard, American Express, or Discover

Expiration date
−Month− −Year−

4. On the Seller's Account: Verify Information page, review your registration information, make any updates, and click **Continue**. (eBay is constantly upgrading its security, and you might need to add information that wasn't required when you registered.)

5. On the Provide Identification page, provide credit or debit card information to ascertain your identity. Click **Continue**.

6. On the second part of the Provide Identification page, provide checking account information. Click **Continue**.

7. On the Select How To Pay Seller Fees page, choose whether you want your selling fees deducted from the checking account or credit/debit card you entered earlier, as shown in Figure 5-1. Click **Continue** to complete the seller account setup.

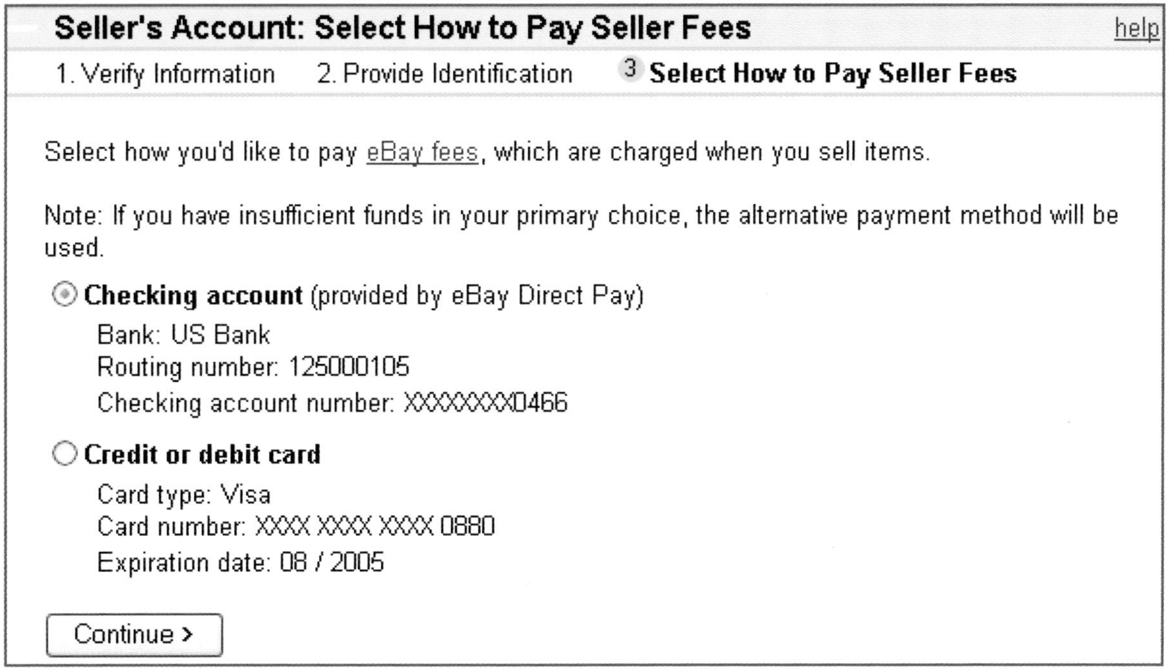

Seller's Account: Select How to Pay Seller Fees *help*

1. Verify Information   2. Provide Identification   3 **Select How to Pay Seller Fees**

Select how you'd like to pay eBay fees, which are charged when you sell items.

Note: If you have insufficient funds in your primary choice, the alternative payment method will be used.

⦿ **Checking account** (provided by eBay Direct Pay)
  Bank: US Bank
  Routing number: 125000105
  Checking account number: XXXXXXXX0466

○ **Credit or debit card**
  Card type: Visa
  Card number: XXXX XXXX XXXX 0880
  Expiration date: 08 / 2005

[Continue >]

Figure 5-1: Choose whether to pay your selling fees by direct withdrawal from your checking account or by charging your credit or debit card.

QUICKSTEPS

SELLING ON THE FAST TRACK

Selling on eBay can be as simple or as complex as you want to make it. If you want to just get going and place an item up for bid, you can do that with a minimum of effort and time. The following information will get you on your way:

1. **Set up your desktop** with the equipment and services you'll need to connect and use eBay. Ideally, have a newer computer, broadband Internet connection, color printer, and picture-capturing devices (digital camera and scanner).

2. **Obtain a seller's account** (necessary step that adds identity verification to your eBay registration and provides a means to pay eBay selling fees).

3. **Review the rules** (know what items are taboo, and read the eBay User Agreement).

4. **Research selling formats** (understand the differences between auction-style and fixed-price selling).

5. **Prepare a title and description** (do research on similar items, and write your description offline with a word processor or other program).

6. **Arrange for a picture-hosting site** (use your own web site, a third-party site, or eBay's Picture Services).

7. **Acquire a picture of your item** (use a digital camera, scanner, or drawing program; and then save the photo as a JPG, GIF, or PNG file).

8. **Obtain accounts for payment methods you will accept** (set up PayPal).

TIP

When looking for items to sell, you can quickly become overwhelmed with the quantity of items and available sources to check out. Approaching each venue with the mindset, "There's a deal here somewhere, I just need to find it," will help keep you motivated to carry on!

Find Items to Sell

Unless you are connected to retail channels, you will need to acquire items to sell at the best below-market price you can get.

- **Basements, attics, and closets** provide the most readily available and lowest-cost items (you already own them). Include items of friends and relatives that can be had for nothing or next to it.

- **Thrift stores** contain hidden treasures that can be ferreted out with a sharp, experienced pricing eye and persistent scouring. Go (early) on promotion days to obtain even deeper discounts.

- **Garage sales and estate sales** are typically announced in your local paper and on your nearest telephone pole. Get up early, map out your route, and be done before brunch.

- **Live auctions** provide great experience in the world of bidding and overall auction psychology. Check out your Sunday paper for upcoming events. Most cost very little, if anything, to attend and provide invaluable pricing data, networking, and generally entertaining auctioneers. (eBay lets you get in on the action of live auctions from its Live Auctions site. See Chapter 4 for information on bidding in live auctions and Chapter 10 to learn how to sell items on them.)

- **Tickets** are a hot seller on eBay (over $250 million in tickets alone were sold in 2003). Sell in the Tickets category, and use the Item Specifics feature to provide key information for buyers (both categories and the Item Specifics feature are described in this chapter).

Calculate Insertion Fees

eBay charges a fee for listing an item for sale, called an insertion fee. The amount you are charged depends on the type of listing (or auction). See Chapter 1 for information on the different auction types.

(A number of calculators that help you determine selling fees are available from third parties. Nucite (www.nucite.com/calculators), a maker of several auction selling tools, offers several calculators for free online use.)

TABLE 5-1: INSERTION FEES DETERMINED

PRICING OPTIONS	INSERTION FEE BASED ON
Standard (single-quantity item)	Starting price of item
Multiple item (Dutch)	Starting price or fixed price times the number of items (maximum insertion fee is $4.80)
Reserve	Reserve price

TABLE 5-2: COMMON LISTINGS INSERTION FEES

ITEM PRICE	INSERTION FEE
$.01 - $.99	$.30
$1.00 - $9.99	$.35
$10.00 - $24.99	$.60
$25.00 - $49.99	$1.20
$50.00 - $199.99	$2.40
$200.00 - $499.99	$3.60
Greater than or equal to $500.00	$4.80

VIEW INSERTION FEES FOR COMMON AUCTIONS

The insertion fee eBay charges for common listings depends on how you initially price the item in the selling form, as shown in Table 5-1.

Table 5-2 displays the insertion fee amount for common listings.

VIEW INSERTION FEES FOR OTHER LISTING TYPES

Table 5-3 lists specialty listings and insertion fees.

TABLE 5-3: SPECIALTY LISTING INSERTION FEES

SPECIALTY LISTINGS	INSERTION FEE
Vehicles (other than motorcycles)	$40.00
Motorcycles	$30.00
Residential, Commercial, and Miscellaneous Real Estate	$100 (1-, 3-, 5-, 7-, or 10-day listings) $150 (30-day listing)
Timeshares and Land	$35 (1-, 3-, 5-, 7-, or 10-day listings) $50 (30-day listing)

Start a Sale

There are three ways you can use eBay to present your items to potential customers: auctions, selling at a fixed price, and real estate advertising. (If you have an eBay Store, you will be provided a fourth option for adding store inventory; Chapter 10 describes eBay Stores.) Before you can start selling, you have to let eBay know which direction you want to go.

NOTE

You can choose to list real estate as a typical auction or use an ad format in which no bidding takes place and the buyer contacts you for more information. A 30-day ad listing is $150; a 90-day ad listing is $300 for real estate, timeshares, and land. **$1,100,000.00**

⊙ **Sell item at online Auction**
Allows bidding on your item(s). You may also add the Buy It Now option. Learn more.

○ **Sell at a Fixed Price**
Allows buyers to purchase your item(s) at a price you set. Learn more.

○ **Advertise your Real Estate**
Allows advertising of property to generate multiple leads. Real estate sellers may also sell at an online Auction or Fixed Price. Learn more.

QUICKFACTS

UNDERSTANDING THE SELLING FORM

eBay divides the Sell Your Item form into five steps:

1. **Category** is where you select a place to catalog your item. Use a search box, or choose from a hierarchical list the primary (or main) category or second category for your item. (*main category* required)

2. **Title, Subtitle, & Description** is where you catch the bidder's attention with words, first in a short title, then in a secondary subtitle, and finally in a more detailed description. (*title* and *description* required)

3. **Picture & Details** is where you visually catch the bidder's attention with pictures (photos, scanned images, and graphics) and other visual enhancements; and provide pricing, auction duration, and item location details. (*starting price*, *quantity*, *duration*, and *item location* required)

4. **Payment & Shipping** is where you indicate to buyers the types of payments you accept and how you want to handle shipping costs and options. (*locations you will ship to* required)

5. **Review & Submit** lets you preview your listing as it will look to bidders and make any last-minute changes before you submit the listing to eBay. (clicking *Submit Listing* required)

TIP

Selling at a fixed price is better known by the associated label that appears in auction listings—Buy It Now. You will only see this option on the Choose A Selling Format page if you qualify for this sales format; that is, you have a feedback rating of 10 or greater or you have proved your identity by using ID Verify. See Chapter 1 for more information on ID Verify. **≡Buy It Now**

1. From any eBay page, click **Sell** on the menu bar at the top of the page. If you are not already logged on to eBay, you need to provide your User ID and password.

2. Click **Sell Your Item** on the Sell hub page. On the Sell Your Item: Choose A Selling Format page, select the selling format you want for the item.

Sell Your Item >

3. Click **Continue** at the bottom of the page. The first page in the selling process, Select Category, is displayed, as shown in Figure 5-2.

Sell Your Item: Select Category

| 1 Category | 2. Title & Description | 3. Pictures & Details | 4. Payment & Shipping | 5. Review & Submit |

Main Category * Required

Choose the best category to help buyers find your item. Select a _previously used category_ or browse from all categories.

Enter item keywords to find a category

[   ] Find Tips

For example, "gold bracelet" not "jewelry"

Select a Previously Used Category

Click to select

Browse categories

Click a category in each box until the last box turns gray   Category #[   ]

Antiques -->
eBay Motors
Art -->
Books -->
Business & Industrial -->
Cameras & Photo -->
Clothing, Shoes & Accessories -->
Coins -->
Collectibles -->

Clear selection

Having difficulty viewing the category selector? Try this one .

Figure 5-2: After you have chosen to list your item, you have to select a category—the first step in submitting an item for bid or sale.

Select a Category

All items on eBay are catalogued into categories, which provide a hierarchical listing of general-to-specific organization of the millions of items listed in auctions. As there are currently approximately 35,000 categories to choose from (as of summer 2004), you want to ensure your item is catalogued in a logical place where buyers would most intuitively look for it. eBay provides several paths you can use for assistance in selecting a category. You can use keywords that relate to your item and have eBay display a list of categories of similar items that you can choose from, or you can start from a *top-level category* and work your way down into more specific subcategories, ultimately choosing your *main category*. Also, for an additional fee, you can elect to list the item in a *second* category.

> ① **Category**

LOCATE A CATEGORY (KEYWORDS)

You can find a category (or *main category*) to list your item in by providing keywords that relate to your item and having eBay search its listings inventory and seeing where other sellers are listing like items.

1. On the Sell Your Item: Select Category page, type one or more keywords in the Enter Item Keywords To Find A Category text box.

> **Enter item keywords to find a category**
>
> | classics junior | **Find** Tips |
>
> For example, "gold bracelet" not "jewelry"

2. Click **Find**. A window opens that contains one or more category hierarchies, listed in order by an estimate of the percentage of items found in each, as shown in Figure 5-3.

3. Either:

   • Select the category you want to use from the list.

   –Or–

   • Reenter a keyword in the text box, and click **Find** to try again using different key-words.

4. Click **Sell In This Category** to establish your main category and return to the Category page.

5. Do one of the following:

- Alter your choice of main category by using a category selector (see "Locate a Category (Selector)" in this chapter).

- Choose a second category (see "Choose a Secondary Category" in this chapter).

- Click **Continue** at the bottom of the page to move to the next step in the selling form.

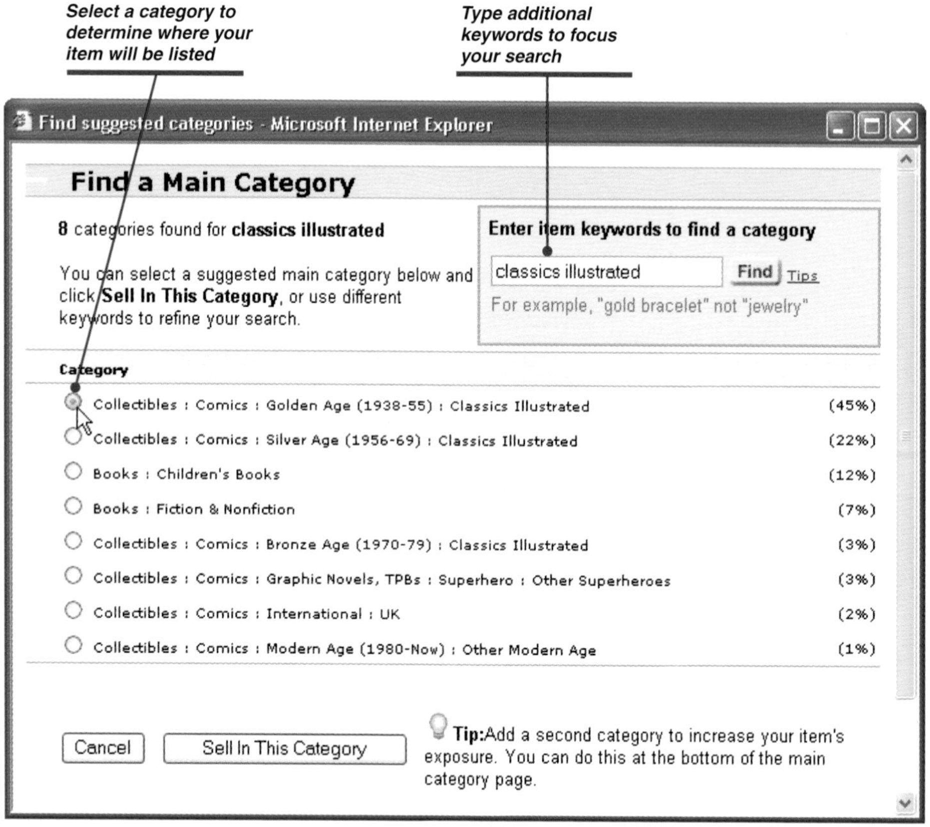

Select a category to determine where your item will be listed

Type additional keywords to focus your search

Find suggested categories - Microsoft Internet Explorer

Find a Main Category

8 categories found for **classics illustrated**

You can select a suggested main category below and click **Sell In This Category**, or use different keywords to refine your search.

Enter item keywords to find a category

classics illustrated   [Find] Tips

For example, "gold bracelet" not "jewelry"

Category

- ⊙ Collectibles : Comics : Golden Age (1938-55) : Classics Illustrated (45%)
- ○ Collectibles : Comics : Silver Age (1956-69) : Classics Illustrated (22%)
- ○ Books : Children's Books (12%)
- ○ Books : Fiction & Nonfiction (7%)
- ○ Collectibles : Comics : Bronze Age (1970-79) : Classics Illustrated (3%)
- ○ Collectibles : Comics : Graphic Novels, TPBs : Superhero : Other Superheroes (3%)
- ○ Collectibles : Comics : International : UK (2%)
- ○ Collectibles : Comics : Modern Age (1980-Now) : Other Modern Age (1%)

[Cancel]   [Sell In This Category]

💡 **Tip:** Add a second category to increase your item's exposure. You can do this at the bottom of the main category page.

Figure 5-3: eBay suggests categories in which to list an item based on a percentage of found keywords.

LOCATE A CATEGORY (SELECTOR)

You can manually move through the category hierarchy to find a main category for your item by using a category selector.

ebY®

The World's Online Marketplace®

Specialty Sites
eBay Live!
eBay Motors
eBay Stores
The Half Zone on eBay
PayPal

Categories
Antiques
Art
Books
Business & Industrial
Cameras & Photo
Cars, Parts & Vehicles
Clothing, Shoes & Accessories
Coins
Collectibles
Computers & Networking
Consumer Electronics
Crafts
Dolls & Bears

1. On the Sell Your Item: Select Category page, under Browse Categories, select the category in the list box to the left. (If your screen doesn't show Browse Categories, click **Try The Enhanced, Easier Category Selector** to use the newer category selector.) The next level of subcategories is displayed in the box to the right, as shown in Figure 5-4.

2. Select the subcategory you think best applies, and either a new list of more focused subcategories is displayed in a list box to the right, or you will see a final subcategory indicator (shaded list box), letting you know there are no more subcategories below the one you have chosen. You also know you have reached a final category when the Category # indicator contains a number, as shown in Figure 5-4.

3. Continue moving through the subcategories until you reach a final (main) category indicator and Category number, or click **Clear Selection** to restart the process.

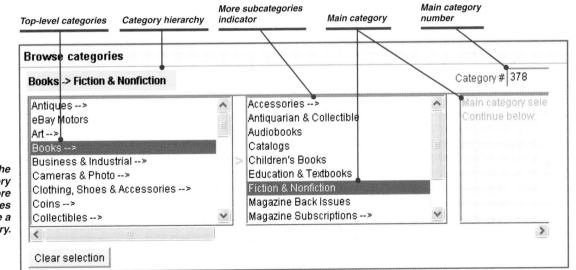

Top-level categories   Category hierarchy   More subcategories indicator   Main category   Main category number

Browse categories

Books -> Fiction & Nonfiction   Category # | 378

Antiques -->   Accessories -->   Main category sele
eBay Motors   Antiquarian & Collectible   Continue below.
Art -->   Audiobooks
Books -->   Catalogs
Business & Industrial -->   Children's Books
Cameras & Photo -->   Education & Textbooks
Clothing, Shoes & Accessories -->   Fiction & Nonfiction
Coins -->   Magazine Back Issues
Collectibles -->   Magazine Subscriptions -->

Clear selection

Figure 5-4: The enhanced category selector provides more focused subcategories after you choose a higher-level category.

CAUTION

Choosing a secondary category will double your insertion fee as well as certain upgrade fees, such as those incurred when having eBay bold your title. The final value fee, however, will not be increased, nor will the fees increase for Scheduled Listings and Home Page Featured upgrades. Also, you cannot include a secondary listing for adult items, Dutch auctions (a special type of auction used for selling multiple items where the winning bidders all pay the same price; that is, the price of the bidder who got the last remaining item), eBay Motors, and real estate.

TIP

If you don't plan on using secondary categories for your listings, you can remove the Second Category area from your screen. In the second category Browse Categories name bar, select the **Minimize Second Category Selection Area Next Time I List** check box. The next time you use the Sell Your Item form, you will only see a link in the Second Category area.

> **Second category**
> List your item in a second category! (Fee varies)
> Listing in two categories has been shown to increase final price on average by 18%.

CHOOSE A SECONDARY CATEGORY

To make your item more accessible to buyers, you can have the item listed in a secondary category, increasing your exposure and potentially increasing the final price by as much as 18 percent (according to information presented at eBay Live! 2004).

1. In the Second Category area (below the Main Category selector), use keywords, a previously used category, or the category selector to find a second category (see

> **Second category**
> Listing in two categories has been shown to **increase final price on average by 18%.** Learn more
>
> Insertion and most listing upgrade fees will be doubled. Final value fees will not be doubled.
>
> **Select a Previously Used Category**
> Click to select
>
> **Browse categories**   ☐ Minimize second category selection area next time I list
>
> **Enter item keywords to find a second category**
> [   ] Find Tips

   "Locate a Category (Keywords)" and "Locate a Category (Selector)" in this section).

2. Click **Continue** at the bottom of the page to move to the next step in the selling form.

> ## Sell Your Item: : Choose a Listing Option
> 1 **Category** 2. Title & Description 3. Pictures & Details 4. Payment & Shipping 5. Review & Submit
>
> **List with Pre-filled Item Information**   or   **List the standard way**
>
> Save time writing your description and adding pictures with this new feature. Learn more.
>
> --
>
> Create your own item description without any Pre-filled Item Information.
>
> [Continue >]
>
> **Search for:**
> [   ] [ISBN ▾]
>
> [Continue >]
>
> 065425364X
> **ISBN** 0-654-25364-X
>
> How to enter all 10 digits of an ISBN number.

Figure 5-5: Pre-filled item information is available for certain categories.

NOTE

There are several categories that are tied to product identifiers, which provide pre-filled item information and pictures for you. For example, if you choose a book category, you are given the opportunity to enter an ISBN number, title, or author's name, as shown in Figure 5-5. You can use the information provided or create your own item description.

NOTE

As a web application, the eBay selling form must conform to the rules and syntax that govern how text, pictures, and just about anything is used on the Web. The basic "language" used to format text and insert photos is HTML (Hypertext Markup Language). You don't need to be conversant in HTML to use eBay, but a rudimentary understanding of how HTML works and knowing how to do some simple techniques will reap great rewards. See Chapter 6 for more information on using HTML in eBay.

Title and Describe the Item

The second section in the eBay selling form covers how the items are titled and described. As with most aspects of eBay, there is a default set of features and there are options and upgrades.

2 Title & Description

Create the Item Titles

Quickly, in 55 characters or less, tell The Donald (Trump) why he should hire you for a $250,000-a-year position. Keeping that metaphor in mind will help you craft titles for your items that bring bidders to them and entice bidders to take the subsequent steps of viewing your pictures, reading your description, and submitting a bid. Bidders will be scanning lists looking for interesting titles. You will only have a few seconds of a bidder's time to entice him or her to look at your item in more detail.

ADD THE ITEM TITLE

In the Sell Your Item: Describe Your Item page, shown in Figure 5-6, type your title in the Item Title text box. You cannot use HTML to enhance your 55-character (including spaces) title, nor can you use asterisks or quotation marks.

Figure 5-6: Type an accurate title (and perhaps a subtitle) that clearly describes your item and includes keywords you think a bidder would use to find the item.

QUICK**FACTS**

CREATING A GOOD TITLE

- Clearly describe your item, using keywords that a bidder might typically use to find the item.

- Place the more important keywords toward the beginning of the title.

- If your item has associated branding, model names, or other unique descriptors, be sure to include them. "KitchenAid 5-qt Artisan 325-watt Mixer, Black" provides a whole lot more information and potential keyword hits than just "Mixer." This is also a good example of using both specific (KitchenAid, Artisan, 325-watt) and general (Mixer, Black) keywords for searchers who know exactly what they want and those who only kind of know what they are looking for.

- Don't waste valuable characters by including buzzwords that no one would use in a search. You might consider your item a "fantastic" item, but unless your item is associated with the Fantastic Four, forget it.

- Don't assume the category name will carry over and support finding your item by a bidder. For example, if you are selling Classics Illustrated Juniors comic books and place them in the Books | Children's | Classics category, make sure you repeat "Classics" in your title.

TIP

Good item titles follow generally accepted protocols that have stood the test of (eBay) time. Search for items similar to yours and see what other sellers are using to describe their items. Also, look at completed auctions to view the titles used by successful sellers. Do an advanced search, and select **Completed Items Only**, or browse to the category you will be selling your item in, and on the left sidebar, under Search Options, select **Completed Listings** and click **Show Items**.

Search Options

Show only:
- ☐ Items listed with PayPal
- ☐ Buy It Now items
- ☐ 🎁 Gift items
- ☑ Completed listings
- ☐ Items priced
  [ ] to [ ]

[Show Items]

ADD A SUBTITLE

Subtitles, for a fee ($.50), allow you to double the 55-character limit imposed by the Item Title box. Subtitles are used to add amplifying information and differentiate your item from a list of similar items, allowing you to load the title

> **FRENCH COUNTRY STAINED GLASS OAK BOOKCASE CURIO CABINET** 🖼️📷
> GOLDEN HONEY CARVED LOUIS XV DISPLAY COCKTAIL BAR CHEST

with keywords the buyer will be using to find the item. Subtitles are governed by the same limitations as titles.

1. In the Subtitle box, type your amplifying information, adhering to the 55-character limit. (If you go over the limit, eBay might do some "editing" for you.)

2. Scroll to the bottom of the page to enter the item description.

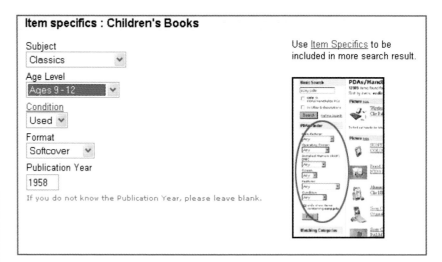

Figure 5-7: Categories that include item specifics allow you to add information about your item that buyers can use to find it.

Create the Item Description

An item description serves at least four basic purposes.

- Captures a bidder's attention
- Clearly describes the item you are selling in terms of what it has to offer and the condition it is in
- Acts as a placeholder for photos and graphics that support the text
- Informs the bidder of transaction details, such as payment and shipping/handling

TYPE THE DESCRIPTION

In addition to the three different interfaces that eBay provides for inserting an item description, you also can use common word-processing techniques to move or copy text (see the QuickSteps "Creating Descriptions outside eBay") or use eBay templates (see "Add Themes and Counters"). The three eBay interfaces allow you to type plain text, enhance it with word processing-like styles to spice up the formatting, or format it using HTML tags you apply. To type an item description using eBay tools, on the Describe Your Item page below the title area (as shown in Figure 5-8), do one of the following:

- Click the **Standard** tab, and start typing your description. Select text by dragging over it, and use the formatting toolbar to apply formatting styles (see the QuickSteps "Using the Formatting Toolbar"). Press **ENTER** to create new paragraphs.
- Click the **Enter Your Own HTML** tab, and type your description. Format the text by typing the applicable HTML tags, or paste text from an HTML editor already tagged. See Chapter 6 for more information on using common HTML formatting tags.
- Click **Use This Alternative** if either of the first two methods proves problematic for you. Your page is reconstructed using a more basic Item Description text box tool, and you can only add formatting using HTML tags.

TIP

Subtitles are not searched when bidders use a Basic Search. If bidders select the **Search Title And Description** check box, however, text in the subtitle will be searched.

NOTE

Some categories offer *item specifics*, or basic information on your item, that you can provide, allowing bidders and buyers to fine-tune their search for items within a category. If your main or second category has item specifics, you will see an additional section on the Describe Your Item page, as shown in Figure 5-7.

TIP

To see how your description will look to prospective bidders, click **Preview Description** below the Item Description text box or **Preview Your Description** from the spelling checker. Click **Close Window** to return to the Sell Your Item template.

QUICKSTEPS

CREATING DESCRIPTIONS OUTSIDE EBAY

As you probably know, word processors allow you to write more accurately, easily, conveniently, and faster than typing text into the text boxes on the eBay auction form. (See Chapter 6 for information on using HTML editors and formatting using HTML tags.)

USE WORD PROCESSORS

There are several programs that can create text for use on the Web.

1. Open a word processor, such as Microsoft Word or WordPad (available in Windows by clicking the **Start** button and selecting **All Programs | Accessories | WordPad**).

2. Type your description and format it using the available styling tools to align and emphasize text.

3. Use grammar and spelling checkers to correct mistakes, and dictionaries and thesauri to assist you in wordsmithing.

4. Save your description in an eBay-related folder so you have a record of your work and can use it again.

TRANSFER TEXT INTO EBAY FROM OTHER PROGRAMS

In order to get the text you've created into the eBay selling form, you need to *cut* or *copy* the text in the originating program and *paste* it into the respective eBay text box. (Paste formatted text onto the Standard tab; place text with HTML tags on the Enter Your Own HTML tab.)

1. Select the text you want to transfer to eBay by dragging over it or using keyboard shortcuts to highlight the text.

Cotntinued…

Figure 5-8: Choose from three different ways to type your description.

Save text for use in future listings · View tips tailored to your category · Click to type and paste text with HTML tags · Use formatting tools

Item description ✳

Be sure to include in your description: Condition (new, used, etc.), original price, and dimensions or size. You may also want to include notable markings or signatures, or its background history. See more tips for Classics Illustrated.

| Standard | Enter your own HTML |

NEW! Select Inserts from the drop-down list below to quickly and easily build your listing.

Font Name ▾ Size ▾ Color ▾ **B** *I* U ...

Inserts ▾ [ABC] [?]

15 cents comics, low HRN (high restock number). All in good-very good condition:

- **Nice color (prior owner's name on each outside cover)**
- **All Color This Picture are uncolored**
- **Completed dot-dots in pencil**

(comments on individual issues are noted below each picture)

Be happy to answer any questions (click "Ask Seller A Question)

Preview description   Can't view our description editor? Use this alternative.

You can add pictures and themes on the next page.

Click to see what your description will look like in a browser · Spell check your title and description · Get toolbar help · Use this method if either the Standard or HTML tabs are problematic

CREATING DESCRIPTIONS
OUTSIDE EBAY *(Continued)*

2. On the program's Edit menu, choose **Cut** to remove the text from the program or **Copy** to retain the text in place (or click their respective buttons on the toolbar). In either case, a copy of the text is placed on a temporary *clipboard* from where it can be retrieved.

3. In the eBay selling form, right-click in the text box where you want the cut or copied text to start, and then click **Paste** from the context menu, or place the insertion point, and choose **Edit | Paste** from the browser's menu bar.

TIP

Accurately describing the condition of an item, or *grading*, and providing proof of authentication can often make or break a sale. Though grading tends more toward the subjective (I say it's in excellent condition; you say it's only very good), and authentication is more empirical (the item is, or isn't, what it's advertised to be), you need to do your homework and research the item to provide the most accurate and legitimate information you can. See Chapter 3 for more information on determining grading and how to authenticate items, including using authentication services.

SPELL CHECK YOUR WORK

Bidders are not typically interested in whether you have an English degree, although a poorly constructed description will raise some eyebrows.

1. To use the built-in eBay spelling checker, in the Item Description area, below the Standard and Enter Your Own HTML tabs, click the **Spell Check** button. If the spelling checker finds any problems, it will highlight potential errors, suggest alternatives, and allow you to accept or ignore any changes, as shown in Figure 5-9.

2. Do one of the following:

   ● Select an alternative spelling from the Suggestions list box, and click **Change** to replace the current instance of the word, or click **Change All** to replace all occurrences of this word.

   ● Click **Ignore** to the leave the current instance as is, or click **Ignore All** to keep the spelling checker from highlighting any subsequent occurrences of this word.

   ● Click **Save Changes** to have any changes you selected be made in the Sell Your Item form.

   ● Click **Cancel Changes** to remove any changes you made to your original text.

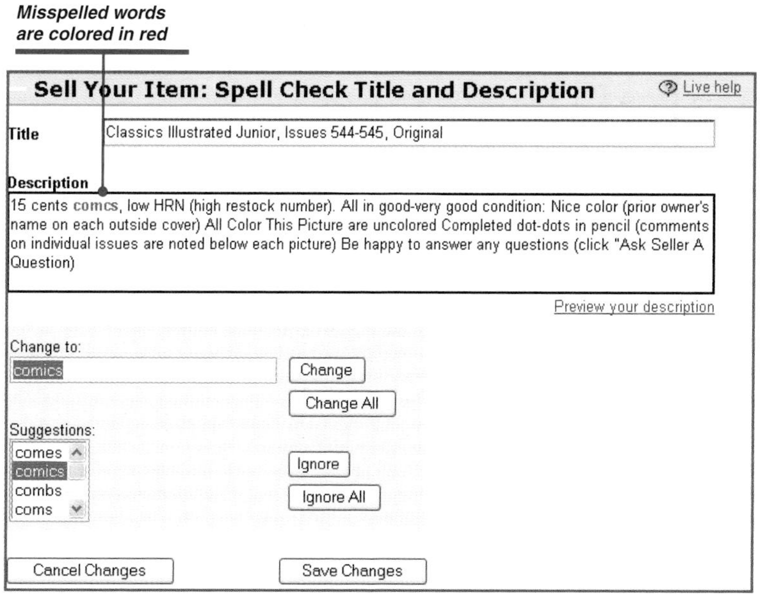

Misspelled words are colored in red

Sell Your Item: Spell Check Title and Description   Live help

Title   Classics Illustrated Junior, Issues 544-545, Original

Description
15 cents comcs, low HRN (high restock number). All in good-very good condition: Nice color (prior owner's name on each outside cover) All Color This Picture are uncolored Completed dot-dots in pencil (comments on individual issues are noted below each picture) Be happy to answer any questions (click "Ask Seller A Question)

Preview your description

Change to:
comics   Change
              Change All

Suggestions:
comes
comics
combs
coms   Ignore
              Ignore All

Cancel Changes   Save Changes

Figure 5-9: The eBay spelling checker reviews your title and description for misspelled words.

Select an insert...   **...to add saved text and HTML**

| Inserts | ⌄ | ABC |

Inserts
Create an Insert...

Sellers Other Items
Add to favorites list

About this feature...

(comments on individual is

Be happy to answer any qu

Check out my <u>other items</u>!

CAUTION

Step 4 of the eBay Sell Your Item form, "Payment and Shipping," is where you select payment and shipping options, and provide instructions to the buyer or bidder that appear in the View Item page. Many sellers also add the instructions to the item description. We don't recommend you do this since the instructions can become buried in the item description, and often they are in conflict with the instructions that appear in the Shipping And Payment Details section of the View Item page.

USE INSERTS

Inserts allow you to create and save text segments for use in future item descriptions. You can have up to five inserts of 1,000 characters or less each. Click the **Insert** down arrow, and either:

- Click **Create An Insert** to name and type (or paste) the text for the insert. For example, you could make an insert out of shipping and handling instructions, a logo, or text formatted with HTML tags.

  –Or–

- Click the insert you want. (Ensure you place your insertion point in the item description where you want the insert to be placed.) eBay provides pre-built inserts for links to your other items for sale and a link that adds you to the buyer's Favorite list.

Insert Pictures and Add Details

In the third step in the process to set up a listing on eBay, "Pictures & Details," you make decisions that frame your sale. For example, you set a starting price; choose whether to have a reserve and its price; determine the length of time the sale is live; choose when to start the sale; and choose whether you want to purchase optional features, such as themes, words in bold, and Gallery participation, to try and accentuate your listing. This section also allows you to link to pictures of your item.   ③ **Pictures & Details**

(When you first open the Pictures & Details page, or if you choose to add pictures using eBay Picture Services, you will see a Security Warning dialog box asking if you want to install a small program from eBay. The program speeds up uploading pictures in eBay Picture Services and provides a few other features. You can click **No** and continue with the process, but you might continue to see the dialog box in future selling forms.)

1 2 3 4 5 6 7 8 9 10

Price the Item

Pricing is an art as old as the history of the first buy-sell transaction, balancing what a seller thinks he or she can obtain for an item against what a buyer thinks it is worth in monetary terms. eBay pricing can be even more interesting as you add the complexity of bidding to the mix. Figure 5-11 shows the three prices you set within the following Sell Your Item formats:

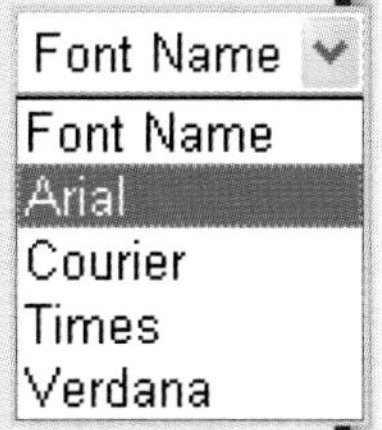

- The standard online auction starting price (required) and possible reserve price
- A fixed-price format (Buy It Now price)
- A blend of online and fixed-price formats

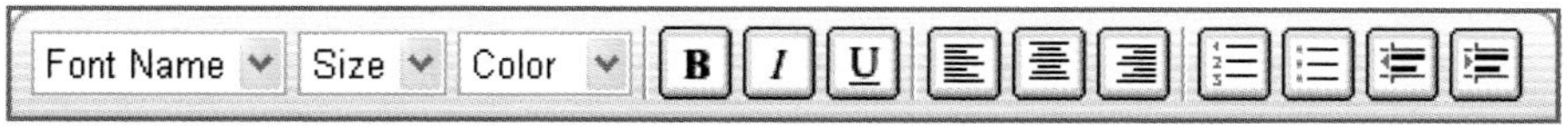

Font Name ▼	Size ▼	Color ▼	**B**	*I*	<u>U</u>							

Figure 5-10: The Standard tab of the Item Description text box provides a formatting toolbar similar to that found in word-processing programs.

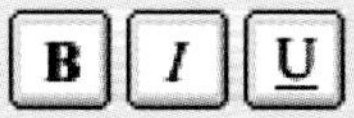

Click here to enter
a reserve price

Pricing and duration

Starting price ✱ Required

$ [   ]

Bidding will begin at your starting price.

Buy It Now price ($0.05)

$ [   ]

Sell to the first buyer who meets your Buy It Now price.

Reserve price (fee varies)
No reserve price. Add

Figure 5-11: You have up to three choices to make in setting auction pricing, depending on the auction format you choose.

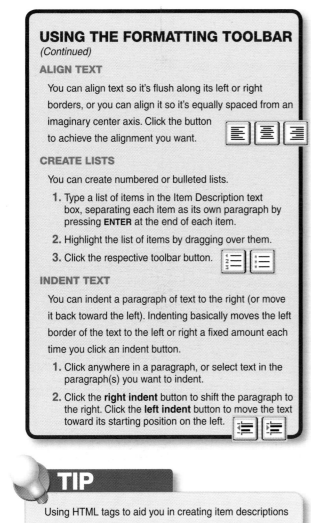

USING THE FORMATTING TOOLBAR
(Continued)

ALIGN TEXT

You can align text so it's flush along its left or right borders, or you can align it so it's equally spaced from an imaginary center axis. Click the button to achieve the alignment you want.

CREATE LISTS

You can create numbered or bulleted lists.

1. Type a list of items in the Item Description text box, separating each item as its own paragraph by pressing **ENTER** at the end of each item.

2. Highlight the list of items by dragging over them.

3. Click the respective toolbar button.

INDENT TEXT

You can indent a paragraph of text to the right (or move it back toward the left). Indenting basically moves the left border of the text to the left or right a fixed amount each time you click an indent button.

1. Click anywhere in a paragraph, or select text in the paragraph(s) you want to indent.

2. Click the **right indent** button to shift the paragraph to the right. Click the **left indent** button to move the text toward its starting position on the left.

TIP

Using HTML tags to aid you in creating item descriptions can greatly enhance the look of your listing. For example, using the formatting toolbar provided by eBay, you have five color choices to select from. If you know the HTML tags for text colors, you would have over 200 colors to choose from. See Chapter 6 for more information on using HTML in your auctions.

SET ONLINE AUCTION PRICING

You need to establish the price where bidding will begin for your item. This is also the lowest price you will accept for your item—unless you decide to use a *reserve* price, which is a price unknown to the bidders until the bidding action has reached that pricing threshold.

On the Pictures & Details page, in the Pricing And Duration section:

1. In the Starting Price text box, type the price where you want the bidding to start (for multiple items or Dutch auctions, the minimum starting price is $0.99).

2. If you elect to establish a reserve price, type the price in the Reserve Price text box. (You may have to click **Add** to get the text box.) The reserve fee is refunded if your item sells. For items that do not sell:

   - Priced up to $49.99, you pay $1.00

   - Priced between $50 and 199.99, you pay $2.00

   - Priced $200 and over, you're charged 1 percent of the reserve price up to a maximum of $100.00

SET FIXED-PRICE LISTING PRICING

If you qualify (you have a feedback rating of 10 or greater or you have proved your identity by using ID Verify), you can establish a fixed *Buy It Now* (or in eBay shorthand: BIN) price ($0.05 fee) that lets a bidder purchase the item at that price. To have a fixed-price listing, you need to make that choice in the first stages of the selling process. See "Start A Sale," earlier in the chapter, for more details. On the Pictures & Details page, in the Pricing And Duration section, type the sales price in the Buy It Now Price text box.

COMBINE ONLINE AND FIXED-PRICE FORMATS

You can blend a bidding-style and fixed-price listing by starting with an auction format and then adding a Buy It Now price (if you're qualified to be a fixed-price seller). The Buy It Now price is only available until the first bid is made. At the point of the first bid, the icon will no longer appear on your live auction page and the auction will continue on a bidding basis only.

NOTE

In order to use the Start Time feature to schedule a start time other than when the listing is submitted, you must have a credit card on file with eBay. To schedule a one-day sale, you must adhere to the same requirements as those for choosing a fixed-price auction: a feedback rating of 10 or higher or have your identification verified by ID Verify (see Chapter 1 for more information on ID Verify).

ID Verify: Successful

You have successfully completed the ID Verify process.

Check your ID Verify icon ✅ in your feedback profile.

NOTE

There is a lot of debate over the optimal duration to sell an item. Unless you have a specific reason to use the one-day option (such as the time-sensitive expiration date of an event ticket, or if you have a large inventory of the same item that you just want to turn over quickly), you're probably better off gaining more exposure for your item with a longer duration. On the other hand, will a ten-day auction deter bidders who want their purchase sooner rather than later? A seven-day auction gives potential bidders a week to find your auction and doesn't cost you any extra—our vote!

Duration ✱

7 days ▾
1 day
3 days
5 days
7 days
10 days ($0.20 fee)

TIP

The heaviest traffic days are on the weekends (Sunday evening seems to be the hottest) because more people look at new listings and those that are closing. So if you time your sale to start and end on a weekend, more people will look at your item.

1. Ensure you selected the default **Sell Item At Online Auction** option on the Choose A Selling Format page. If you didn't, return to that page, and change the Sell Your Item format.

2. On the Pictures & Details page, set your starting price, add a reserve price (if you want one), and in the Buy It Now Price text box, type your price.

Schedule and Locate a Listing

You can schedule your listing to last for one of five different durations and determine when to start the sale. Also, you can inform bidders and buyers where you are located and receive a free eBay benefit of being found by bidders when they search by geographic region.

TIME YOUR SALE

1. Click the **Duration** down arrow, and select the number of days you want your auction to last.

2. In the Start Time area, either:

   - Leave the default (and free) option, **Start Listing When Submitted**, selected. The sale will start when you submit the listing and end the number of days later you chose as the duration. For example, if you submit a seven-day listing at 8:35 P.M. on Sunday, October 3, 2004, the listing will be scheduled to end at 8:35 P.M. on Sunday, October 10, 2004.

     –Or–

   - Click **Schedule Start Time** ($0.10 fee), click the **Select A Date** and **Select A Time** down arrows, and choose the day and time you want the listing to start. You can schedule up to three weeks in advance, in 15-minute increments.

3. If you don't want the User IDs of bidders displayed, in the Private Auction area, click **Add** and then select the **Private Auction** check box. A private auction cannot be used if you are selling multiple items. Private auctions are typically used to sell adult products, items of high value, and those items that might otherwise embarrass bidders if others knew they bid on them.

Private auction
No private auction. Add

UNDERSTANDING QUANTITY

For most sellers, you will use the default in the Number Of Items text box, but if you sell more than one of the same or similar item, you need to understand how multiple items and lots are handled.

SELL MULTIPLE ITEMS

Multiple-item bidding is handled differently depending on the auction format: online auction or fixed price (Buy It Now):

- Multiple-item listings for online auctions (or Dutch auctions) require bidders to specify a quantity and bid amount, resulting in a final bid amount by multiplying the two values. All bidders pay the same amount, that of the lowest successful bidder (determined when the quantity has been bid to zero).

- Fixed-price listings handle multiple-item purchases by simply multiplying the quantity the buyer wants by the price of the item.

- On the Individual Items tab, type the quantity in the Number Of Items text box if you are selling multiple items. To sell multiple items, you must have a minimum feedback rating of 30 or be ID Verified.

SELL LOTS

Lots are packages, groups, or collections of the same or similar item. To sell lots:

1. Click the **Lots** tab in the Quantity area.

2. Fill out the **Number Of Lots** and **Number Of Items Per Lot** text boxes with your applicable number of lots and items for sale.

Individual Items	NEW! Lots
Number of lots *	**Number of items per lot** *
1	
Enter "1" if you have one group, collection, or lot. Learn more about lots.	Example: If you have 5 books in your collection, enter 5

DISPLAY YOUR ITEM'S LOCALITY

1. In the Item Location area, click the **Country** down arrow, and select where your item is located. (If you have an established location, you will see that location and a Change option to allow you to change to a different site if needed.)

Item location *
Country
United States
Zip Code   **Location** *
98201   Look up >   Everett, Washington
Shown on item listing
☑ Include my item in distance-based searches
Requires Zip Code

2. Provide a more specific location (the location that the buyer or bidder will see) by either:

- Typing the ZIP code where the item is, and clicking **Look Up**. A region (typically a city and state) is entered in the Location text box

Zip Code	**Location** *
98201 Look up >	Everett, Washington
	Shown on item listing

   –Or–

- Typing your own description of the item location in the Location text box

3. Select the **Include My Item In Distance-Based Searches** check box if you want to do this (typically for large items where the buyer will come to pick up them up).

Add Pictures

As the saying goes, a picture is worth a thousand words. *Pictures* (which include photos, scans, and graphics) can go a long way in supplementing the descriptive text of your item. Your picture options depend on how you *host*, or store, your pictures. Pictures are not physically added or copied to the selling form—you type a link to where the picture is hosted. Hosting options include:

- Your own hosting site
- eBay Picture Services
- A third-party service

There are two basic steps to using pictures in your listing:

1. Create the JPG, PNG, or GIF file using a digital camera, scanner, or drawing program.

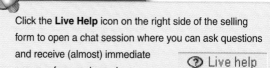

NOTE

Pictures used in eBay, and on the Internet in general, are digital files that have to be in JPG, PNG, or GIF file format—for example, Dresser.jpg.

TIP

You are limited to one free picture using the Add Pictures section; however, you can link to as many as you want (for free) using HTML tags in the Item Description, or you can combine several pictures into one using photo-editing software. Chapter 6 describes both of these techniques.

TIP

Click the **Live Help** icon on the right side of the selling form to open a chat session where you can ask questions and receive (almost) immediate answers from real people.

⟨?⟩ Live help

2. Link the picture to the selling form. In the Add Pictures section:

Add pictures

| eBay Picture Services Let eBay host your pictures | **Your own Web hosting** Enter your picture URL |

Picture Web address

http://mywebsite.verizon.net/xxx/yyy/armoire2.jpg

For example, URLs ending in .jpg or .gif

☐ The description already includes a picture URL for my item.

- Type the hosted picture's location address, or *URL* (uniform resource locator), in the Your Own Web Hosting tab—for example, http://mysite.net/ebay/books/SleepingBeauty.jpg. Use either a hosting URL of your own or one provided by a third-party service. Select the **The Description Already Includes A Picture URL For My Item** check box if you added one or more URLs in the Item Description text box.

–Or–

- Use eBay Picture Services, shown in Figure 5-12, and browse to the pictures you want on your computer by clicking the **Add Pictures** button(s). eBay will store the pictures and create the URL link for you.

(See Chapter 6 for more information on the actual mechanics of hosting and enhancing pictures, including eBay Picture Services options.)

Figure 5-12: Enhanced eBay Picture Services is the most common way to get your pictures to appear in a listing.

Add Themes and Counters

You can easily (and cheaply) add visual enhancements to your listing and employ a counter to let you know how often your listing is viewed.

USE THE LISTING DESIGNER

In the Listing Designer section of the selling form ($0.10 fee), you can easily add some flair and choose how your description and pictures are arranged. *Themes* provide a template of color and graphics that support a design, a topic of interest, or an eBay category. *Layouts* let you choose how to locate pictures of your item in relationship to your listing description.

1. In the Listing Designer area, click the **Select A Theme** down arrow, and select a category of available themes. After web page refreshes, the themes within the selected category are displayed in the associated list box.

2. Select one or more themes. (There are over 100 themes in all categories!) A miniature representation (or *thumbnail*) of each theme appears to the right of the list box.

3. In the Select A Layout list box, select how you want to arrange your description and pictures. A sample of each choice is displayed to the right of the list box as you click it.

4. Click **Preview Listing** to see how your theme and layout choices will look together in your auction listing, as shown in Figure 5-13. Click **Close Window** at the bottom of the page to return to the listing.

USE A COUNTER

A counter keeps track of the number of times a page has been viewed, providing a reasonable measure of how many bidders and buyers have viewed your listing. (We say "reasonable" measure because if the same bidder viewed your item ten times, the counter would add ten to the total count, skewing the statistics.) You can choose to display the count or keep the count hidden from everyone but yourself. To do either, in the Page Counter area:

Figure 5-13: This listing shows an enhanced item description using theme and layout features.

- To add a visible counter, click **Change** to choose a new or alternate counter. Select either of the number styles.

  –Or–

- To add a hidden counter, click **Thanks For Looking!**. The Thanks For Looking! graphic is displayed instead of the counter.

Use Visibility Upgrades

There are several options you can employ to attract attention to your listing. Whether their cost justifies their advertising potential to bring more bidders to your auction is one of those great philosophical questions for the ages, although eBay is quick to provide statistics that support they do, as shown in Figure 5-14.

In the Increase Your Item's Visibility area, select the upgrades that you want for your item.

- **Gallery** ($0.25) provides a thumbnail picture you choose of your item next to your auction listing and lists your item and picture in Gallery View.

- **Gallery Featured** ($19.95) supersizes the basic Gallery features by adding your listing to the Featured Item section in Gallery pages (as well as in the standard Gallery list) and increasing your picture size.

- **Bold** ($1.00) accentuates your item title with boldface type.

- **Border** ($3.00) adds a purple frame around the listing.

- **Highlight** ($5.00) surrounds your auction details with a colored background in auction listings.

- **Featured Plus!** ($19.95) adds your listing to the Featured Items (beginning) area of its category list and in the list generated by a search (as well as in the standard auction and search listings).

Figure 5-14: There is no bigger promoter of eBay than eBay!

- **Home Page Featured** ($39.95 single listing/$79.95 two or more listings) provides a randomly selected exposure to your listing under the Featured Items list on the eBay home page (listings are rotated, and there is no guarantee) as well as on the Featured Items list on the Browse Hub page and on the item's category page.

Featured Items *all featured items...*
- NEW 14x70 Redman Mobile Home
- *FIBERSYN Carbohydrate Blocker* ~Only $12.95~ SAVE $66
- TUMMY TUCK ? my MOM lost 37 LBS #t Diet Aid *BioFFEINE*
- MEDITERRANEAN STYLE-FORT LAUDERDALE, FLORIDA
- Greenhouse, Store Front, Trailer sites & more, 3 acres
- BABY G WATCHES, WHOLESALE PRICE, BLOWOUT WATCH SALE!

- **Gift Services** ($0.25) adds a Gifts And Services icon next to your item title, lists your item in Gifts view, and attracts bidders and buyers to your gift services, such as gift wrapping and direct shipping to the gift's recipient.

Enter Payment and Shipping Information

The "Payment & Shipping" step of the selling form does exactly as it says, outlining choices you have for receiving payment and how and where you are willing to ship the item to the successful bidder.

4 Payment & Shipping

Figure 5-15: Make payment-acceptance choices, and eBay transfers those choices to the listing the bidder sees.

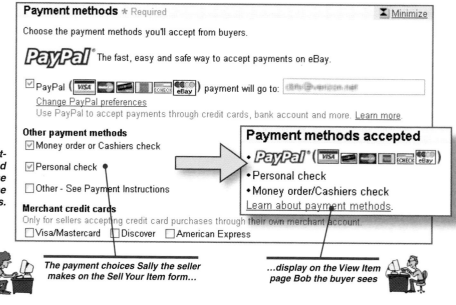

Payment methods * Required ⚊ Minimize

Choose the payment methods you'll accept from buyers.

PayPal The fast, easy and safe way to accept payments on eBay.

☑ PayPal (VISA ▭▭▭ ECHECK eBay) payment will go to: [_____]
Change PayPal preferences
Use PayPal to accept payments through credit cards, bank account and more. Learn more

Other payment methods
☑ Money order or Cashiers check
☑ Personal check
☐ Other - See Payment Instructions

Merchant credit cards
Only for sellers accepting credit card purchases through their own merchant account.
☐ Visa/Mastercard ☐ Discover ☐ American Express

Payment methods accepted
- *PayPal* (VISA ▭▭▭ ECHECK eBay)
- Personal check
- Money order/Cashiers check
Learn about payment methods.

The payment choices Sally the seller makes on the Sell Your Item form...

...display on the View Item page Bob the buyer sees

TIP

If you accept PayPal as a payment choice (highly recommended), you have several options you can use. In the Payment Methods PayPal area, click **Change PayPal Preferences**, sign in, and review the **Pay Now Button** and **PayPal Preferences** options. Select the ones you want, and click **Submit** at the bottom of the page. The last option, **Show My Buyers Low Monthly Payments Possible With PayPal Buyer Credit**, allows you to offer standard (free) or promotional financing (for an additional fee) on higher-priced items. See www.paypal.com/offercredit for more details.

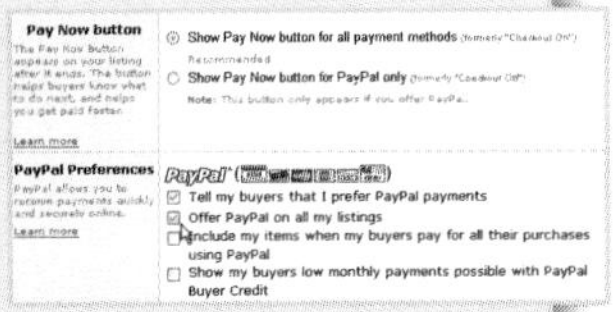

Financing available NEW!

Only $75 per month
if you use PayPal Buyer Credit. Subject to credit approval. US residents only. See repayment details.
See details | **Apply now**

Payment instructions & return policy   ⚏ Minimize

Give clear instructions to assist your buyer with payment, shipping, and returns.

Increase sales by offering a shipping discount in your description for multiple item purchases.

Describe your return policy and earn buyer confidence. Learn more.

```
Cashier's Check, or personal check. Will ship within 2-3 weekdays
after receiving payment (exceptions: holidays and personal checks
will be held until cleared by local bank). Returned items accepted
within 2 weeks of payment received. Buyer pays shipping for returned
items unless othewise negotiated with seller.
```

Add Payment Information

You have several choices in how you inform successful bidders how to pay you and how to take care of returned items.

CHOOSE PAYMENT METHODS

In the Payment Methods area, select the check boxes next to the methods you accept. The options you choose will appear in the Payment Methods Accepted section in the View Item form the bidder or buyer sees, as shown in the right side of Figure 5-15.

DESCRIBE PAYMENT INSTRUCTIONS

In the Payment Instructions And Return Policy area (below the Shipping Costs section), type your payment instructions, ensuring the text is "in synch" with the payment methods you selected.

CREATE A RETURN POLICY

A clearly stated return policy in the auction listing may save you money and hours writing e-mails to a disgruntled buyer and avoid more severe actions (see Chapter 9 for information on handling problem transactions). Points to cover in a return policy include:

● **Who will pay** for shipping the item back to you

● **Degree of package opening/use of the item** you will accept

● **Returned checks** if not written to proper Pay To The Order Of

● **Restocking fee** a merchant charges to return the item to inventory

● **Grace period** that you accept returns

In the Payment Instructions & Return Policy area, add your return-policy instructions to any payment instructions you might have added previously, as shown in Figure 5-16.

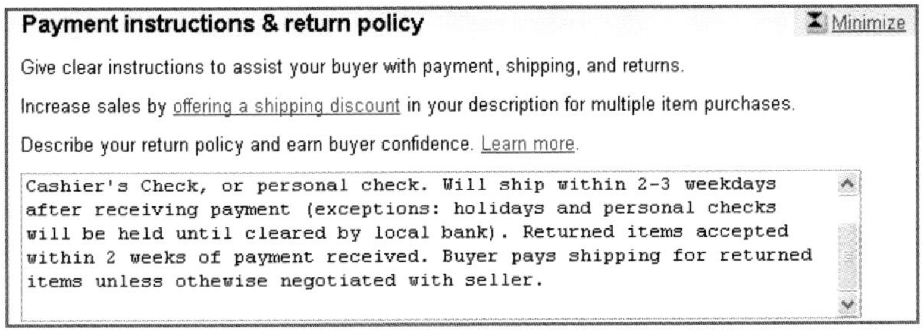

Figure 5-16: Adding a return policy to your payment instructions can save headaches down the road.

QUICKSTEPS

ENHANCING A PAYPAL ACCOUNT

You can sell items with your Personal PayPal account, described in Chapter 4, but if you are planning on being a successful seller, you will need to perform enhancements to it. There are a couple paths you can take:

- **Verification**, shown in Figure 5-17, confirms that the checking account PayPal members have added to their account actually belongs to them, which adds to the overall security of the system. (You can get verified without confirming a bank account, but it's geared toward corporations and other non-personal accounts.) Once verified, sending and receiving limits are raised and you can send payments from the checking account.

- **Premier Accounts** allow you to retain your Personal account identity and accept credit card payments, although you will incur a fee for receiving funds (for most members: $0.30 plus 2.9 percent). Sending funds, as with Personal accounts, is free for U.S. bank accounts. You also receive other benefits, such as expanded access to the customer service call center and selling tools.

- **Business** accounts provide the same benefits and fees as Premier Accounts, but you must register them in a business name.

To enhance your PayPal account:

1. On the eBay home page, click **PayPal**, either in the Specialty Sites area or on the links bar at the bottom of the page.

2. In the Member Log In area, type your password and click **Log In**.

3. On the Account Overview page, in the Enhance Account sidebar, click **Get Verified** or **Upgrade Account** to change your Personal account.

Figure 5-17: During verification, you first add a bank account to your PayPal account and then you confirm it.

Calculate Shipping Costs

You have three methods of telling your bidders and buyers how much (if any) shipping charges will be.

Shipping costs * ⌧ Minimize

Specify Domestic Shipping Costs Now?
- ○ Yes, describe my package and let the shipping calculator show the correct costs to my buyers (based on ZIP Code)
- ◉ Yes, provide flat costs to my buyers
- ○ No, have buyers contact me later

LET EBAY AND THE BUYER CALCULATE SHIPPING

eBay can calculate shipping for most packages using United States Postal Service (USPS) and UPS services. All you have to do is provide basic shipping information, and eBay will add a section to your listing where the bidder or buyer can see the cost.

Calculate shipping
Enter your US ZIP Code: [   ]
[Calculate]

Learn more about how calculated shipping works.

Buyers outside US: If seller ships to your country, see item description or contact seller for details.

PayPal®   Log Out | Help

| My Account | Send Money | Request Money | Merchant Tools | Auction Tools |

| Overview | Add Funds | Withdraw | History | Profile |

Bank Account Successfully Added!

US Bank, XXXXXX0466 has been added to your PayPal account.

You can now **withdraw** funds electronically from your PayPal account and have these funds deposited into this bank account.

To use this bank account to add funds or Send Money, you will need to confirm it. An email with instructions on how to Confirm this bank account has been sent to your email address. Press Continue to start using PayPal.

Confirm Your Bank Account!

While your bank account has been successfully added to your PayPal account, it has not been confirmed yet. By confirming this bank account, you'll get several benefits:

- Payments funded by your confirmed bank account or PayPal account balance will be exempt from your sending limit
- You will be able to send money instantly with your bank account
- You will be able to add funds to your PayPal account

Plus, you'll be automatically entered to **win $1,000.00 USD** in our weekly sweepstakes!

1. Click **Yes, Describe My Package And Let The Shipping Calculator Show The Current Costs To My Buyers**.

2. Enter the following information, as shown Figure 5-18:

- **Package Weight** (in pounds and ounces)

- **Package Size** (letter, small package, large package)

- **Shipping Service** (USPS or UPS) and **Level Of Service** (Priority Mail, Ground, 2nd Day Mail)

- **Packaging & Handling Fee** (buyers will not see this as a separate cost; it's integrated into the overall shipping cost)

- **Shipping Insurance** (not offered, optional, or required; free insurance up to a $100 package value for UPS and USPS Express Mail)

- **Seller ZIP code** (establishes where package will be sent from)

- **Sales Tax** (select **Apply Sales Tax To The Total Which Includes Shipping And Handling** if your state requires it)

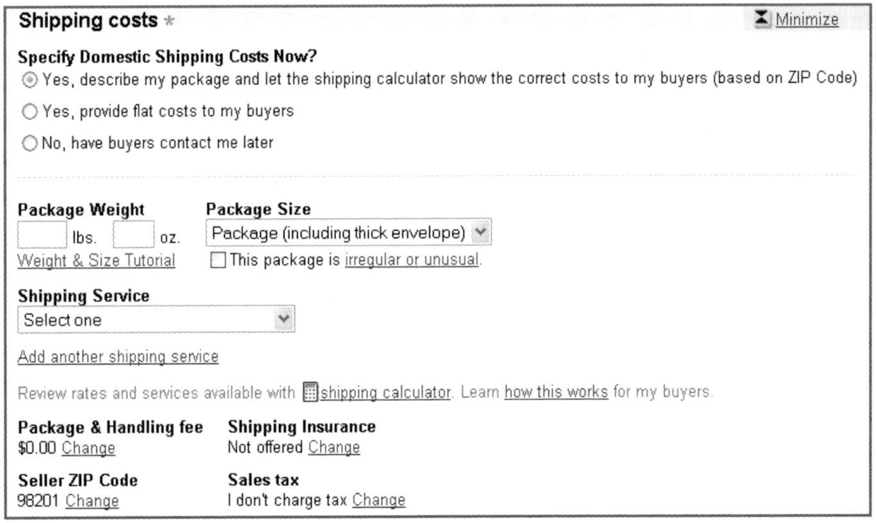

NOTE

Calculated shipping costs are available to the bidder during the listing. All that's needed is the bidder's ZIP code; however, any insurance costs are based on the final value price, so a final shipping cost may not be available until the listing is completed.

NOTE

Calculated shipping is only available for U.S. addresses. If you want to offer shipping to areas outside the U.S., make your choices in the Ship To Locations area at the bottom of the Payment And Shipping page, or describe them in the Payment Instructions & Return Policy section.

Shipping costs *   ⏳ Minimize

Specify Domestic Shipping Costs Now?

◉ Yes, describe my package and let the shipping calculator show the correct costs to my buyers (based on ZIP Code)

○ Yes, provide flat costs to my buyers

○ No, have buyers contact me later

Package Weight   **Package Size**

[   ] lbs. [   ] oz.   Package (including thick envelope) ▾

Weight & Size Tutorial   ☐ This package is irregular or unusual.

Shipping Service

Select one   ▾

Add another shipping service

Review rates and services available with 🖩shipping calculator. Learn how this works for my buyers.

Package & Handling fee   **Shipping Insurance**
$0.00 Change   Not offered Change

Seller ZIP Code   **Sales tax**
98201 Change   I don't charge tax Change

Figure 5-18: Provide basic shipping information and let the buyer see what his or her shipping costs will be.

SPECIFY FLAT-RATE SHIPPING

1. Click **Yes, Provide Flat Costs To My Buyer**.

2. Click the **Shipping Service** down arrow, and select the service you want to offer.

3. In the Shipping And Handling text box, type the amount you will charge. (Don't know what to charge? See "Run the Shipping Calculator.")

4. To offer up to three services and charges, click **Add Another Shipping Service**.

Shipping Service		Shipping & Handling
US Postal Service Priority Mail ▾	$	3.85
US Postal Service Media Mail ▾	$	1.42 Remove
Add another shipping service		

5. Under Shipping Insurance, click **Change**, select the applicable option from the drop-down list, and add any cost. (UPS offers free insurance for items valued up to $100).

6. If you need to charge sales tax, under Sales Tax, click **Change**, select your state from the drop-down list, and type the tax percentage your state charges for your locale. If your state requires tax on both shipping and handling costs, select that option.

RUN THE SHIPPING CALCULATOR

If you want to know what rates are for USPS and UPS levels of service to a specific area or determine an average you can charge all buyers, try running the shipping calculator.

1. Click **Yes, Provide Flat Costs To My Buyer.**

2. Below the Shipping Service and Shipping & Handling areas, click **Shipping Calculator**.

   📠 shipping calculator

3. In the Describe Your Package area, provide the basic shipping information.

4. In the Shipping Calculator Rates area, run the calculator (select a city or type a ZIP code, and click **Show Rates**) twice to get an idea of U.S. shipping charges, first in a city near you, and then again in a city as far away as possible. Use the two extreme values to derive an averaged cost (or charge any value that you feel is warranted—just be sure to defend your decision if queried by a questioning buyer!). Service rates for both the USPS and UPS are displayed, as shown in Figure 5-19.

TIP

See Chapter 8 for descriptions of shipping options and strategies for using them. Also, add shipping instructions to the Payment Instructions And Return Policy area in the selling form (tell the buyer how long after the listing closes you will ship the item, and provide tracking data when you ship it so he or she can tell when it will arrive).

5. Either:

- Close the **Seller Shipping Calculator** window.

  –Or–

- Select up to three services, and click **Offer These Services** at the bottom of the window.

  Offer These Services

6. On the selling form, accept the shipping service(s) and shipping and handling costs imported from the calculator, or change them to what you want.

7. Add insurance and state tax, as applicable (see "Specify Flat-Rate Shipping" in this section).

Figure 5-19: The Shipping Calculator provides shipping costs for USPS and UPS services based on your description of the package, your ZIP code, and the item destination.

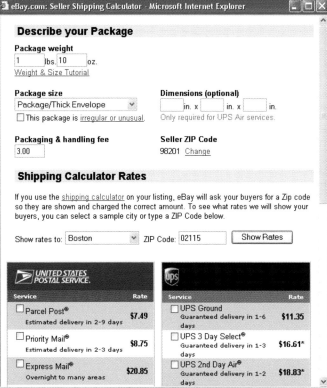

NOTE

If you decide to ship outside the United States and choose an alternate option in the Ship To Locations section (last section in the "Payment & Shipping" step), there are a few pointers to keep in mind: fully explain how you determine shipping costs, provide an estimate of how long the delivery will take, use PayPal so exchange rates will be automatically calculated, and include custom forms. You can also offer local pickup only in the Ship To Locations section. Use this option for items that that are awkward to ship, such as large, heavy items or extremely fragile items.

DELAY CALCULATING SHIPPING COSTS

If you want to wait and communicate with the buyer before you commit to shipping costs, select **No, Have Buyers Contact Me Later**. After the listing closes, you will know where the item is to be shipped, whether the buyer has any input, and can determine an exact cost. Be aware that many buyers are leery of listings that have vague shipping costs as they see that as a way for the seller to tack on "hidden" fees.

Review and Submit the Selling Form

The last step in placing a listing, "Review & Submit," provides you with the opportunity to see your listing as a bidder or buyer will see it, review your inputs, make any changes before you submit it, and review your listing fees.

> 5 **Review & Submit**

Correct Errors and Omissions

There are a few ways you can approach your review.

- Preview your listing (see it as the bidder will), and then move back and forth to the selling form to make any corrections.

- Review your Review & Submit page, make corrections as you find them, and then do a final preview.

- Blend both methods.

1. Click any of the **Edit** links to the right of the section you want to change. You will return to the selling form step/page where that particular feature was located.

> Edit title
>
> Edit subtitle
>
> Edit description

2. Do either:

- Click **Save Changes** at the bottom of the page to return to the Review & Submit page with your changes reflected.

–Or–

- Click **Cancel Changes** at the bottom of the page to return to the Review & Submit page with your changes ignored.

3. Preview the listing by clicking **Preview How Your Item Will Look To Buyers** at the top of the page. Click **Close Preview** at the top of the preview page to return to the listing.

TIP

It's easy to make errors in the selling form if you use a mouse that has a scroll wheel. When you think you're scrolling down a page, you find that you're actually rotating your selection in a drop-down list you just used. Try to avoid using the scroll wheel whenever filling out an online form, and use the scroll bars on the side of the page instead.

Step 1: Review your listing

Preview how your item will look to buyers
Click an 'Edit page' link to make changes.

Sally the seller views and closes the listing preview before submitting the listing…

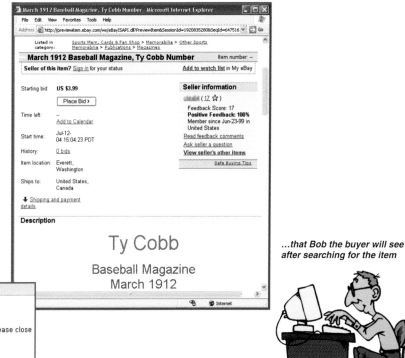

Sell Your Item: Preview Your Listing

Buyers will see the page below when they view your item. Please review the listing before submitting.

This listing is a preview only. This item has not been submitted. To submit or edit your listing, please close the preview window.

Close Preview

…that Bob the buyer will see after searching for the item

TIP

Now that you've submitted an item for auction, you can give yourself the rest of the month off, right? Don't even think about it! There are several actions that can, and need, to take place, both during the sale and after. See Chapter 7 for information on managing listings when they are live and Chapter 8 for actions to take after the sale is completed.

Review Fees and Submit

The final decision in the selling form is to make sure you're comfortable with the fees you've acquired throughout the selling form process.

1. In the **Review The Fees And Submit Your Listing** area, review your listing fees, and add or remove features.

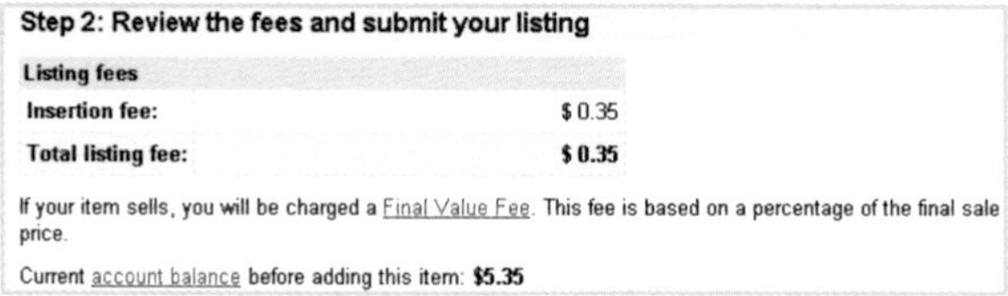

Step 2: Review the fees and submit your listing

Listing fees	
Insertion fee:	$ 0.35
Total listing fee:	$ 0.35

If your item sells, you will be charged a Final Value Fee. This fee is based on a percentage of the final sale price.

Current account balance before adding this item: **$5.35**

2. Verify the details of your account by clicking **Account Balance**. (See "Get a Seller's Account" in this chapter for information on eBay payment options.)
3. Click **Submit Listing** when your listing is as you want it. As shown in Figure 5-20, eBay will congratulate you (as it should!) and will send you a listing confirmation e-mail.

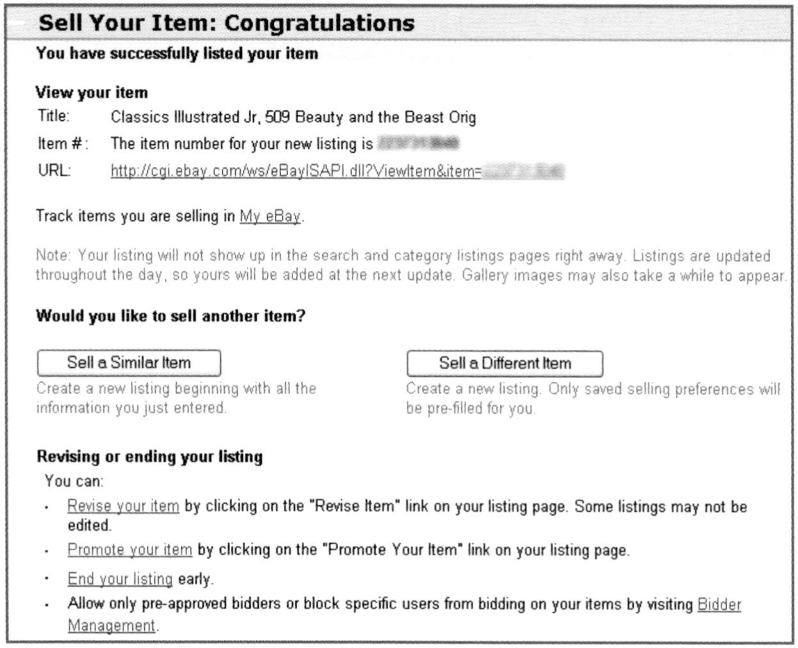

Sell Your Item: Congratulations

You have successfully listed your item

View your item

Title: Classics Illustrated Jr, 509 Beauty and the Beast Orig

Item #: The item number for your new listing is

URL: http://cgi.ebay.com/ws/eBayISAPI.dll?ViewItem&item=

Track items you are selling in My eBay.

Note: Your listing will not show up in the search and category listings pages right away. Listings are updated throughout the day, so yours will be added at the next update. Gallery images may also take a while to appear.

Would you like to sell another item?

Sell a Similar Item — Create a new listing beginning with all the information you just entered.

Sell a Different Item — Create a new listing. Only saved selling preferences will be pre-filled for you.

Revising or ending your listing

You can:

- Revise your item by clicking on the "Revise Item" link on your listing page. Some listings may not be edited.
- Promote your item by clicking on the "Promote Your Item" link on your listing page.
- End your listing early.
- Allow only pre-approved bidders or block specific users from bidding on your items by visiting Bidder Management.

Figure 5-20: After you complete the listing, you'll receive a congratulatory page and an e-mail with all the pertinent links and numbers.

How to...

Chapter 6
Making Your Listing Stand Out

In this chapter you will learn how to add visibility to your selling listing so that it can successfully compete with other listings on similar items as well as stand out from the crowd. You don't need dancing bears or talking heads to help draw attention to your listing—you just need to become comfortable with a few techniques that center on your display: taking, enhancing, organizing, and hosting pictures of your item; and using HTML to format your item's description. You can include as many pictures of your item as you want and add links to other material that supports the sale of your item.

According to eBay Live! 2004, buyers ranked pictures and the item description as the two most important pieces of listing information in their buying decisions.

QUICKSTEPS

GETTING PICTURES DISPLAYED ON THE FAST TRACK

There are really only a few steps you need to do to get one decent (and free) picture of your item displayed in your auction listing:

1. Obtain a digital camera or scanner.

2. Take a picture of your item.

"Sally, the seller, transfers her digital images into her computer."

3. Download the picture from your digital device to your computer.

4. From Sell on the menu bar, sign in and step through the Sell Your Item form.

5. In the "Pictures & Details" step of the selling form, choose to use eBay Picture Services (see "Use eBay Picture Services," later in this chapter).

> **3 Pictures & Details**

6. Browse to the location of the picture on your computer, and select it.

7. Submit your auction listing.

(For many sellers, this is all that's needed; for others—well, that's what the rest of the chapter is for.)

TIP

You might be able to use a scanner for many two-dimensional-like items as well as truly flat items. For example, we used one to take a picture of a portable CD player—the picture produced was great.

Include Pictures

If Cuba Gooding, Jr. is an eBay-buying enthusiast, I can see him shouting, "Show me the pictures!" every time he pulls up a listing. *Pictures* (a term that includes photographs, scanned images, and designed graphics) are often what sell an item. eBay has even devoted an entire way of looking at listings (Gallery view) that focuses on the visual image of an item. This section shows you how to take photos with a digital camera, use a scanner to take pictures of two-dimensional items, enhance your pictures with editing programs, organize your pictures in folders, and place your pictures on your own web site or one provided by eBay.

You are not selling your walls and blinds...

...you are selling a light!

Figure 6-1: Focus on the item you're selling.

Use a Scanner to Capture Digital Pictures

Nothing beats a flatbed scanner for obtaining a JPG file of two-dimensional items such as comic books, magazines, box covers, traditional photos, and even 35-mm slides. Scanners are generally cheaper than digital cameras, and many are included in the all-in-one home office devices that provide your printing, copying, and faxing functions. The newer scanners are simple to use, requiring only a few steps to obtain a digital picture.

TAKING QUALITY PHOTOS WITH DIGITAL CAMERAS

The fastest, cheapest, safest, and easiest way to obtain pictures for use on a selling form is to use a digital camera. For images that are designed to be displayed online, even a low-cost digital camera will be adequate (and thousands are for sale on eBay!).

You don't need to be a professional photographer or own a studio to produce quality pictures that capture a bidder's interest. There are several basic photographic pointers, however, that you can use to separate your listings from the pack.

THINK COMPOSITION

Photographic composition defines the detail, orientation, and symmetry of the picture. In eBay parlance, this boils down to taking pictures that focus on the item you are selling (see Figure 6-1). If you are selling a silver place setting, concentrate on the silverware itself, not on how well you can set a dining room table. Close-up pictures show details a buyer will be interested in; save the panoramas for your next trip to the Grand Canyon!

THINK SIZE

That new gazillion-megapixel camera takes great pictures, evidenced by the striking print that comes off your inkjet printer. Most bidders and buyers, however, don't want to wait the two and a half hours it would take to download that picture. Also, size relates to composition—a small picture makes it hard to see detail. Consider using eBay Picture Services to "supersize" pictures, or use HTML to create thumbnails and large-size offerings of the same picture.

Continued...

1. Place the item to be scanned on the flatbed, ensuring that the item is aligned with the origin of the scanner, as shown in Figure 6-2 (see "Straighten a Picture" in this chapter for techniques to correct skewed scans).

Figure 6-2: A good scan starts with proper alignment of the item to the origin of the flatbed.

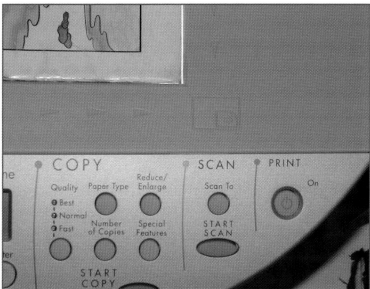

2. Start the scanner using controls on the device or from a scanning software program on your computer.

3. Choose to scan a picture (many software programs provide the choice of scanning a picture/photo or a document). Document scans are typically for OCR—optical scanning recognition—that converts text from the item into an editable word-processing file.

TAKING QUALITY PHOTOS WITH DIGITAL CAMERAS *(Continued)*

UTILIZE GOOD LIGHTING

Dark, backlit, and shadowed pictures show you are either an amateur photographer or haven't taken the time to create a quality picture—neither of which adds to your selling potential. Use a flash unless you have added auxiliary lighting or have good natural lighting. There is no additional cost to take several shots with a digital camera until you have one that provides your item in its "best light."

CREATE A MINI-STUDIO

Even if you are a casual seller, it is worth your time to set up an area that provides a pleasing environment for your pictures. For example, if selling furniture, you might have a kit of backdrop sheets, clamps, floodlighting, and a dolly available. When selling small items, such as glassware, you might line an open box with fabric to create an instant setting.

ENHANCE YOUR PICTURES

Despite your best efforts, sometimes you are just unsatisfied with the results of your picture taking. Fortunately, most digital cameras come with at least rudimentary picture-editing software, and if they don't, you can purchase programs designed for the novice photographer, the professional photographer, and everyone in between. Editing programs allow you to change resolution, sharpen images, adjust color, and otherwise change several other image attributes. See "Enhance Pictures with Photoshop Elements" for steps on how to use one popular program.

4. Drag a bounding box by its selection boxes (or *handles*) to select only the area you want scanned. (You probably won't have to fiddle with these if you want to scan the entire item—the software typically selects the outer border by default.)

5. Use menus to adjust properties. Typical adjustments you can make include:

   - **Resize** an item proportionally down to about half its full size. An approximate 4-inch x 5-inch scanned image provides a good-sized image on most monitors.

   - **Change the number of colors** to a higher setting (greater than 256 colors or 8-bit). Although you gain file size by increasing the color, the results are generally worth it in the eye of the bidder.

   - **Change resolution** to something close to 72 dots per inch, or dpi (see the Tip on resolution on the next page).

   - **Lighten** or **darken** the image, as necessary.

6. Preview the scan, make any further adjustments, and accept the results.

7. If prompted, save the file in an eBay pictures folder as a JPG file with medium-high compression. (There is no degradation at a setting of 7 out of 10, and file size is dramatically reduced from the highest setting.) Although compression shrinks the file size, the downside is that it does so by eliminating many of the pixels that make up the resolution of the picture.

Enhance Pictures with Photoshop Elements

Picture-editing software provides several tools that can be used to improve the quality of pictures you place in listings. These enhancements can be accomplished by most programs, although Adobe Photoshop Elements is used in this section due to its large popularity among non-professional photographers who want to go beyond the basics—but not too far. (The nature of the features

TIP

Resolution, measured in dots per square inch (dpi), is a measure of how well an optical device (digital camera and scanner, in our case) can contrast fine detail in an image. The higher the resolution—the greater density of dpi—the sharper the image, and the larger the file size (in kilobytes or megabits). Computer monitors are generally limited to displaying images at 72 dpi, so any resolution greater than that will not add to your bidder's viewing experience. Actually, higher-resolution pictures may defeat your purpose as they have larger file sizes and take longer to download to the viewer's computer. Large-file-size pictures taken at higher resolutions can be saved at lower resolutions in a photo-editing program (see "Change Picture Size and Resolution" in this chapter).

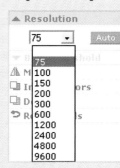

TIP

You can purchase ready-made "boxes" that provide the proper environment for taking pictures of smaller items. Two basic products are made by Cloud Dome (www.clouddome.com) and EZcube (www.ezcube.com).

---

involved is the same for many other programs; the actual procedures will vary slightly from program to program.) The first step in any of these procedures is to open the picture in Photoshop Elements. (For a more in-depth understanding of Adobe Photoshop Elements, see another book in the McGraw-Hill/Osborne QuickSteps series, *Adobe Photoshop Elements 2.0 QuickSteps*.)

1. Open Photoshop Elements.

2. Click **File** | **Browse** to the open the File Browser, shown in Figure 6-3, which locates picture files on your hard drive.

3. Use the folder hierarchy in the upper-left corner to select the folder where your picture is located, find the thumbnail you want in the right pane, and double-click the picture. The picture opens in its own window within Photoshop Elements. (Close the File Browser window by clicking the **Close** button at the right end of the title bar.)

4. Click the **Maximize** button to center the picture on the canvas, as shown in Figure 6-4 (you may not see the same palettes as shown in the figure).

Figure 6-3: The File Browser helps you locate thumbnails and provides properties on selected pictures.

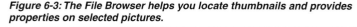
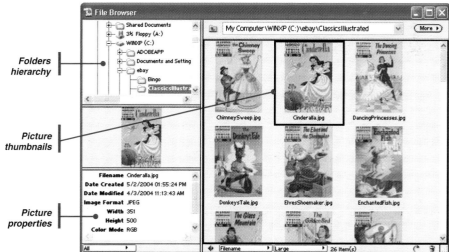

QUICKSTEPS

ROTATING A PICTURE USING A MOUSE

You can freely rotate a picture using a mouse.

1. Click **Select | All** to select the picture.

2. Click **Image | Transform | Free Transform**.

3. Click the **Rotate** button on the options bar.

4. Move your cursor near a corner or border of the selected picture until it becomes a double-headed curved line, and drag your mouse the direction and amount of rotation you want.

5. Click the **Commit Transform (Return)** button on the options bar.

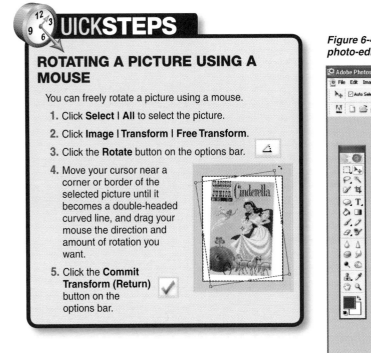

Figure 6-4: Open the picture in Adobe Photoshop Elements or another comparable photo-editing program to enhance pictures and fix common problems.

TIP

Besides straightening a picture, you can use a picture-editing program to *purposely* skew a picture to add a special effect to your composition.

CAUTION

If your photo is already straight and you try to straighten it using Image | Rotate | Straighten Image, it may become skewed, depending on the shape of the object and how Photoshop Elements sees it.

STRAIGHTEN A PICTURE

You can shoot a fairly straight picture with a digital camera, but it's common to skew a magazine, book, or other *ephemera* (paper-based antiques and collectibles) when using a scanner. Either:

- Click **Image | Rotate | Straighten Image** to let Photoshop Elements give its best guess at correcting the problem created by the scanner or other source.

  –Or–

- Click **Image | Rotate** and select a predefined degree of rotation from the submenu to correct a problem or intentionally skew a picture.

REMOVE BLURS

Sharpening increases the contrast between neighboring pixels and tends to bring blurry pictures into focus.

1. Click **Filter | Sharpen | Sharpen**, or press **CTRL+F**. The picture will change, hopefully for the better.

Filter	View	Window	
Sharpen	Ctrl+F		
Artistic		▶	

2. Continue sharpening by choosing **Filter | Sharpen** (the last filter used is displayed at the top of the menu) and pressing **CTRL+F** to sharpen the image or **CTRL+Z** to remove the previous effect. Figure 6-5 shows what too much of a good thing can do to a picture.

3. If the edges remain blurred, try selecting **Sharpen Edges** from the Sharpen submenu.

Sharpen	▶	Sharpen
Sketch	▶	Sharpen Edges
Stylize	▶	Sharpen More
Texture	▶	Unsharp Mask...

Figure 6-5: Overuse of sharpening (and other filters and effects) can cause undesired results.

Original photo

After excessive sharpening

Figure 6-6: By cropping you can remove areas of a picture that don't accentuate your item.

REMOVE UNWANTED AREAS IN A PICTURE

Cropping is the term used for trimming areas from a picture by removing them, as shown in Figure 6-6.

To quickly crop a picture:

1. Click the **Rectangular Marquee** tool in the toolbox, and drag the crosshair pointer over the area of the picture you want to keep.

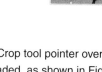 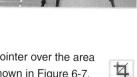

2. Click **Image | Crop**. The area outside the marquee is removed.

To fine-tune a crop:

1. Click the **Crop** tool in the toolbox, and drag the Crop tool pointer over the area you want to keep. The area to be removed is shaded, as shown in Figure 6-7.

2. Point to a border or sizing handle, and drag the bounding box toward or away from the center of the cropped area to adjust the area you want to keep.

3. Press **ENTER** to retain only the area within the bounding box.

TIP

To be more accurate in placing the marquee around the area you want to keep, click **View | Zoom In**, or press CTRL++ (CTRL and the plus sign). Repeat either technique to continue enlarging the picture. Click **View | Zoom Out**, or press CTRL+- (CTRL and a hyphen) to reduce the zoom.

TIP

After using the Crop tool, or other tools, return to the selection cursor by clicking the **Move** tool.

Figure 6-7: The Crop tool lets you refine the area to retain by adjusting the bounding box handles after you make your selection.

Figure 6-8: You can resize a picture and change its resolution by retaining all the original pixels, or you can have the software add or remove pixels as it sees fit.

Image Size

Pixel Dimensions: 703K

Width: 433 pixels

Height: 554 pixels

OK

Cancel

Help

Document Size:

Width: 4.33 inches

Height: 5.54 inches

Resolution: 100 pixels/inch

☑ Constrain Proportions

☑ Resample Image: Bicubic

TIP

The default Image Size dialog box setting lets Photoshop Elements *resample* the picture as you change file size or resolution, which means it adds or removes individual dots (or *pixels*) automatically to increase or decrease the file size. For large changes this can cause undesired effects, but for smaller changes you probably won't see much difference in quality. If you want to retain the original number of pixels (keep the file size the same) as you change file size or resolution, deselect the **Resample Image** check box.

CHANGE PICTURE SIZE AND RESOLUTION

1. Click **Image | Resize | Image Size**. The Image Size dialog box appears, shown in Figure 6-8.

2. In the Document Size area, do one of the following:

   ● Type a new value in the Width or Height text boxes for the dimension you want. Changing one value will automatically change the other as long as you leave the **Constrain Proportions** check box selected. You can click the **units of measure** down arrow and select **Percent** to change the size based on a percentage of the original.

   ● Type a new value in the Resolution text box. In either case, notice the value (file size) next to Pixel Dimensions changing.

3. Click **OK** when through.

CREATE A COMPOSITE PICTURE

Whether you use eBay Picture Services or your own web site in the Add Pictures area of the selling form, you are limited to displaying one picture for free. So in order to show the covers of two comic books you're selling as a group, does that mean you need to purchase an additional picture through eBay Picture Services? Not necessarily. You can use Photoshop Elements to create one digital picture from the two (or you can use HTML to add as many pictures as you want for free, as described in "Create a Custom Item Description," later in this chapter).

1. Click **File | New**. In the New dialog box, type a name for your composite picture, click the **Preset Sizes** down arrow, and choose a size for your picture (4 x 6 should work), or type your own values in the Width and Height text boxes. If necessary, change the resolution to 72 pixels per inch. Click **OK**.

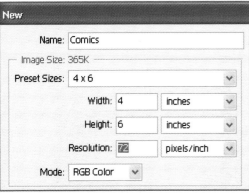

New

Name: Comics

Image Size: 365K

Preset Sizes: 4 x 6

Width: 4 inches

Height: 6 inches

Resolution: 72 pixels/inch

Mode: RGB Color

2. Use the File Browser to open the first picture that will be in your composite in its own window. Modify the picture (see "Change Picture Size and Resolution" in this section) so its resolution is 72 pixels per inch and it is the size you want in the composite picture.

3. Select the **Move** tool, and drag the resized picture onto the composite picture canvas. A *layer* from the original picture is copied.

4. Repeat steps 2 and 3 for the other picture(s) you want in the composite. Do one or more of the following:

   - Use the **Move** tool to shift the pictures on the canvas to the positions you want. (Overlapping the pictures provides a mosaic look to the composite picture.)

   - Make minor resizing changes by clicking the picture to select it, holding down **SHIFT** (to change the size proportionally), pointing to a corner sizing box until the cursor becomes a double-headed angles arrow, and dragging to the size you want.

   - Remove a picture by clicking it to select it, pressing **DELETE**, and clicking **Yes** when asked if you want to delete the layer.

5. When you have the composite looking as you want, as shown in Figure 6-9, save the composite picture (see "Save Pictures for eBay" in this section).

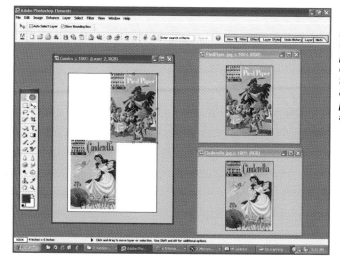

Figure 6-9: Combine several pictures into one composite picture to take advantage of eBay's one-free-picture offer on its selling form.

TABLE 6-1: THE FOUR FILE FORMATS USED FOR PICTURES ON THE WEB

	JPEG Joint Photographic Experts Group	GIF Graphics Interchange Format	PNG-8 Portable Network Graphics	PNG-24 Portable Network Graphics
Best suited for	Photos, broad range of colors/hues/ brightness	Logos, clip art, shape details	Logos, clip art, shape details	• Photos, broad range of colors/hues/brightness • Logos, clip art
Number of colors supported	16 million	256	256	16 million
Background transparency/matting supported (Matting simulates transparency by matching pixels along the edges of a picture to the background on which the picture is placed)		X	X	X (Multilevel transparency supported so you can blend edges better with background color)
Progressive scan support (Low-resolution picture appears as the full picture downloads)	X			
Animation supported		X		
Compression	Lossy (Pixels are discarded, especially at lower-quality settings)	Lossless	Lossless	Lossless
Browser support	Most	Most	Popular browsers (IE/ Netscape), but not all	Popular browsers (IE/ Netscape), but not all

TIP

The numbers (8 and 24) associated with the PNG file formats refer to the maximum number of colors supported by each in the binary number system. For example, PNG-8 supports 8 bits (11111111), or 256 colors, in our standard base-10 terms.

Save Pictures for eBay

You can save your changes to the original file by choosing **File | Save** or pressing **CTRL+S**; however, it's recommended you do not modify the original file(s)—instead, save your changes as a new file that you can optimize for the Web.

CHOOSING A PICTURE FILE FORMAT

Most picture-editing programs, digital cameras, and scanners allow you to save your pictures in one of several file formats, such as JPEG, GIF, PNG, or TIFF. For pictures to be used on eBay, you are limited to the file formats that are supported by web browsers. Each format has features and limitations that make it suitable for particular purposes, as shown in Table 6-1. The best current compromise of size, quality, and support for photos or scans of items used on eBay is JPEG (file extension .jpg). Use GIF if creating clip art or using solid-color logos and other graphics.

1. In Photoshop Elements, click the **Save For Web** button on the shortcuts bar, or choose **File I Save For Web**. The Save For Web dialog box appears, as shown in Figure 6-10.

   Settings: JPEG High

   You can optimize the picture by adjusting the format-specific optimization settings in the right sidebar. For eBay use, the default settings will work just fine—for example, use JPEG High for photos and GIF for logos and graphics (see the QuickFacts "Choosing a Picture File Format").

2. Check the file size and download time for a specific connection speed at the bottom of the right, or optimized picture, pane. Change the picture's dimensions and file size by making adjustments in the **Width**, **Height**, or **Percent** text boxes. Preview any optimized changes by clicking your browser icon in the Preview In box. Click **OK** when finished.

3. In the Save Optimized As dialog box, locate and name the file. Click **Save**.

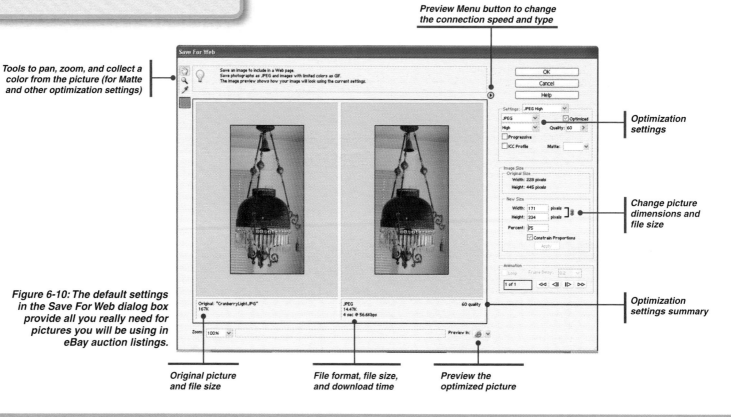

Preview Menu button to change the connection speed and type

Tools to pan, zoom, and collect a color from the picture (for Matte and other optimization settings)

Optimization settings

Change picture dimensions and file size

Optimization settings summary

Figure 6-10: The default settings in the Save For Web dialog box provide all you really need for pictures you will be using in eBay auction listings.

Original picture and file size

File format, file size, and download time

Preview the optimized picture

NOTE

The Save For Web dialog box provides several means to optimize pictures using file formats acceptable on the Web; however, you do not have to use this dialog box to save files for use on the Web. You can use the Save As dialog box and choose one of the file formats listed in Table 6-1, although you won't have as many options available to you.

TIP

Change the connection speed used to calculate the viewer's download time by clicking the **Preview Menu** button above and to the right of the altered photo in the Save For Web dialog box (see Figure 6-10) and selecting **56.6 Kbps Modem/ISDN** from the menu. This is the speed of the majority of dial-up modems and can be used as the worst-case download time scenario; that is, if the speed is acceptable at this setting, it will satisfy all but those who should upgrade their modems.

NOTE

If you want your picture ownership to be brutally obvious to everyone, simply use a picture-editing program to type text directly on your picture. For instance, in Photoshop Elements, click the **Horizontal Type** tool, click the picture, and type the text.

Digitally Sign Your Pictures

To provide some degree of protection against others using your pictures for their purposes, you can affix a copyright notice to your pictures. (A user would need to open your picture in Photoshop Elements or Photoshop to see the copyright information, but the burden of responsibility in using copyrighted material is on the user, not the originator.)

1. Open the picture you want to copyright in Photoshop Elements (or Photoshop).
2. Click **File | File Info** to open the File Info dialog box, shown in Figure 6-11.
3. In the upper part of the dialog box, fill in the **Title**, **Author**, and **Caption** text boxes.
4. Click the **Copyright Status** down arrow, and select **Copyrighted Work**.
5. In the Copyright Notice text box, type a statement, such as Copyright 2004, *yourname*. All Rights Reserved.
6. In the Owner URL text box, type the URL to the owner's web site, where you could have supplementary information on your work.
7. Click **OK** to apply the data to the file.

Figure 6-11: You can provide proof of ownership by adding a digital copyright to your pictures.

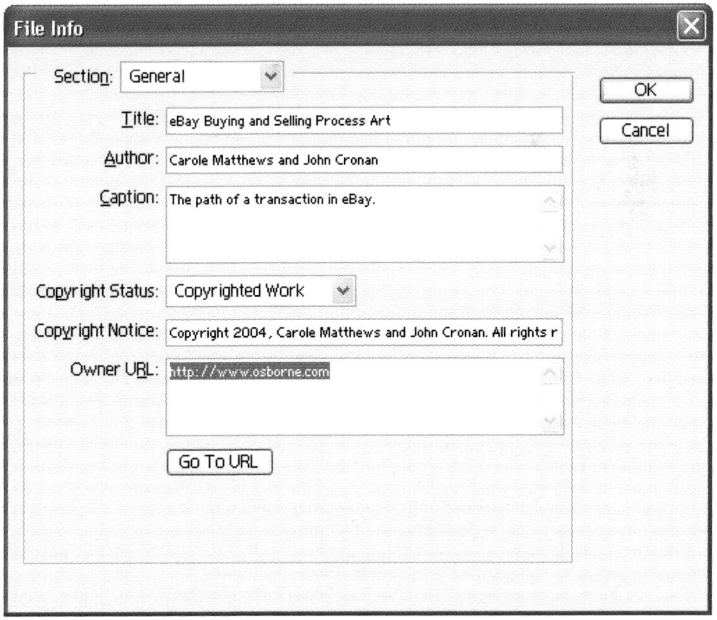

Organize Your Pictures

Regardless of the method you use to create a picture for an eBay auction listing, you will need to provide the picture from a folder on your computer. You can use any folder hierarchy system that makes sense to you, but Microsoft has provided one for you—My Documents | My Pictures. If you find your digital picture-taking needs a higher level of organization, you can use a third-party program that offers picture-friendly features, often integrated with photo-editing programs, such as Adobe Photoshop Album, described in this chapter.

STORE YOUR PICTURES IN ONE FOLDER

The latest Microsoft operating systems have been "training" us for years to use their My Documents folder and underlying subfolders to store our personal files. The My Pictures folder in Windows XP has added features that make working with picture files even easier. Click the **Start** button, and click **My Pictures** on the Start menu. The My Pictures folder opens in Microsoft Explorer, as shown in Figure 6-12. Do one or more of the following:

- Create a subfolder hierarchy so you can organize the pictures you use in listings. (We use the listing number for the folder name, which we also use in Outlook to organize e-mails.)

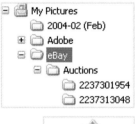

- Create a shortcut to your My Pictures folder on the desktop by using the right mouse button to drag the My Pictures icon from the Start menu to a blank area on your desktop. Click **Create Shortcuts Here** from the context menu that appears.

Shortcut to My Pictures

- Use the Picture Tasks feature on the tasks pane to help you get pictures from your camera or scanner, print the pictures, or add them to a special folder that stores files to be written to a CD. (Your options will depend on your hardware and software configurations.)

| Open |
| Edit |
| Import into Adobe Photoshop Album |
| Preview |
| Print |
| Refresh Thumbnail |
| Rotate Clockwise |
| Rotate Counter Clockwise |

- Right-click a picture file, and use the picture-related options on the context menu.

NOTE

It used to be that the most difficult step in the digital photography process was getting the picture from the camera to your computer. Microsoft Windows XP and software that help you transfer and organize digital pictures make the process as simple as connecting a USB cable (or serial cable for older models) between your camera and the computer and turning the camera on. Windows XP sees the camera as a removable disk and provides a window where you can set up folders and transfer the photos from the camera. Alternatively, you can use the software that came with your camera or third-party programs, such as Adobe Photoshop Album (see "Integrate Storing, Editing, and Sharing" in this chapter), which provides the same ease-of-access capability and more. And if all that fails, get a card reader that Windows also sees as a removable disk, pull the memory card from your camera, and insert it in the card reader.

Figure 6-12:
The My Pictures
folder displays
thumbnails and
offers picture-
related tasks.

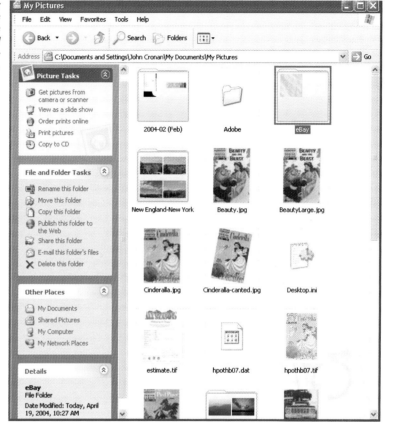

INTEGRATE STORING, EDITING, AND SHARING

There are as many integrated programs available for handling pictures as there are digital camera and scanner manufacturers. Though most provide the basics, a good example of what a better program can do for you is Adobe Photoshop Album. The program offers six elements, as shown in Figure 6-13, at least five of which are key to eBay sellers.

- **Get Photos** provides gateways to transfer your pictures from current locations (hard drive, digital camera and scanner, media such as CDs, and mobile phones) into the program.

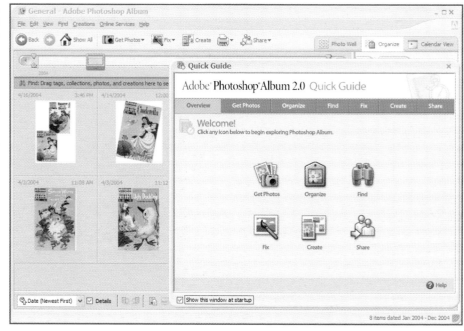

Figure 6-13: Integrated programs are available that combine all the tools you need for working with pictures in eBay.

QUICK**FACTS**

CHOOSING A PHOTO-EDITING PROGRAM

Most eBay sellers are not, nor do they want to become, professional photographers, digital or otherwise. They are generally busy enough placing listings, managing auctions, shipping items, and dealing with bidders and buyers. The quandary, however, lies in the fact that you still need to provide a certain modicum of quality to the pictures you use in your listings. To compensate for this potential lack of talent, what do you do? You cheat! Today's picture-editing software can make the job of improving less-than-perfect pictures relatively painless—to your time, frustration factor, and checking account.

Adobe Photoshop Elements (see "Enhance Pictures with Photoshop Elements" in this section) is a prime example of a reasonably priced middle-of-the road program (it sells for $99.00 at the Adobe Store). Using Adobe's product line as an example, you can use their entry-level program Photoshop Album ($49.95 Adobe Store price), which combines integrated storage with some editing features (see "Integrate Storing, Editing, and Sharing" in this section). Similar products typically come with your digital camera or scanner, although you will eventually bump up against a feature you need that isn't provided. On the other hand, you could purchase Adobe's flagship photo-editing program, Photoshop CS, although the cost ($649.00 Adobe Store price) and steeper learning curve is hard to justify for the type of pictures you need for your items.

- **Organize** lets you tag your pictures by topic for easy retrieval; create collections of similar pictures; and view them in several formats, such as by a timeline, tags, or collections.

- **Find** individual pictures by dates in a calendar view, a date range, tags, and even color similarity by selecting **Find | By Color Similarity with Selected Photo(s)**.

- **Fix** pictures by using basic techniques (such as fix red eye, crop, or rotate), or open the picture in Photoshop Elements for more features.

- **Create** allows you to combine pictures into photo albums, calendars, and other packages. This element of Photoshop Album is not necessary for most eBay sellers, although some might find it useful to create and send a custom eCard to successful bidders or create a slideshow of multiple-item pictures (both eCard and slideshows are saved in PDF format, which requires Adobe Acrobat Reader; a free download is available from http://www.adobe.com/products/acrobat/readstep2.html).

- **Sharing** provides easy-to-use features to transfer pictures for eBay-related areas such as hosting, e-mail, devices such as mobile phones and PDAs; or even your printer.

QUICKSTEPS

CHANGING EBAY PICTURE SERVICES IMAGES

You can perform three actions on pictures you host using Enhanced eBay Picture Services (these actions are not available to pictures you choose using the Basic Picture Services tool). Click the thumbnail you want to change.

ROTATE A PICTURE

Click the **Rotate** button in the upper-right corner of the preview area. Each time you click the button, the picture in the preview area rotates counterclockwise 90 degrees.

TRIM A PICTURE

Click the **Crop** button in the upper-right corner of the preview area. Sizing handles appear on the picture in the preview area. Drag the preview picture's border or corner to the rectangular area you want to display. You can move the crop rectangle by placing your mouse pointer over the area and dragging the four-sided pointer. The shaded area outside the new border will not display in the auction listing.

REMOVE A PICTURE

Click the **Remove Pictures** button in the upper-left corner of the preview area.

Use eBay Picture Services

eBay Picture Services provides one free hosted picture and includes several free and for-fee features:

- **Add additional pictures** ($0.15 each), up to a maximum of 12
- **Supersizing** a picture that, when selected by the bidder, displays an enlargement up to 11 by 8 inches in size ($0.75)
- A **preview picture** that is displayed at the top of your auction, in addition to the standard location farther down in the form, along with the description (free to Picture Services members)
- A **slide show** that lets a bidder cycle through two or more pictures of an item to give a sense of animation ($0.75)
- **Picture Pack** is a package deal of features—up to six pictures, supersizing, and Gallery listing ($1.00, or increase from seven to twelve pictures for $1.50)

1. Following Step 2 of the Sell Your Item form, "Title & Description," after you have clicked **Continue**, you will see an informational message and then a warning to download a small file to improve the speed and functionality of the eBay Picture Services (referred to as *Enhanced eBay Picture Services*). Click **Yes** in the Security Warning dialog box to download the file. (You do not have to install the file to use the *Basic* eBay Picture Services—just click **No** to continue.)

2. In the third step of the selling form, "Pictures & Details," scroll down the screen, and under Add Pictures, click the **eBay Picture Services** tab.

Add pictures

eBay Picture Services
Let eBay host your pictures

3. If you have not done so already, you are given another opportunity to download the Enhanced eBay Picture Services file that improves the speed and functionality of the service. Click **Yes** in the Security Warning dialog box to display the Enhanced eBay Picture Services tab.

CAUTION

eBay Picture Services only hosts pictures for the duration of the auction listing. They will not be available in completed auctions.

4. Click **Add Pictures** in the 1. (Free) box. In the Open dialog box, browse to locate the picture you want to appear in the auction listing. Double-click the picture, and a thumbnail appears in the box. A larger view of the selected picture displays in the preview area to the right of the tab, as shown in Figure 6-14.

5. Add additional pictures or select options from the preview area (see the QuickSteps "Changing eBay Picture Services Images"). The picture(s) will be uploaded to eBay through your Internet connection when you leave the Picture Services tab or click **Continue** at the bottom of the page.

Figure 6-14: eBay provides picture-hosting services for free or at minimal cost using basic or enhanced options.

Rotate and crop previewed pictures (Enhanced eBay Picture Services only)

Add up to 12 pictures; the first one is free

Choose from several picture upgrades

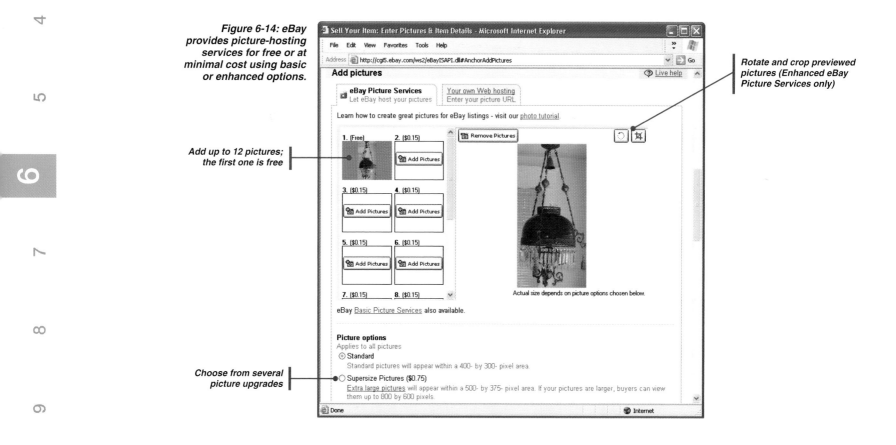

Host Your Pictures

You can arrange to have your pictures hosted on a web site outside of eBay. While adding a few more steps to the process than required by eBay Picture Services, you have more flexibility, can use multiple pictures, and have greater control over where they are located on the auction listing. All you need to do is transfer the picture(s) from your computer to the hosting web server and provide the URL of the hosting web server in the selling form. There are three typical methods to hosting your own pictures.

RUN YOUR OWN WEB SERVER

If you are a total "do-it-yourselfer," you can have a web server sitting in your den that stores the pictures that appear in your auction listings—simply type your URL and picture location, for example, http://mywebsite.com/ ebay/2237301954.jpg, in the Your Own Web Hosting tab in Step 3 of the selling form. Unless you have a web server for other pursuits, however, it is not practical to create one just for hosting eBay pictures (common expenses include a computer, software, static IP address, constant Internet connection, and firewall—not to mention your time).

USE A THIRD-PARTY WEB SITE

Most ISPs (Internet service providers) offer some limited (and often free) space on a web server where you can set up a personal web site as part of your service contract. You can use this same location to host your eBay pictures. Also, you can rent web server space from many web hosting companies. The steps to using this method include:

1. Set up a folder for eBay use on your web site by obtaining from your ISP or web server administrator the FTP (file transfer protocol) address and logon data to access your web site. Use an FTP program, such as CuteFTP (www.cuteftp.com) or WS_FTP Pro (www.ipswitch.com), to connect to the web site.

2. Transfer the picture from your computer to the web site using the FTP program, as shown in Figure 6-15.

3. Click the **Your Own Web Hosting** tab in Step 3, "Pictures & Details," of the selling form.

> **NOTE**
>
> One of the biggest advantages to hosting your own pictures is you have a virtually unlimited number of pictures you can display in your auction listing—and free from any eBay fees. The trick is that you have to include them in your Item Description; otherwise, you are limited to one free picture using the Your Own Web Hosting tab in Step 3, "Pictures & Details," of the Sell Your Item form. See "Create a Custom Item Description" in this chapter for techniques on using HTML to spice up your descriptions by formatting text, adding pictures and logos, and providing links to other web sites and your e-mail address.

4. Type the URL to your picture (different from the FTP address) in the Picture Web
Address text box.

Folders and files on web server

Local folders

**Select files and click
direction arrows to
transfer files**

```
WS_FTP95 Pro ftpmysite.verizon.net

Local System
c:\Documents and Settings\John Cronan\My D

    Name              Date       Size    ChgDir
    ..                                    MkDir
    2004-02 (Feb)    040303 08:15
    Adobe            040414 10:02
    eBay             040419 10:27
    New England-N~   040225 09:23         View
    Beauty.jpg       040407 15:58    1
    BeautyLarge.j~   040414 16:25    3    Exec
    Cinderalla-ca~   040414 12:00
    Cinderalla.jp~   040403 11:13    1    Rename
    Desktop.ini      031106 11:25         Delete
    estimate.tif     040303 08:15   10
    hpothb07.dat     040419 07:14         Refresh
    hpothb07 tif     040419 07·14    5
                                          DirInfo

Remote System
/ebay

    Name              Date       Size    ChgDir
    ..                                    MkDir
    24_Whitehorse~   040417 21:59    71912
    Beauty.jpg       040407 22:58   125308
    BeautyLarge.j~   040414 23:28   360676
    BK-greyish.gi~   040417 22:36    10624  View
    SleepingBeaut~   040405 16:34   118437
    UglyDuck.jpg     040407 17:04   129318  Exec
                                            Rename
                                            Delete
                                            Refresh
                                            DirInfo

    ASCII      Binary    Auto

Received 439 bytes in 0.1 secs, (30.77 Kbps), transfer succeeded
226-Transfer complete.
226 Quota: avail(84.4%)=4425453.0 used(15.6%)=817427.0 limit=5242880.0 bytes

Close    Cancel    LogWnd    Help    Options    About    Exit
```

*Figure 6-15: FTP programs let you drag and drop files
between your local computer and a remote web site.*

USE A SERVICE

For a small fee (a few dollars a month), or even for free, you can use a service
similar to eBay Picture Services that provides hosting, a transfer service (an
online form that lets you browse for pictures on your computer and FTP), and
editing features. For sellers with limited computer experience or who want the
ease of eBay Picture Services but with more features, this is probably the way to
go. A Google search displays services you can choose from, as shown in Figure
6-16. The service you choose will provide instructions on what to type in the
selling form to access your pictures.

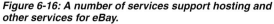

Figure 6-16: A number of services support hosting and other services for eBay.

Create a Custom Item Description

eBay gives the seller a lot of latitude in creating an item description outside the boundaries of the tools and features on the Sell Your Item form described in Chapter 5. With only minimal knowledge, you can put together what is essentially your own web page using HTML editors or adding the HTML code yourself. You can create eye-catching listings that include backgrounds, multiple pictures, a logo, and links to other web pages that support the item, you as the seller, and your other eBay activities, as shown in Figure 6-17.

Figure 6-17: Create listings that showcase your item with additional pictures and hyperlinks.

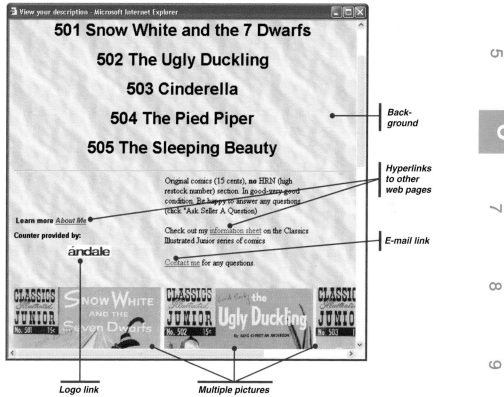

NOTE

eBay has strict guidelines on the type and number of links you can use in the item description in Step 2 of the selling form. You should review the links policy in its entirety (click **Help** on the links bar at the top of a page and search for "links policy"); however, eBay pretty well sums it up by saying auction listings can only contain "…text descriptions, graphics, pictures, and other content relevant to the sale of that item." In other words, you cannot link to web sites outside of eBay "or any page that has items for sale outside of eBay."

Use a WYSIWYG HTML Editor

The easiest way to create a web page that you can use as your item description in Step 2 of the selling form is to purchase a WYSIWYG (What You See Is What You Get) HTML editor, such as Microsoft FrontPage, that lets you use word processor-type controls to format text, add pictures, and create links.

1. Open the HTML editor (Microsoft FrontPage is used here as an example).

2. Type your description, using the tools and features of the editor (shown in Figure 6-18) to format the text.

3. When you have the page looking the way you want it, switch from the WYSIWYG view to the view that shows the HTML code.

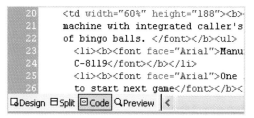

4. Press **CTRL+A** to select all the text, and then press **CTRL+C** to copy it to Windows Clipboard. Save the HTML file for future use.

5. Open your selling form, and in the second step of the form, "Title & Description," click the **Enter Your Own HTML** tab, click the text box to place the cursor there, and press **CTRL+V** to paste the text into the text box.

Item description

Describe your items features, benefits, and condition. Get tips on writing a great item description in Toys & Hobbies.

| Standard | Enter your own HTML |

* Spell Check

```
<html>
<head>
<meta name="GENERATOR" content="Microsoft FrontPage 6.0">
<meta name="ProgId" content="FrontPage.Editor.Document">
<meta http-equiv="Content-Type" content="text/html; charset=windows-1252">
<title>Vintage Bingo Game</title>
</head>
<body background="./0">
<p align="center"><font size="7" color="#008080">Vintage<br>
Bingo Game</font></p>
```

6. Click **Preview Description** below the text box to see how your text will look in the live listing. Return to your editor to make any corrections.

Microsoft Word lets you save the text you type and format as an HTML page. This is fine if you are using it as a separate page that you will host along with your pictures and link to it—for example, a page you use for more information on your item where a bidder can click a link in the listing that reads "For More Information." However, if you are using Word as an editor to create text where you would copy and paste the text into the item description in the Sell Your Item form, it's better to paste the formatted text from Word onto the Standard tab and let eBay convert it to HTML for you. If you paste the text onto the Enter Your Own HTML tab, the HTML code isn't copied from Word, only the text.

Use HTML to Format Text

HTML employs a series of tags that identify the elements in a web page. Tags consist of a tag name enclosed in angle brackets, and normally come in pairs. Tags are placed at the beginning and end of an element, usually text, that you want to identify, with the ending tag name preceded by a slash. For example, "Buy Now!" uses the bold tag to identify the word "Now." The phrase would display as Buy **Now**!

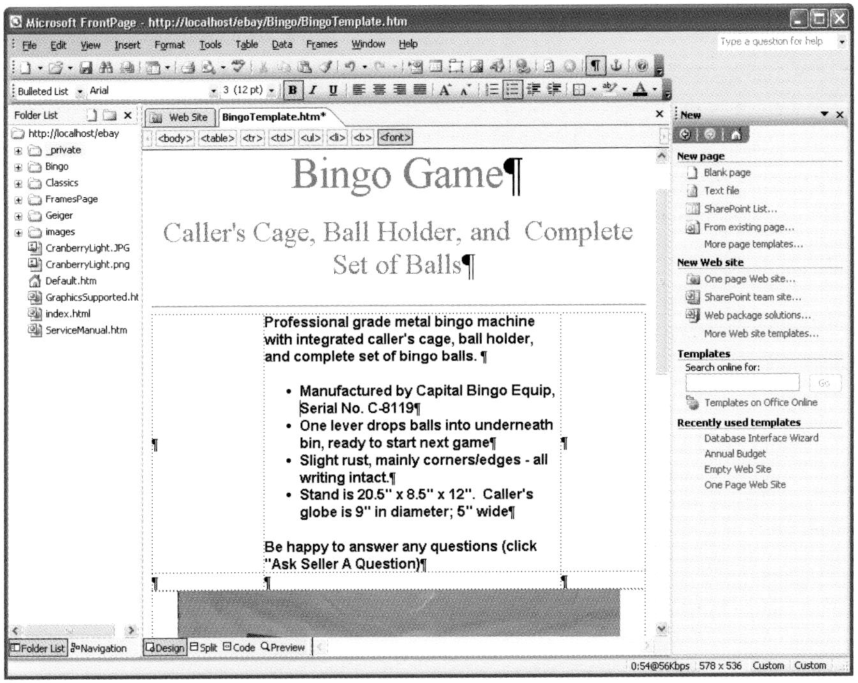

You can type your own tags in the Enter Your Own HTML tab of the item description in the second step of the selling form (see Chapter 5), or you can use a text editor, such as Notepad, shown in Figure 6-19.

1. Click the **Start** button, and select **All Programs I Accessories I Notepad**.

2. Type or paste your text into Notepad.

3. Use HTML tags to format the text as you want it to appear in your auction listing.

4. Press **CTRL+A** to select all the text, and then press **CTRL+C** to copy it to Windows Clipboard. Save the text file for future use.

5. Open your selling form, and in the second step of the form, "Title & Description," click the **Enter Your Own HTML** tab, click the text box to place the cursor there, and press **CTRL+V** to paste the text into the text box.

6. Click **Preview Description** below the text box to see how your text will look in the live listing. Return to Notepad to make any corrections.

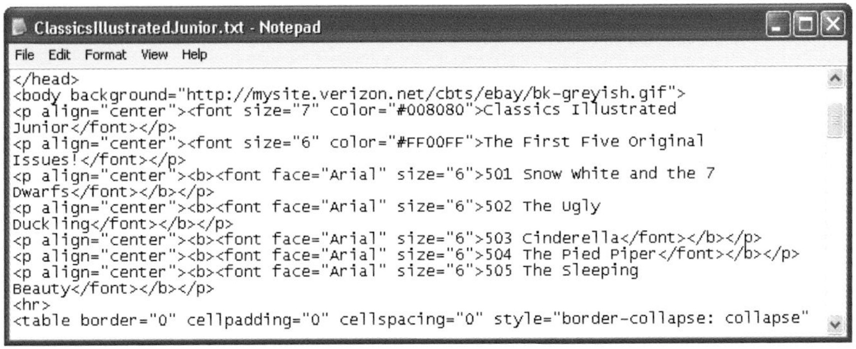

Figure 6-18: WYSIWYG HTML editors let you use word processor-like tools to create a web page.

Figure 6-19: You can type or paste text into a text editor, such as Notepad, and add HTML tags.

QUICK**FACTS**

LEARNING ABOUT HTML

To learn more about HTML, the language of the Web, you can check out eBay's listings of commonly used tags and use other readily available resources.

VIEW COMMON TAGS

eBay provides a "starter kit" of tags you can reference to get started typing your own descriptions.

1. Click **Help** in the links bar at the top of a page.
2. On the eBay Help page, type html in the Search Help text box, and click **Search Help**.
3. Click the **HTML Tips To Improve The Look Of Your Item Description** link. Tags are listed by usage categories.
4. Alternatively, click **Site Map** on the links bar, and under Help, click **Images/HTML Board**.

Many HTML tags are combined with one or more *attributes* that modify what the tag does—for example, in the Use Color section of the HTML Tips page,

Use Color
Liven type up with built-in colors like purple, red, silver, teal, yellow, or
Tag
`<font color=color> </font>`

the <FONT> tag is modified by the color attribute to add color to text. Other attributes for the <FONT> tag include size, the font family (for example, Arial), weight (how bold), and style (italic, oblique, or normal). The <TABLE> tag has well over a dozen attributes, as you'll see in the "Check Out Online HTML Resources" QuickFacts.

KEEP GOOD HABITS

HTML is a forgiving language, which can lead one to be a bit sloppy in the application of HTML tags and attributes. Adhering to the generally accepted rules of other languages used for web pages might prevent

Continued...

Add Pictures using HTML

Pictures in the eBay selling form (and in web pages in general) are not actually an integral part of the page; they are hosted, or linked, to the web page from the web server where they are located. All you have to do is add some HTML to your item description that points to the stored location.

You can link to as many pictures of your item that you want.

1. In the selling form's Enter Your Own HTML text box or in a text editor, use the IMG tag and SRC attribute (see the QuickFacts "Learning about HTML" for descriptions of HTML terms, such as tag and attribute), and type <IMG SRC="*URL to picture*">. For example, if your picture, ParlorLight.jpg, is hosted on acmehosting.com in a folder named Jones, you would type <IMG SRC="http://acmehosting.com/Jones/ParlorLight.jpg">.
2. Preview your description, and make any desired changes, such as combining an alignment tag to shift the picture on the page (for example, adding <CENTER> before the IMG tag will center the picture horizontally on the page).

ADD A LOGO

Logos give acknowledgement to third parties that assist you in listing a particular item. eBay limits logos for an item description to:

Counter provided by:

ándale

- Text no larger than HTML Size="3"
- Text containing no more than ten words
- Graphic or picture sized no greater than 88 x 33 pixels
- Only one logo per description being *hyperlinked* so a bidder can click it and jump to a third party's web page that describes the services used in the listing

Use the IMG tag to provide a static logo. See "Hyperlink to an Amplifying Page" to see how to create a hyperlink.

TIP

If you want the bidder to see text when he or she moves the mouse pointer over the picture, add the ALT attribute to the IMG tag. For example, <IMG SRC="http://acmehosting.com/Jones/ParlorLight.jpg"ALT="Hanging Oil Parlor Light w/Gorgeous Red Shade"> will cause the words "Hanging Oil Parlor Light w/Gorgeous Red Shade" to appear when the mouse pointer is moved over the picture.

ADD A BACKGROUND

You can add a picture to the background of your listing to give contrast to the text and pictures of your items. (An example of a textured background is seen in Figure 6-17.) The BODY tag is used with the BACKGROUND attribute. The picture you choose will be repeated, or tiled, to fill the area in the selling form. Background images are usually small files, typically GIFs, with patterns that can be repeated into a seamless backdrop.

1. Transfer the background you want to use to a hosting web server.

2. In the Enter Your Own HTML text box in the second step of the selling form, or in a text editor, type <BODY BACKGROUND="*URL to background picture*">.

Add Hyperlinks to Other Web Pages

Hyperlinks are a type of link that make an object on a web page "clickable." eBay only allows limited hyperlinking from the item description.

HYPERLINK TO AN AMPLIFYING PAGE

You can have one hyperlink to a page that provides extra information on the item for bid or sale. After you create the hyperlink, the clickable text will be colored blue and underlined.

```
mythical "Ashley Lake" claimed
  This non-existent lake
06 map of Virginia based on
  New York all the way to what is
  map of the region, and Wells
red on so many maps so as to
s 1672 account of his voyages
```

1. Transfer the HTML page that contains your amplifying information to a hosting web server.

2. In the Enter Your Own HTML text box in the second step of the selling form, or in a text editor, type <A HREF= "*URL to information HTML file*">*text you want to be clickable*</A>. For example, if your information file is named OlympusD-460 More.htm, located on a web server at http://www.acmeserver.com, and you wanted "See More Details" to be hyperlinked, your entry would be similar to: <A HREF="http://www.acmeserver/yourusername/olympusd-460 More.htm">See More Details</A>.

CREATE AN E-MAIL HYPERLINK

You can have one hyperlink that opens the bidder's e-mail program with your e-mail address displayed in the To box so he or she can contact you for more information on the item.

In the Enter Your Own HTML text box in the second step of the selling form, or in a text editor, type <u><A HREF= "mailto:*e-mail address you want to appear in To block*">*text you want to be clickable*</A></u>. For example, if your e-mail address is CamerasOnTheCheap@acme.com, and you wanted "Contact Me" to be hyperlinked, your entry would be similar to: <A HREF="mailto:camerasonthech eap@acme.com">Contact Me</A>.

HYPERLINK TO YOUR ABOUT ME PAGE

You can add a hyperlink to your item description that takes a bidder directly to your About Me page. (The eBay-provided About Me icon does the same thing.) See Chapter 10 for additional information on how to create an About Me page.

In the Enter Your Own HTML text box in the second step of the selling form, or in a text editor, type <u><A HREF="http://members.ebay.com/aboutme/ *youruserid*">*text to be the hyperlinked*</A></u>. For example, if your User ID was "littlebuddy" and you wanted "Come see more about me!" to be hyperlinked, your entry would be: <A HREF="http://members.ebay.com/aboutme/ littlebuddy">Come see more about me!</A>.

Chapter 7
Managing Your Sale

In this chapter you will learn what to do after you click the Submit button on the Sell Your Item form until the listing closes. The real work of selling on eBay starts when you submit that selling form. There are several actions you can take to monitor active sales while the listings are live, including communicating with bidders; changing a listing; adding to the item's description; or canceling a bid, a scheduled listing, or even the entire sale. Also, you might want to learn as much as you can about your prospective buyers.

Fortunately, eBay provides My eBay, shown in Figure 7-1, a great tool to help you manage and keep track of the most common things that are required during the auction or sale. (See Chapter 8 for information on what to do after the listing closes.)

NOTE

The management activities described in this chapter are designed for the casual eBay seller. If you have dozens of items for bid at a time, see Chapter 10 for techniques and tools that are geared toward selling on eBay on a volume or business basis.

Organize My eBay Selling Views

You can customize a great deal in the My eBay views that is associated with selling items, making your management of multiple listings that much easier. See Chapters 1 and 2 for additional information on using My eBay.

View Selling Activities

There is no better place to start managing sales than from the My eBay All Selling page, shown in Figure 7-2. Selling activities are divided into *views*. Two views pertain to working with current auctions; one provides reminders for current and completed listings; and two more display information related to listings after a sale is completed. Open the All Selling page by clicking **My eBay** on the menu bar at the top of any eBay page, and then clicking **All Selling** on the My eBay Views sidebar.

Figure 7-1: From My eBay you can monitor listings and act upon most live-sale management issues.

- **Scheduled Items** lists items that are scheduled to start at a future time (up to three weeks from the time you submit each selling form).

- **Items I'm Selling** displays those items that are currently for sale or bid.

- **Selling Reminders** act as constant "nags" to ensure you don't forget key selling points, such as listings that will be closing soon, feedback yet to be provided to buyers, and items to be shipped.

- **Items I've Sold** displays listings and activities (such as filtering and sorting listings) and provides actions you can perform for completed sales with a winning bidder or buyer (such as leaving feedback and checking on payment and shipping status).

- **Unsold Items** displays listings and provides actions for completed sales that closed without a winning bidder or buyer.

TIP

You can add or remove selling (and other) views that are displayed on the My Summary page (see Chapter 1 for more information).

TIP

Items for sale on your My eBay page that are in "play" and will sell when the auction closes are displayed in bold green text. Items that are waiting for that first bid are shown in red. Fixed-price (and eBay Store) items are displayed in black.

NOTE

Listings don't always stay put. Items that initially appear in the Items I'm Selling view will move to the Items I've Sold or Unsold Items view after the auction or sale is completed. Also, scheduled auctions that first are displayed in the Scheduled Items view will appear in the Items I'm Selling view after the auction starts.

Figure 7-2: The All Selling page in My eBay is a great central locator to view any items that are for sale, will go on sale, or that have been for sale recently.

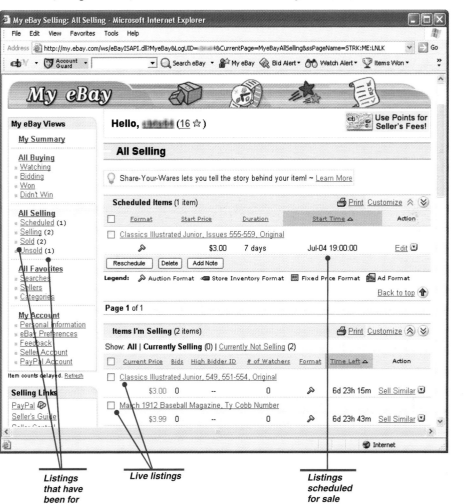

Listings that have been for sale

Live listings

Listings scheduled for sale

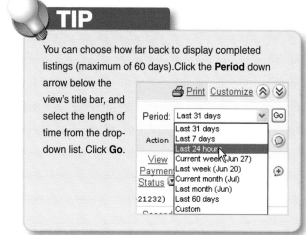

You can choose how far back to display completed listings (maximum of 60 days).Click the **Period** down arrow below the view's title bar, and select the length of time from the drop-down list. Click **Go**.

Make a Selling View Your Home Page

You can access any of the selling pages each time you open your browser or by clicking your browser's home page button.

1. Click **My eBay** on the menu bar at the top of any eBay page, and then click the view you want as your home page on the My eBay View sidebar.

2. Open your browser's **Options** or **Preferences** dialog box (Internet Explorer: **Tools | Internet Options**; Netscape Navigator: **Edit | Preferences**).

3. In the Home Page section of either browser, click **Use Current** (**Page**) to set the view you currently have open in My eBay as your home page. Click **OK**.

Change Selling Form Preferences

The options you chose the first time you used the Sell Your Item form to create a listing are retained and appear as default preferences when you use the selling form again. You can change these options so they are displayed the next time you sell an item.

Figure 7-3: You can change the default settings that appear in the Sell Your Item form.

Seller Preferences		
Sell Your Item picture preference:	**Your Own Web Hosting**	change
Payment preferences		change
Display Pay Now button:	**For all items**	
PayPal Preferred:	**On**	
Offer PayPal on All Listings:	**Yes**	
Payment Address:		
	Everett WA 98201	
	United States	
Shipping preferences		
Offer combined payment discounts:	**Yes**	change
Offer UPS Daily Rates:	**No**	change
Unsuccessful bidder notices:	**Display both similar items and my items**	change
Participate in eBay merchandising:	**Yes**	change

1. On the My eBay sidebar, under My Account, click **eBay Preferences**.

2. In the Seller Preferences section, click **Change** next to the preference you want to change, as shown in Figure 7-3. (You will need to sign in since you're accessing personal features.)

3. Make your preference changes, and click **Submit**.

4. Review the confirmation page to ensure your changes are correct.

TIP

Scheduled listings were formerly referred to as *pending items.*

Manage Current Selling Activities

While completing the Sell Your Item form, you are in total control of the process, but once the sale goes live, bidders and buyers pretty much run the sale. So would this be a good time for that seven-day vacation to Maui? Not unless you have wireless Internet access from your beach cabana. It's still your listing, and a number of things can crop up that might require timely attention.

Reschedule a Scheduled Listing

You can reschedule a listing up until the time it starts.

1. Click **My eBay** on the menu bar at the top of any eBay page. Either:

   - Click **All Selling** on the My eBay Views sidebar, and scroll down the All Selling page to the Scheduled Items view.

   –Or–

   - Under All Selling on the My eBay Views sidebar, click **Scheduled**.

2. Select the listing you want to reschedule, and click **Reschedule**.

3. On the Reschedule Items page, shown in Figure 7-4, click the **Reschedule To Start On** down arrows, and select a new date and time for the listing to start.

4. Click **Reschedule**.

Figure 7-4: Scheduled listings can be rescheduled as long as the listing has not started.

Find Your Listings Outside of My eBay

There are several methods you can use to find and view your current listings outside of My eBay.

FIND WHERE YOUR AUCTIONS AND SALES ARE LISTED

You can find out where a listing is located, including which page it is on within a category.

1. On the links bar at the top of a page, click **Site Map**.
2. Under Services, in the Buying And Selling area, click **Where Is An Item**.
3. Type the item number of the auction you want to locate, and click **Submit**.
4. Click the item description to open the listing, or click any of the levels in the category hierarchy, as shown in Figure 7-5.

Figure 7-5: Quickly find where your listing is located, and open it or any of the pages in its category hierarchy.

FIND LISTINGS BY ITEM NUMBER

You can quickly view a listing by searching for the item number. A Search text box is displayed on the Basic Search and Advanced Search tabs on the Search page and on many other pages.

1. Type the item number in the Search text box. (The item number can be retrieved from your listing confirmation e-mail, one of the views in My eBay, or an individual View Item page for a listing.)
2. Click the **Search** button.

BOOKMARK A LISTING

You can easily display any of your listings anytime you have your browser open by creating a *Bookmark* or *Favorite* link to the listing page.

To always have the My eBay page available to you, open **My eBay** and press CTRL+N. A second browser window opens. Keep your My eBay page open in one window while using the second window for other eBay purposes. To quickly arrange the two windows side-by-side, close or minimize all programs except the two eBay browser windows, right-click a blank area of the

Windows taskbar, and select **Tile Windows Vertically**.

If you are using eBay Toolbar (strongly recommended, see Chapter 3), you can easily record favorites (different from Favorites and Bookmarks used in browsers) using the Bookmarks button. Display the View Item page you want to record, and click the **Bookmark** button. eBay fills in the title and address of the current view, using the item title, item number, and ending date for a Bookmark Title, and the web address. Click **OK** to accept it. Now when you click the Bookmark button, the item can be selected from a list. The Bookmark feature also lets you organize your bookmarks, rearrange their order, or remove items from your list.

1. Open the eBay listing View Item page that you want to be able to view quickly.

2. Your actions will depend on your browser.

- In Internet Explorer, click **Favorites** on the menu bar, and select **Add To Favorites**. In the Add Favorite dialog box, click **OK** to accept the name and locate the link in the main Favorites list, or first click **Create In** to select an existing folder, or click **New Folder** to create one.

- In Netscape Navigator, click **Bookmarks** on the menu bar, and select **Bookmark This Page** to accept the name and locate the link in the main Bookmarks list, or first click **File Bookmark** to open the File Bookmark dialog box and select an existing folder, or click **New Folder** to create one.

Get Daily E-Mail

To assist you in keeping track of your current auctions, you can have eBay send you a daily status e-mail that lets you know how things are going with your sales (and purchases).

1. Click **My eBay** on the menu bar at the top of any eBay page. On the My eBay Views sidebar, under My Account, click **eBay Preferences**.

2. In the eBay Preferences section, click **View/Change** to the right of Notification Preferences.

3. In the Transaction Emails section (you will need to sign in), scroll down the list of notifications, and select the **Bidding And Selling Daily Status** check box.

4. Click **Save Changes** at the bottom of the page.

View selling totals

Gauge interest in your item

Figure 7-6: The Items I'm Selling view is your best place to monitor and manage listings that are currently for sale.

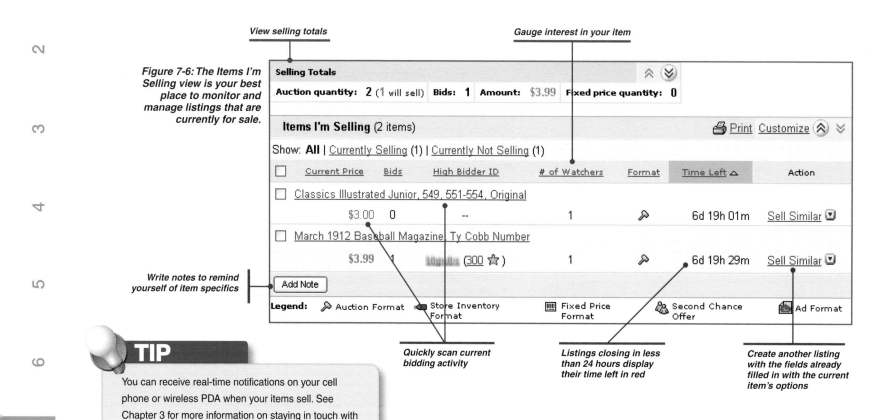

Selling Totals

Auction quantity: 2 (1 will sell)   **Bids: 1**   **Amount:** $3.99   **Fixed price quantity: 0**

Items I'm Selling (2 items)   🖨 Print Customize ⊗ ⊗

Show: **All** | Currently Selling (1) | Currently Not Selling (1)

☐	Current Price	Bids	High Bidder ID	# of Watchers	Format	Time Left △	Action
☐	Classics Illustrated Junior, 549, 551-554, Original						
	$3.00	0	--	1	⚒	6d 19h 01m	Sell Similar ⊡
☐	March 1912 Baseball Magazine, Ty Cobb Number						
	$3.99	1	10pmbz (300 ☆)	1	⚒	6d 19h 29m	Sell Similar ⊡

Add Note

Legend: ⚒ Auction Format   🏪 Store Inventory Format   ▥ Fixed Price Format   👥 Second Chance Offer   📧 Ad Format

Write notes to remind yourself of item specifics

Quickly scan current bidding activity

Listings closing in less than 24 hours display their time left in red

Create another listing with the fields already filled in with the current item's options

TIP

You can receive real-time notifications on your cell phone or wireless PDA when your items sell. See Chapter 3 for more information on staying in touch with your listings.

TIP

The Items I'm Selling view provides key information about listings that have items currently for sale or bid, as shown in Figure 7-6. Display the Items I'm Selling view by clicking any of these links on the My eBay Views sidebar: My Summary, All Selling, or Selling. (See Chapter 1 for more information on using the basic features of My eBay, such as creating notes.)

Change a Listing

You can revise the auction listing up to the point the auction is completed. Table 7-1 shows the situations that dictate to what extent you can make changes.

To change a listing (see "Add to the Item Description" in this chapter for information on how to add to it):

1. Click **My eBay** on the menu bar at the top of any eBay page. On the My eBay Views sidebar, click **Selling**.

2. Click the **Action** column down arrow in the listing you want to change, and click **Revise**.

The Action column in the Items I'm Selling view provides links to several pages that let you modify a particular listing. You can reach the same pages from other areas in eBay. Particularly useful is the Site Map (see Chapter 1 for more information on using Site Map). Click **Site Map** on the links bar at the top of a page, and find the action you're interested in in the Buying And Selling area. Since this approach is not listing-specific, you will need the item number for the listing you want to modify.

QUICKSTEPS

FINDING CURRENT LISTINGS WITH NO ACTIVITY

You can quickly see which auctions have yet to have a bid in the Items I'm Selling view. Click **My eBay** on the menu bar at the top of any eBay page. On the My eBay Views sidebar, click **Selling**. Either:

- Click **Currently Not Selling** below the Items I'm Selling title bar to view only listings with no bidders.

Items I'm Selling (2 items)

Show: **All** | Currently Selling (1) | Currently Not Selling (1)

☐ Title   Current Price   Bids

–Or–

- Click **Bids** in the column headers row. Click once to sort all current listings with those having the greatest number of bids listed first (ascending sort); click a second time to sort all current listings having those with the least number of bids listed first (descending sort).

TABLE 7-1: CONDITIONS UNDER WHICH YOU CAN MAKE CHANGES TO AUCTION LISTINGS

	Not within 12 hours of auction closing and received no bids	Within 12 hours of auction closing (no bids)	Received a bid (not within 12 hours)	Within 12 hours of auction closing and received a bid
Do anything (except change selling format)	X			
Add to the item description		X	X	
Add a second category		X	X	
Add selling features ($$$)		X	X	X

3. Review the Revise Your Item page caveats, and click **Continue**.

4. On the Review & Submit Listing page, click any of the **Add** or **Edit** links that are available to you (your limitations are listed at the top of the page). Make the change on the page to which you are redirected.

Revise Your Item: Review & Submit Listing

Item you are revising:

Listed on:
Classics Illustrated Junior, First 5 Issues! 501-505 (#2240318844)
Item HAS BIDS/PURCHASES or less than 12 hours left

5. Click **Make Changes** to return to the Review & Submit Listing page.

6. Repeat step 4 for any other changes you want to make. Click **Submit Revisions** at the bottom of the Review & Submit Listing page when you are finished. You are congratulated on your revision.

Revise Your Item: Congratulations

You have successfully revised your listing

View your item

Title: Classics Illustrated Junior, First 5 Issues! 501-505

Item # :   The item number for your new listing is ▬▬▬

URL: http://cgi.ebay.com/ws/eBayISAPI.dll?ViewItem&item=▬▬▬

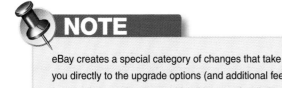

NOTE

eBay creates a special category of changes that take you directly to the upgrade options (and additional fees) for your listing. What we would call just another listing change (see "Change a Listing"), eBay calls "Promote Your Item." To "promote" your listing, use My eBay to find the listing, and click its title to display it. On the View Item page, click **Promote Your Item** under the item's title bar. Click **Continue** on the upgrades description page. Make your upgrade choices, and click **Continue** a second time. Click **Submit** after reviewing the summary of upgrades.

> **You are signed in**
>
> NEW! Change your cross-promoted items
>
> Revise your item
>
> Promote your item
>
> Sell a similar item

TIP

Revised listings alert bidders and buyers to changes by placing a Revised link next to the Description label on the View Item page. Clicking the link opens an Item Revision Summary page that lists when revisions were made and what information was changed.

> **Description** (revised)

Add to the Item Description

Once you have bidders or are within the 12 hours of a listing closing (see Table 7-1), you cannot change a description—you can only add to it. The bidder or buyer will see the original description, and added text will be shown in a separate area on the listing, as shown in Figure 7-7. To change the item description:

Figure 7-7: Text added to an item description is time- and date-stamped and added after the original description.

> On May-06-04 at 12:21:19 PDT, seller added the following information:
>
> I think every home these days should have a Geiger counter. They also make great entertainment. For example:
>
> 1. Dress up in a yellow jumpsuit, don a paint respirator, go up to some large panel truck stuck in traffic, and pretend your monitoring it (sweep the wand a few inches from the sides of the truck).
> 2. At some point, go into a panic and run as fast as you can from the scene.
> 3. Go home and watch the pandemonium on the 5 o'clock news.
> 4. Wait by the phone for the call from the FBI and Tom Ridge.

1. Click **My eBay** on the menu bar at the top of any eBay page. On the My eBay Views sidebar, click **Selling**.

2. Click the **Action** column down arrow in the listing whose description you want to annotate, and click **Add To Description**.

   > Sell Similar
   > Revise
   > Add To Description
   > End Item
   > Edit Promotions

3. On the first Add To Description page, review the editing limitations to make sure your listing is eligible to be changed, and click **Continue**.

4. On the second Add To Description page, type unformatted text or text formatted with HTML tags in the Add To Description text box, as shown in Figure 7-8 (see Chapter 6 for information on adding HTML tags to format item descriptions). Click either of the links, above or below the text box, to view your current or added description, respectively.

5. Click **Save Changes** when finished. Your added text appears below your original description.

   > Save Changes >

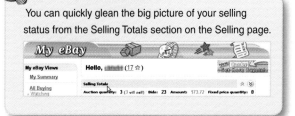
Sell Similar Items

eBay provides a slick feature to keep you from having to re-create a Sell Your Item form from scratch when selling items that share common details. For example, if you are selling anything in a series where the only thing that changes is the issue or series number, you only have to update that particular number instead of slogging through the steps of the selling form. To quickly sell an item similar to one currently for sale:

1. In My eBay, display the **Items I'm Selling** view from the My Summary, All Selling, or Selling pages.

2. Scroll through your list of items that are currently for sale, and locate the item whose details you want to use in another listing.

3. Click **Sell Similar** under the item's Action column. (If Sell Similar isn't shown in the item's Action column, click the **Action** column down arrow, and choose it from the drop-down list.)

4. The Category step of the Sell Your Item form is displayed, as shown in Figure 7-9, with the same category as the currently selling item.

5. Change the main or second category, and click:

- **Selling Format** to change the selling format from, for example, an auction to a Buy It Now, fixed-price sale.

- **Continue** to move to the subsequent steps in the Sell Your Item form, where you can keep or change your previous entries. (See Chapter 5 for how to fill it in.)

- **Go To Review** to jump to the fifth and final step in the Sell Your Item form, where you can preview the listing and return to any of the earlier selling form steps. This is also where you submit the new listing.

Figure 7-8: You can add text, either plain or HTML-tagged, to your item description.

Figure 7-9: The Sell Similar Item option pre-populates the Sell Your Item form with details from a currently selling item.

TIP

Sell Similar can also be found on the View Item page of an item that did not sell. This is another useful way to change some things about the similar item before listing it.

QUICK**FACTS**

CHECKING ON YOUR BIDS AND BIDDERS

The Bid History page, shown in Figure 7-10, provides access to a wealth of information on the progress of your auction as well as information on your bidders. As a plus to the seller of the item, you can also obtain the e-mail addresses of your bidders. To open the Bid History page, first open the listing from My eBay, and then click the **number of bids** link next to History.

Current bid:	**US $31.00**
	Place Bid >
Time left:	**3 days 3 hours**
	7-day listing
	Ends May-09-04 15:41:46 PDT
	Add to Calendar
Start time:	May-02-04 15:41:46 PDT
History:	1 bid (US $31.00 starting bid)

VIEW THE AUCTION SUMMARY

The top section of the Bid History page provides a snapshot of the auction, similar to what you see in the My eBay Items I'm Selling section and on the View Item page of the actual auction.

Continued...

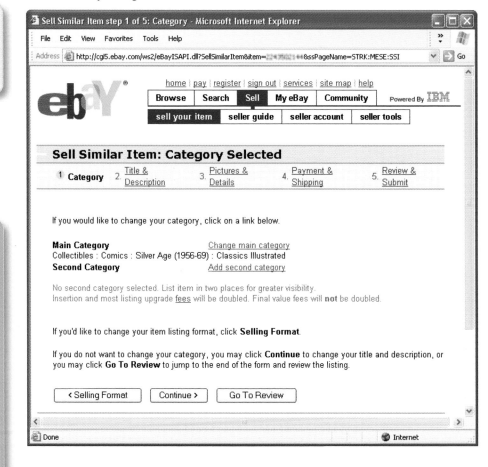

CHECKING ON YOUR BIDS AND BIDDERS (Continued)

INVESTIGATE A BIDDER

There are several sleuthing techniques you can employ to feel comfortable with the people you are about to do business with. In the Bidding History section, click a bidder's **User ID**. On the Member Profile page, do one or more of the following:

- In the Feedback Score section, review the recent feedback statistics and note any bid retractions.

- Note how long the bidder has been an eBay member.

- Click the **ID History** link to see if the bidder has a high number of identity changes.

> Member since: Jul-20-02
> Location: United States
> • ID History
> • Items for Sale
>
> [Contact Member]

- Review any negative feedback to see if there is a trend.

- See if a **New ID** icon or **Changed ID** icon is displayed next to the bidder's User ID. (The New ID icon signifies the bidder has been a registered eBay member for fewer than 30 days.) Multiple changes of a User ID could mean someone is trying to bury his or her past.

Don't take any individual piece of potentially negative data as reason to cancel a bid. There can be legitimate reasons for just about anything, and one or two disgruntled persons leaving negative feedback among hundreds of transactions shouldn't necessarily raise a red flag unless it's coupled with other warning signs.

CONTACT A BIDDER

You can contact bidders by e-mail from several pages:

- **My eBay | All Selling | Selling and View Item pages** let you contact the high bidder by clicking his or her User ID.

Continued...

Continued...

Figure 7-10: The Bid History page provides a wealth of information on prospective buyers.

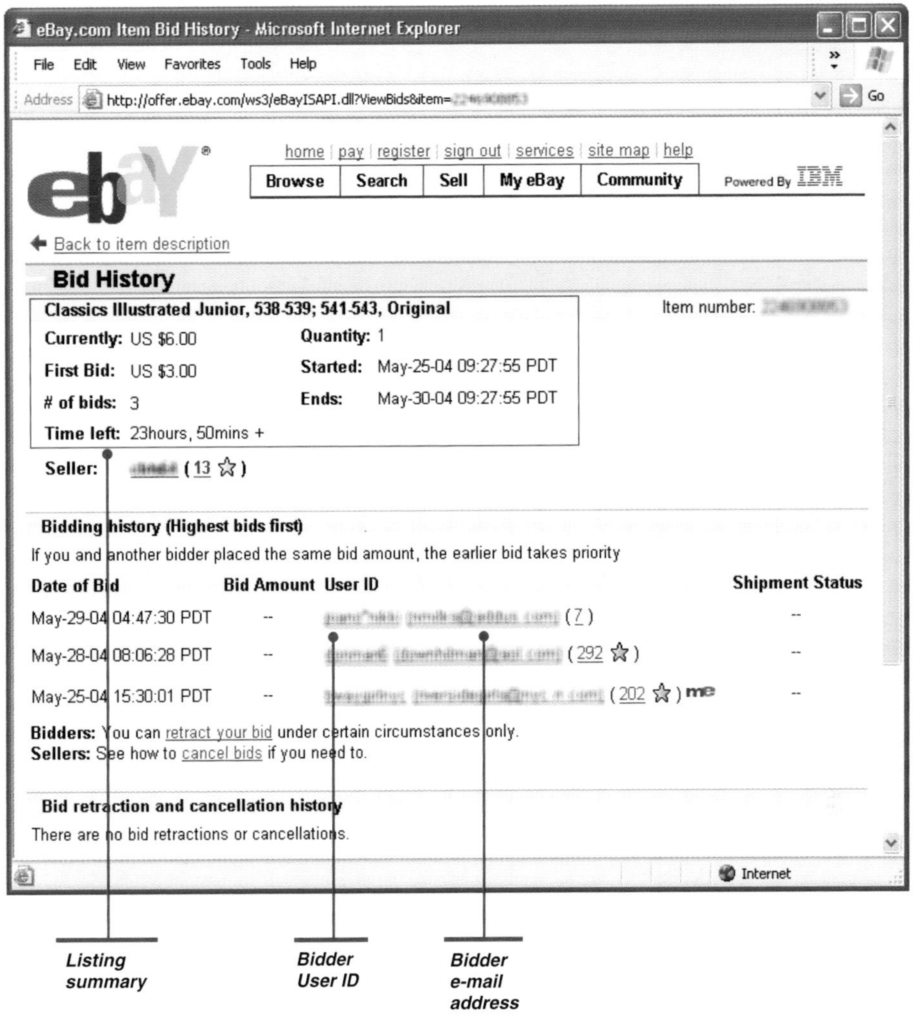

Listing summary

Bidder User ID

Bidder e-mail address

Cancel a Bid

Hmmm, why would you want to take potential money out of your pocket? Typically, you wouldn't, but there are a few instances where you might have to—for example, you might find a bidder's feedback record to be questionable or his or her identity unverifiable. Also, a bidder might ask you to retract his or her bid. Furthermore, if you need to cancel an auction, you will need to cancel all outstanding bids unless you're willing to sell to the current high bidder (see "End a Listing Early" in this chapter).

 (A seller's *canceling* of a buyer's bid doesn't have the same negativity attached to it as when a buyer *retracts* a bid.)

1. Click **My eBay** on the menu bar at the top of any eBay page, and then under All Selling, click **Selling**.

2. In the Items I'm Selling section, click the link for the listing that contains the bidder you want to cancel.

3. Click the **number of bids** link next to History to display the Bid History page.

4. Select and copy the item number by dragging over it and pressing **CTRL+C**, and note the bidder's User ID.

5. At the bottom of the bidding history, click **Cancel Bids**.

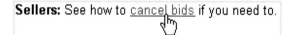

Sellers: See how to cancel bids if you need to.

6. On the Bid Cancellation page:

   ● Click the **Item Number** text box, and press **CTRL+V** to paste the number in the box. (Copying and pasting is faster and less prone to typing mistakes.)

   ● Type the **User ID** of the bidder in the text box provided.

   ● Type your explanation for the bid cancellation in the Reason For Cancellation text box. eBay's legitimate reasons are when a bidder asks you to remove his or her bid, when you need to close a listing early, or when you cannot verify the identity of the bidder (though you can type any reason you want).

7. Click **Cancel Bid** when finished.

Limit Bidders and Buyers for a Listing

You can conduct a private sale by limiting the buyers or bidders who can participate. You simply create and maintain a list of User IDs for eligible members and attach an auction or Buy It Now sale to that list on an item-number basis. Members who try to bid or buy on the listing will receive a notification from eBay that they are not on a list of approved bidders or buyers for the item. Ineligible members can contact you by e-mail and request to be placed on the list.

1. Open **My eBay**, and locate the listing you want to limit from the Items I'm Selling view.

2. Click the title to display the listing on the View Item page. Select and copy the item number by dragging over it, right-clicking the selection, and selecting **Copy** from the context menu.

    Item number: 8813609437

3. Click **Site Map** from the links bar at the top of the page.

4. Under Buying And Selling, click **Pre-Approved Bidder/Buyer List**.

5. In the Pre-Approved Bidder/Buyer List section, click **Continue.** (If you already have a list of eligible members, you can just add an item to be included in the restriction and add or remove User IDs; if you do not have a list of members, create one and add a participating item number.)

6. Under Items With Pre-Approved Bidders, click **Add A New Item** to add to a current list of restricted sales or create the first one.

Items with Pre-Approved Bidders

Currently, you have no items with pre-approved bidders

+Add a new item with pre-approved bidders

7. In the table under Add Item, right-click the **Item No.** text box, and select **Paste** from the context menu.

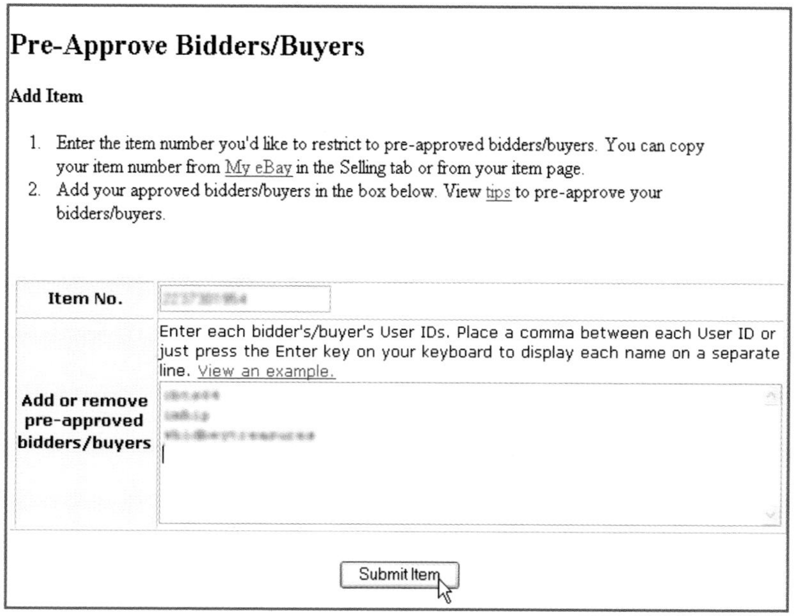

Figure 7-11: Enter an item number and a list of approved User IDs to conduct a private sale or auction.

Pre-Approve Bidders/Buyers

Add Item

1. Enter the item number you'd like to restrict to pre-approved bidders/buyers. You can copy your item number from My eBay in the Selling tab or from your item page.
2. Add your approved bidders/buyers in the box below. View tips to pre-approve your bidders/buyers.

Item No.	[item number]
Add or remove pre-approved bidders/buyers	Enter each bidder's/buyer's User IDs. Place a comma between each User ID or just press the Enter key on your keyboard to display each name on a separate line. View an example.

Submit Item

8. Type or paste the User IDs of members who you want to be able to bid on the listing. Type a comma after an entry, or press ENTER to separate the User IDs, as shown in Figure 7-11.

9. Click **Submit Item** when finished.

Cancel a Scheduled Listing

You can cancel a listing you've scheduled to start at a future time without incurring any listing fees.

1. Click **My eBay** on the menu bar at the top of any eBay page, and then click **All Selling | Scheduled** on the sidebar.

2. Under Scheduled Items, select the check box to the left of the listing(s) you want to cancel, and click **Delete**, as shown in Figure 7-12.

Figure 7-12: You can cancel a scheduled listing up until the time it goes live.

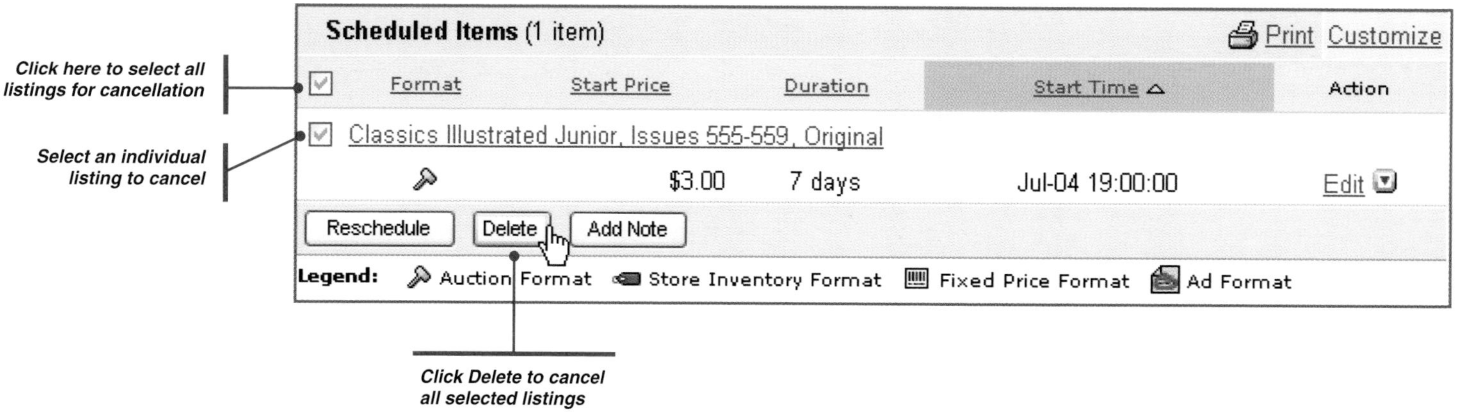

Click here to select all listings for cancellation

Select an individual listing to cancel

Scheduled Items (1 item)   🖨 Print Customize

☑	Format	Start Price	Duration	Start Time △	Action
☑	Classics Illustrated Junior, Issues 555-559, Original				
	🔨	$3.00	7 days	Jul-04 19:00:00	Edit ▼

Reschedule   Delete   Add Note

Legend: 🔨 Auction Format   📦 Store Inventory Format   ▦ Fixed Price Format   🖼 Ad Format

Click Delete to cancel all selected listings

End a Listing Early

There are several legitimate reasons why you might need to end a listing before its natural conclusion (item is no longer for sale, item is broken, family emergency prevents shipping, you discovered the item is a fake, and so on), and there are many illegitimate or unethical reasons to stop a sale (a buyer contacts you and offers to buy the item off eBay, you're just "testing the market" to relist at a higher price, and so on). There is no penalty for ending a listing early (eBay cannot force you to sell an item), but repeated premature endings will get bidders' attention and ultimately eBay's. Early endings are differentiated on whether a bid has been made and whether you want to sell to the current high bidder.

1. Click **My eBay** on the menu bar at the top of any eBay page. On the My eBay Views sidebar, click **Selling**.

2. Click the **Action** column down arrow in the listing you want to end early, and click **End Item** (you will need to sign in).

   | |
   | Sell Similar |
   | Revise |
   | Add To Description |
   | End Item |
   | Edit Promotions |

3. The action you need to take depends on one of three scenarios you can choose from, as outlined in Table 7-2. Figure 7-13 shows your choices when you have bids.

TABLE 7-2: ACTIONS TAKEN WHEN ENDING AN AUCTION

Actions you need to take...	No Bidders	Bidders	Sell to Highest Bidder
Cancel bids		X	
Select a reason for ending early: • Item no longer available for sale • Error in minimum bid or reserve amount • Error in listing • Item lost or broken	X	X	
Click...	End Your Listing	1. Cancel Bids 2. End Your Listing	Sell Item
Notification placed at top of Closed Item page		Your selected reason for ending the auction	"The seller ended this listing early to sell to the highest bidder(s) at current bid price"

Figure 7-13: To cancel an auction once a bid is made, you must cancel any outstanding bids or sell to the next-highest bidder.

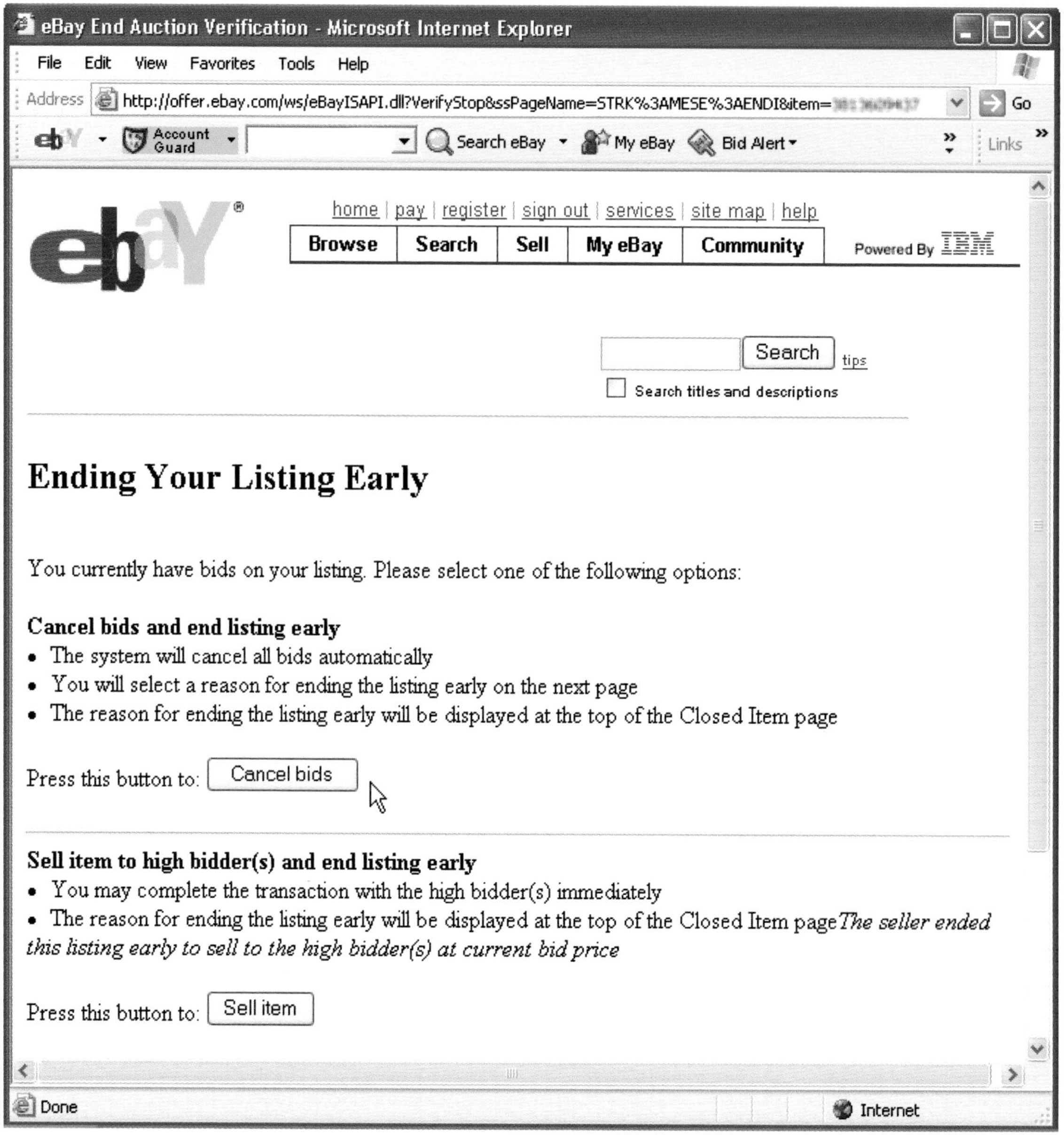

eBay End Auction Verification - Microsoft Internet Explorer

File   Edit   View   Favorites   Tools   Help

Address   http://offer.ebay.com/ws/eBayISAPI.dll?VerifyStop&ssPageName=STRK%3AMESE%3AENDI&item=▓▓▓▓▓▓▓   ⌄   → Go

ebaY ▾   Account Guard ▾   [   ] ▾   🔍 Search eBay ▾   My eBay   Bid Alert ▾   »   Links »

home | pay | register | sign out | services | site map | help

Browse   **Search**   **Sell**   **My eBay**   **Community**   Powered By IBM

[   ]   Search   tips

☐ Search titles and descriptions

Ending Your Listing Early

You currently have bids on your listing. Please select one of the following options:

Cancel bids and end listing early
- The system will cancel all bids automatically
- You will select a reason for ending the listing early on the next page
- The reason for ending the listing early will be displayed at the top of the Closed Item page

Press this button to: Cancel bids

Sell item to high bidder(s) and end listing early
- You may complete the transaction with the high bidder(s) immediately
- The reason for ending the listing early will be displayed at the top of the Closed Item page*The seller ended this listing early to sell to the high bidder(s) at current bid price*

Press this button to: Sell item

Done   🌐 Internet

How to...

Chapter 8
Closing Out Your Sale

In this chapter you will learn how to close out a sale. After the sale is completed, there are still many things to do (or at least monitor), including following up with the winning bidder or buyer with payment instructions, receiving payment, shipping the item, taking actions to avoid future issues with problem bidders, and relisting items that didn't produce a sale the first time around.

Fortunately, eBay—and to a large degree PayPal (owned by eBay)—provide several features and tools to help you along the way and make the process typically painless. Some of these features and tools come at a cost, however, so it will be up to you to decide if convenience and some built-in degree of safety are worth the added expense.

Evaluate the Sale

After a sale ends, it's worthwhile to take a few minutes and review the specifics of the sale that were unknown until the highest bidder won at auction or a buyer purchased a Buy It Now item. For example, you can now determine the full amount you owe eBay for listing an auction item, as its winning bid amount (or final value) is now known. Also, you now know the winning bidder or buyer and can research his or her eBay standing to help you make possible decisions on receiving payment (see Chapter 7 for information on researching bidders and buyers). To help manage the overall process of closing out the sale, the Items I've Sold view in My eBay as well as associated Reminders provide great tools to guide you along the way.

Determine Final Value Costs

In addition to the insertion and possible upgrade fees you incurred when listing an item, eBay charges an additional fee based on the closing bid of the auction or sale price, known as the *final value fee* (the fee is charged whether or not you and the buyer actually consummate the sale). The fee is cumulative, based on the following tiers (for Dutch auctions, use the final value fee for the lowest successful bid and multiply it times the total number of items you sold):

- Items with a closing bid price up to $25 are charged 5.25 percent of the closing price.
- Items between $25 and $1,000 are charged:
  - 5.25 percent on the first $25 (or $1.31); and
  - 2.75 percent of the closing price above $25.
- Items over $1,000 are charged:
  - 5.25 percent on the first $25 (or $1.31); and
  - 2.75 percent of the closing price between $25 and $1,000 (or $26.81); and
  - 1.50 percent of the closing price above $1,000.

COMPLETING A SUCCESSFUL SALE STEP-BY-STEP

As the seller, you are responsible for only one element of the transaction: delivering the goods. How you go about satisfying that requirement with your buyer will go a long way towards ensuring you have the opportunity to do it again with other buyers. eBay and PayPal cover several of these aspects in their automated e-mails to the buyer, but you need to monitor what's being communicated—and it's good eBay practice to give the buyer a more personal touch with your own e-mail. (Each of these points is covered in more detail later in this chapter.)

ENSURE THE BUYER KNOWS WHAT IS OWED

Monetary information includes such details as shipping/handling and insurance costs, the final value cost of the item, applicable tax, and a total of all costs. Send the buyer an e-mail invoice after the auction. (See "Invoice the Buyer" in this chapter.)

ENSURE THE BUYER KNOWS HOW TO PAY YOU

Include the payment types you accept, how the buyer can most easily accomplish them, and where to send paper-based instruments. For example, remind the buyer to click the **Pay Now** button on the winning confirmation he or she receives from eBay (if you accept PayPal and have chosen to display it); and, if you accept checks and money orders, reiterate your billing address. (See Chapter 5 for information on preparing payment instructions in the Sell Your Item form.)

Continued...

Not all sales incur final value fees. For example, you are not charged a fee if no bid was made or no bid met your reserve price, you listed a *non-binding* real estate item or a real estate listing other than timeshares or property (the final value fee for timeshares and property is $35), or you used an ad format instead of an auction or fixed-price format.

View Your Sales Fees

You can see how much eBay is charging you for each current or sold listing.

1. Click **My eBay** on the menu bar at the top of any eBay page.

2. On the My eBay Views sidebar, click **Seller Account**.

3. Under My Seller Account Summary, click **View Account Status** (you will need to sign in).

4. On the Account Status And Invoices page, determine whether to view recent (View Your Account Status) or dated (View Your Previous Invoices) transactions.

> **My Seller Account Summary**
>
> Last invoice (03/31/04): (View invoice)
>
> Payments and Credits since last invoice:
>
> Fees since last invoice: (View account status)

> **View your account status**   **or**   **View your previous invoices**
>
> ⦿ Since last invoice
>
> ◯ For a period (up to 4 months)
>
> From: ☐ / ☐ / ☐
>
> To: ☐ / ☐ / ☐
>   MM DD YYYY
>
> ☑ Organize invoices in page format
>
> [View Account Status]
>
> May 2004 ▾   Invoices will be available for 18 months.
>
> Note: Invoices dated after November 2003 may have a new look.
>
> [View Selected Invoice]

5. Click the **Date** column header to sort the transactions in ascending order (earliest dates first). Click it again to sort in descending order (latest dates first).

6. Locate all transactions for a particular item number to see the fees you were charged, as shown in Figure 8-1.

COMPLETING A SUCCESSFUL SALE STEP-BY-STEP *(Continued)*

PROVIDE POSITIVE FEEDBACK

Be sure to give positive feedback when you're satisfied payment is received. Remember: you get paid first and the buyer gets the item last. Don't expect a glowing feedback report from your buyer if you haven't done the same for him or her. (See Chapter 4 for more information on how to give feedback.)

PROVIDE SHIPPING DETAILS

Let the buyer know when the item is on its way. Provide the shipping service used; tracking information, if available; and estimated delivery time. (See "Ship the Item" in this chapter.)

CLOSE OUT THE TRANSACTION

Send a final e-mail letting the buyer know you appreciate the business. Inform him or her you left feedback, and ask if the item arrived satisfactorily and if there's anything you can do to improve the experience.

Figure 8-1: You can see all the eBay selling fees for a particular listing in the My eBay Account Status page.

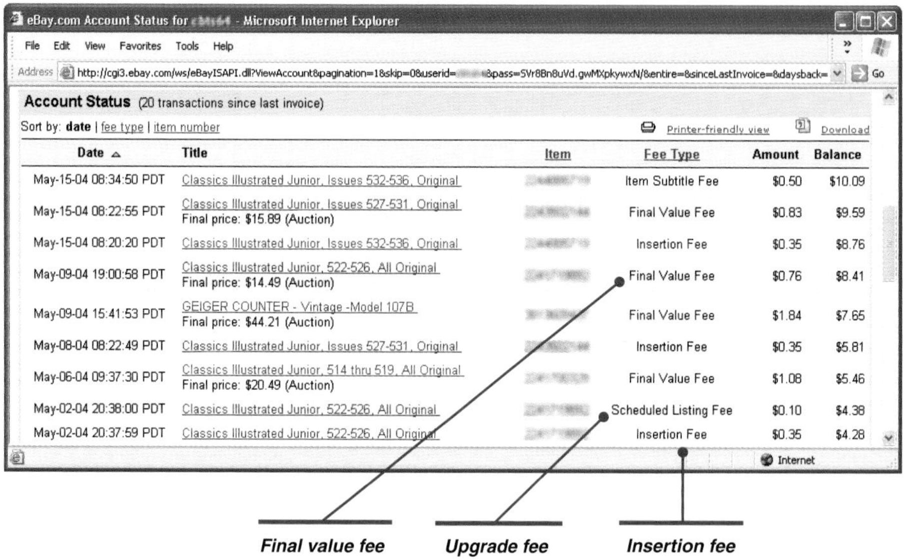

Final value fee   Upgrade fee   Insertion fee

Manage Completed Sales

You can monitor the status of completed sales from either eBay or PayPal.

MONITOR AND TRACK COMPLETED SALES FROM MY EBAY

The Items I've Sold view in My eBay, shown in Figure 8-2, provides a great overview of your recently completed sales. Key features of the view include:

- Sort listings by column headings
- Group listings by progress status (All, Awaiting Payment, Awaiting Shipment, Awaiting Feedback)
- Variable durations of listings from the previous 24 hours up to 60 days
- Status icons for completed checkout, payment, shipping, and feedback (both provided to others and received from others). See Chapter 2 for an explanation of the icons.

- Menu options to quickly change a listing's status or perform actions on listings that did not sell

View the Items I've Sold view in My eBay from one of these pages:

- My Summary
- All Selling
- Sold

Figure 8-2: The Items I've Sold view in My eBay is a great way to manage sold items.

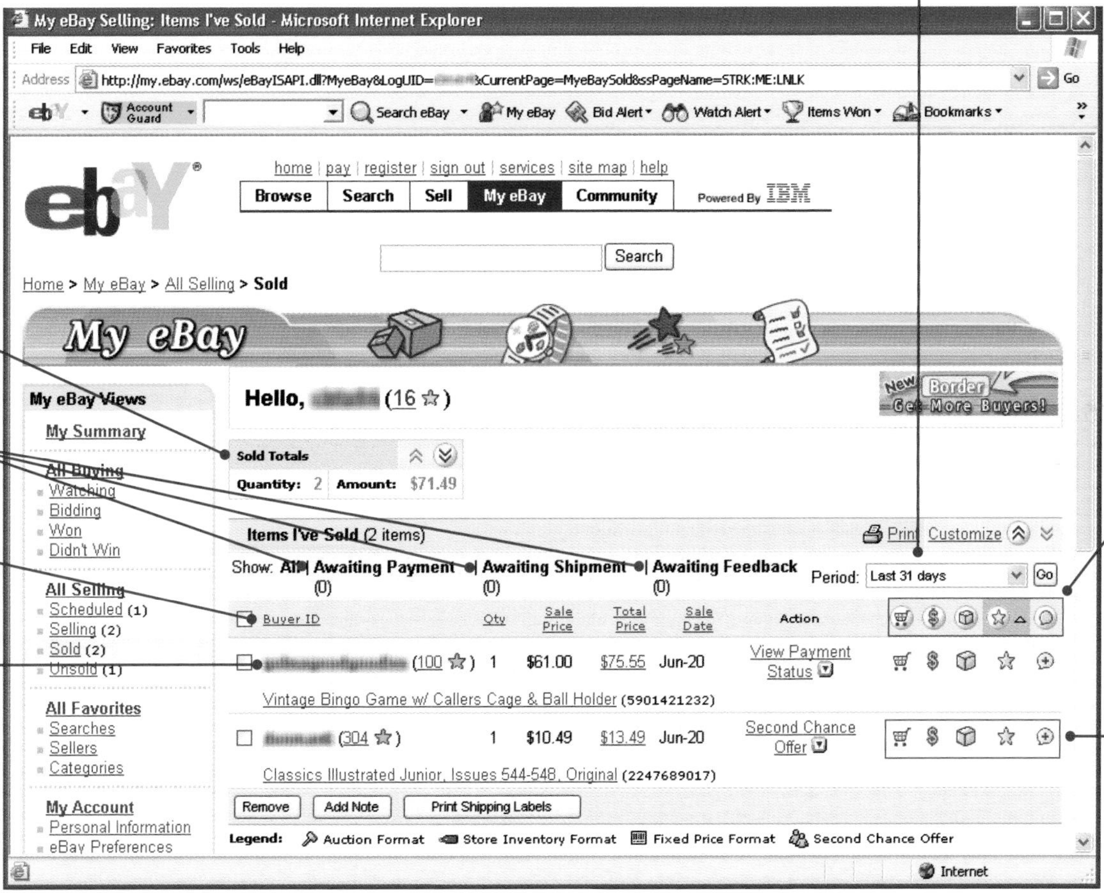

Change how far back you want to see listings

View Sold Totals summary

Arrange listings by categories

Click to sort by columns

Click to view the buyer's/bidder's profile and feedback

Click to sort by actions completed or not completed

See what actions in a transaction have yet to be accomplished or have been accomplished

MONITOR AND TRACK COMPLETED SALES FROM PAYPAL

PayPal (assuming you have a PayPal account) offers Post-Sale Manager, a free (as of summer 2004) service that lets you quickly see the results of sales for the prior 30 days.

1. On the eBay home page, click **PayPal** under Specialty Sites, or type www. paypal.com in your browser's address bar, and press **ENTER**.

2. Log in to PayPal, and open your account(s) overview page.

3. Click the **Auction Tools** tab on the upper row to open the Auction Tools page.

4. Under Manage eBay Items Sold, click **Post-Sale Manager**. A table of your recent sales is displayed, as shown in Figure 8-3.

5. Customize which transactions to display by doing either or both:

- Click the **View** down arrow to switch between multiple PayPal accounts.

- Click the **Show** down arrow to filter your list of transactions based on several criteria.

6. Click an action button, such as **Track** (a shipment), **Invoice** (send a payment request), or **Leave** (feedback), to perform the stated action.

7. Click **Submit**.

TIP

The My eBay Items I've Sold view and the PayPal Post-Sale Manager provide similar post-sales reporting metrics and features. The main difference between the two is that the Items I've Sold view provides a better date filter, including allowing you to display listings back 60 days versus 30 days for the Post-Sale Manager. Also, you can be confident My eBay will remain a free service of eBay, while Post-Sale Manager leaves the door open for a future cost for its use.

Post-Sale Manager is currently a free service. PayPal reserves the right to charge a fee for this service in the future, with appropriate advance notification.

Figure 8-3: Use PayPal's Post-Sale Manager to see the status of completed sales and perform any pending actions.

Change accounts

Filter listings

Sort items by clicking the respective hyperlinked column heading

Select individual sales (or click the column heading to select all listings) to invoice or remove them from the table

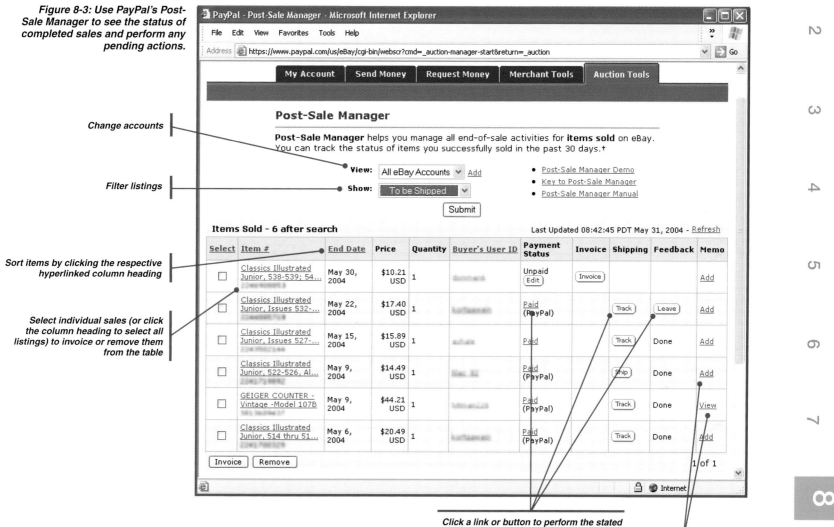

Click a link or button to perform the stated action or review a completed action

Add or view notes you made about a sale

Receive Payment

When the auction ends, both the seller (shown in Figure 8-4) and the buyer receive automated e-mails from eBay that let each know who the other party is, restate the closing price and any fixed shipping costs, and start the end-of-auction process. What happens next depends on two factors:

- **Is your payment amount final?** That is, are your shipping costs predetermined by a fixed cost or a calculated amount, or have you chosen for the buyer to contact you after the sale to negotiate shipping costs? If the latter, can the buyer pay immediately through PayPal or let you know an alternative payment method is on its way? If the final amount isn't known to the buyer, you will have to let him or her know the details by sending an invoice.

- **Who's quicker to the draw?** Has the buyer or bidder clicked the Pay Now button that appears in his or her end-of-auction e-mail in the completed listing form **Pay Now** and acknowledged payment using PayPal or one of your other accepted payment means, or do you need to send an invoice to request payment? (You can still send an invoice after a buyer acknowledges payment, but it's not necessary if all payment details are known and correct.) See Chapter 4 for details on the buyer's side of the end-of-auction experience.

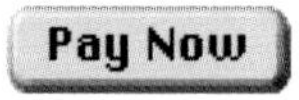

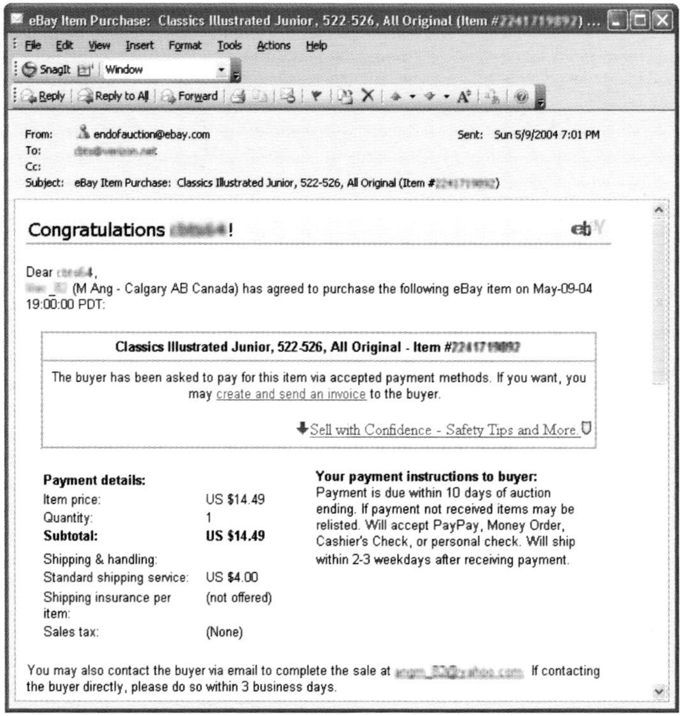

Figure 8-4: eBay sends the seller an end-of-auction e-mail providing the final sales price and links to send an invoice through either eBay or private e-mail.

QUICKSTEPS

COMBINING PURCHASES ON AN INVOICE

You can offer to combine multiple purchases from a buyer into one invoice and offer a discount. If you choose this feature, you will see the option in the shipping area of your next Sell Your Item form (giving you the choice of excluding certain items). Successful bidders and buyers will see the other items you have for sale on the congratulatory e-mail they receive from eBay.

1. From My eBay, click **eBay Preferences** on the My eBay Views sidebar.

2. Under Seller Preferences | Shipping Preferences, click **Change** to the right of Offer Combined Payment Discounts.

3. On the Combined Purchases Preference page, select the **Yes, Allow Buyers To Combine Items** check box, and select within how many days of purchase you want to provide the offer.

Combined Purchases Preference

Shipping discounts allow your buyers to save on shipping when they purchase more items from you. You can exclude individual items from being discounted.

☑ Yes, allow buyers to combine items purchased within 7 days ▾ and send a single payment.

○ I will specify discounts for Flat Rate Shipping **now**
○ I will specify discounts for Actual Rate Shipping **now**
◉ I will specify shipping discounts later

[Save Settings]   Cancel

---

4. Specify the type of discount you will provide, and click **Save Settings**.

Invoice the Buyer

An invoice is a document sent by you, the seller, stating the amount owed by the buyer who is receiving the goods or services. Invoicing used to be a personal e-mail from the seller directly to the buyer (and still can be) in which payment and shipping details were reiterated; however, the ease-of-use features in the eBay and PayPal system-generated invoices make the automated process hard to beat. (Whether you use eBay or PayPal to send the invoice is mostly a personal choice, usually dependent on how much time you spend in PayPal. Some sellers don't even accept PayPal, so the choice is clear for them.)

USE EBAY TO SEND AN INVOICE

1. Send an eBay invoice by:

   • Clicking the **Create And Send An Invoice** link in the end-of-auction e-mail a seller receives (see Figure 8-4).

   • Clicking the **Send Invoice** button in the View Item form at the end of a sale. The page looks like that shown in Figure 8-5 (open the listing by clicking the item title in My eBay).

   • Selecting the **View Payment Status** option from the Action drop-down list in the Items I've Sold view (and clicking **Send Invoice**).

2. On the Send Invoice To Buyer page, shown in Figure 8-6, make any changes to your Shipping And Handling, Insurance, Sales Tax, or Payment Instructions/Personal Message settings. Select **Copy Me On This Invoice** at the bottom of the page to get a copy of the invoice e-mail, and click **Send Invoice**.

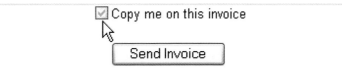

☑ Copy me on this invoice

[Send Invoice]

After you click this button, your buyer will be emailed an invoice.

Figure 8-5: Opening the View Item form after a sale has been completed and before payment has been made informs you that the next action to take is to send an invoice.

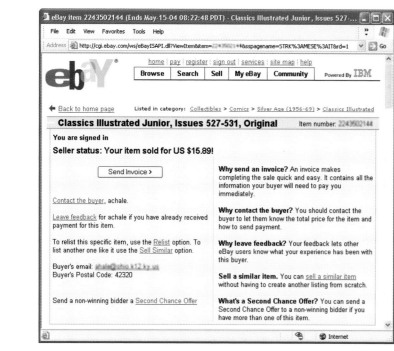

PayPal offers a free option to send an automatic invoice within an hour of a completed sale if you use PayPal as a payment method.

1. In My eBay, on one of the All Selling views, click **PayPal** in the Selling Links sidebar, beneath My eBay Views sidebar.

2. On the PayPal Seller Overview page, click **Log In To Your PayPal Account**, and log in.

PayPal Help Center
Log in to your PayPal account

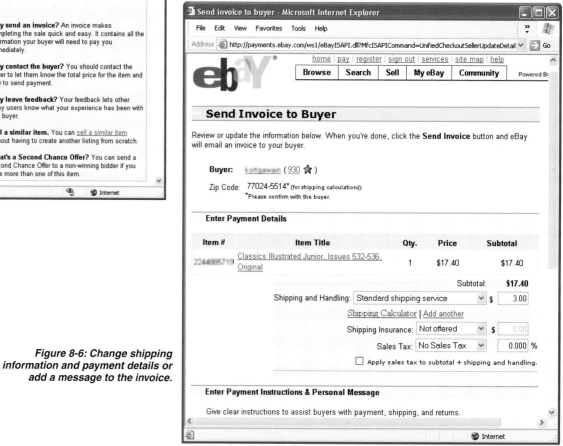

Figure 8-6: Change shipping information and payment details or add a message to the invoice.

Figure 8-7: PayPal lets you set up an automatic invoice, which is best if you are using PayPal as your only payment method.

3. On the PayPal home page, click **Invoice Your Winning Buyers** in the Enhance Account sidebar.

4. On the Winning Buyer Notification Registration page, shown in Figure 8-7, verify your eBay User ID and eBay e-mail address, customize a message to the buyer, provide a URL to a 150 x 100 pixel logo (if you want to include one), and click **Submit**. The buyer receives an e-mail invoice.

Enhance Account

Money Market

PayPal Preferred

ATM/Debit Card

Invoice your winning buyers

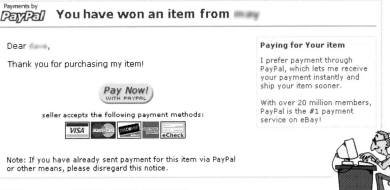

SEND YOUR OWN INVOICE

To create a more personal feel to your transaction, you can create your own invoice and have complete control over what you say to your buyer. Also, an invoice of your own is a more flexible tool if you have left shipping costs and other details open for negotiation until after the sale is completed.

1. Create the text of your invoice in a word-processor program, such as Microsoft Word. Include at a minimum:

   ● A description of what was bought and its item number

   ● Your mailing address if you accept paper currency, such as checks or money orders

   ● A reiteration of payment and shipping instructions that appears in the listing (make sure the two sets of instructions are the same), including shipping method, insurance costs, when you expect to be paid, and when you will send the item

If you want to get more creative with your invoice than your e-mail program allows, you can use more advanced formatting features in your word processor and attach the invoice as a file attachment to the e-mail you send the buyer. You do run the risk, however, that a small number of buyers might have problems opening the file, either because they have their security settings set up to block attachments or because they don't have a compatible word-processor program on their computer. Have a toned-down version of your invoice available to send just in case.

Let buyers know that you have received payment by dropping them a quick e-mail. Even when paying through secure methods, such as credit cards and PayPal, it's a nice touch to let the buyer know that his or her part of the transaction has gone through successfully. Also, this is a good time to indicate you'll be leaving him or her feedback and remind the buyer to do the same for you after the item arrives. Don't pass up the chance to solicit positive feedback for yourself!

- A mention that you will leave feedback when paid (recommended) and you would appreciate the same from the buyer when the item is received

- A "thank you" for the opportunity to do business with the buyer

2. Copy and paste the text into your e-mail program, and send the invoice. (Ensure you have the buyer's e-mail address correctly spelled in the To field of the e-mail.)

3. Save the word-processor document for use in future sales.

4. In My eBay, update the item's status when you get paid. In the Items I've Sold view, select **Mark Paid** in the item's Action drop-down list.

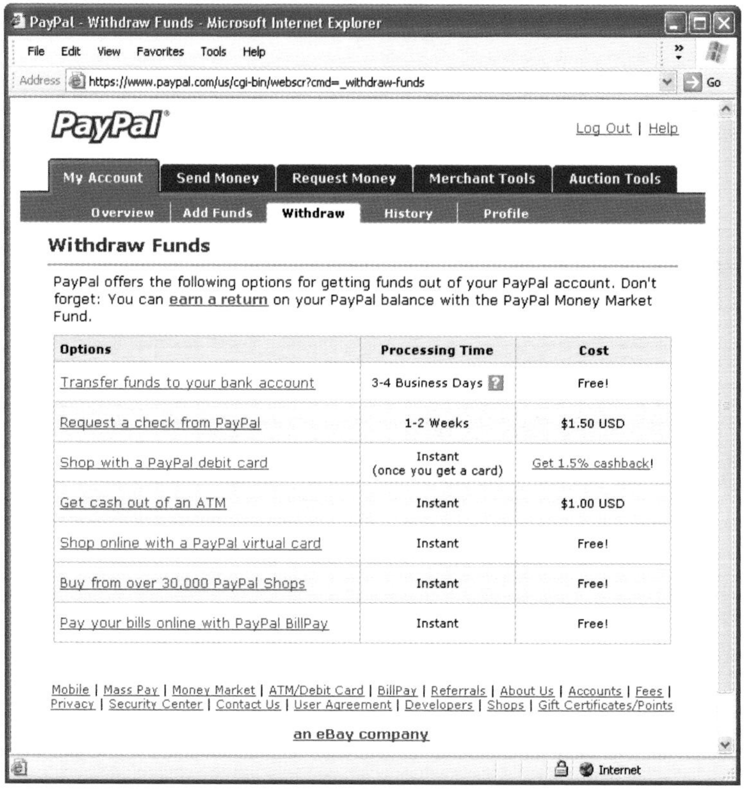

Figure 8-8: You have several options to choose from when using the money received from your sold items in your PayPal account.

Leave Buyers and Bidders Feedback

eBay has a social contract between buyers/bidders and sellers based on the feedback concept that helps ensure the integrity of the overall system. Consider providing feedback to buyers after a transaction is completed as a mandatory part of the sale. eBay recognizes we are all busy people and makes the action as easy as possible for us. (See Chapter 3 for information on writing feedback for both good and bad experiences.)

To quickly find sales that need feedback, do one of the following from My eBay:

- Check the **Selling Reminders** view on My Summary to see if you have any recent sales for which you haven't submitted feedback. Click the link to open the Items I've Sold view with only those listings awaiting feedback displayed. Click the **User ID** to open the Member Profile page where you can leave feedback.

- Display the **Items I've Sold** view (accessed from the My Summary, All Selling, or Sold pages), and click the **Feedback Left Status** icon to sort recent sales so all listings you haven't attended to are listed first.

- Click **Feedback** under My Account on the My eBay Views sidebar. Click **Leave Feedback** to leave feedback for all of your listings lacking feedback, as shown in Figure 8-9.

Figure 8-9: All of your listings that require feedback are displayed on one page.

Ship the Item

The most critical phase of the eBay transaction is moving the sold item from the custody of the seller to the buyer. Not only are you giving up complete control to a third party (the shipper), but you also are putting faith in your buyers that they will be reasonable people and accept the delivered item despite any number of potential problems: unforeseen delays in delivery, misinterpretations as to shipping instructions, or good-faith assumptions on your part. By performing the actions you do have control over (for example, using sound packaging and choosing tracking features your shippers offer), you will alleviate many headaches (and late-night e-mails).

Package the Item

As the saying goes, you only have one shot at a first impression. For your buyer, the appearance of the packaging he or she receives from you generally qualifies as that one opportunity. Even if your item arrives undamaged, an obviously poorly packaged item will leave a bad impression in the buyer's mind; whereas even when an item arrives damaged, if it's obvious you took all necessary precautions in your packaging to prevent it, the buyer will generally only be interested in getting a refund and will vent his or her angst toward the shipper instead of you. The dos and donts of packaging include:

- If you don't want to turn your house into a shipping center, pay a commercial packing outfit, such as the UPS Store (formerly Mailboxes, Etc.), to do the packaging (and mitigate your responsibility in any insurance claims that might arise).

- Use only sturdy, clean boxes with old labeling and markings removed or covered. Don't exceed the maximum gross weight a box is designed for (this is often indicated on a bottom flap), especially when reusing a box.

- When in doubt, double-box. I was amazed years ago that outfits like Dell could ship relatively fragile items, such as computer and monitors, through normal channels without major breakage problems. Their secret to success (besides custom-fit Styrofoam) was to suspend the item in a well-packaged box of its own within a larger box full of cushioning material (allow at least three inches on all sides).

GETTING FREE PACKAGING

You can get a lot of free packaging items from the three main eBay shippers delivered to your door (packaging material is labeled for its intended level of service, for example, USPS Express Mail tape or UPS Next Day Air boxes):

- **USPS** (United States Postal Service) provides limited materials from their local post offices. Order from http://shop.usps.com. On the Postal Store page, under the Browse Store sidebar, click **Shipping Supplies** and choose **Personal** or **Business Use**.

>>**Browse Store**	**Shipping Supplies**
▸ Shipping Supplies	**Business Use**
▸ Stamps by Rate	**Personal Use**
▸ Stamps by Subject	

- **UPS** (United Parcel Service). Order from www.ups.com. On the UPS home page, click the **Shipping** tab, and select **Get UPS Labels, Paks, And More** (requires a UPS account).

- **FedEx** (Federal Express). Order from www.fedex.com. On the FedEx home page, under Manage Your Account, click **Order Supplies** (requires a FedEx account). FedEx is not one of eBay's preferred shipping partners, but when you need to get a package to someone yesterday morning, FedEx is there for you—at a price.

- **eBay.** Check out Seller Central by clicking **Site Map** | **Seller Central** (under Sell) | **Resources** (on sidebar) | **Packing/Shipping Materials** (under Selling Supplies) for "almost free" shipping-supplies listings.

- Use packing tape (clear tape is the most common; the United States Postal Service recommends two-inch), not that roll of leftover masking tape from last summer's painting efforts. Think about getting a tape gun if you are planning on doing more than a few items a year. Tape all seams for added protection.

- Fill hollow items with packing material (Styrofoam or biodegradable peanuts, bubble wrap, crumpled paper, foam, or cardboard) to provide added structural integrity.

- Save quality packing material you receive. As most eBay sellers are also eBay buyers, you should have access to a lot of free boxes, bubble wrap, and Styrofoam peanuts. (A good measure of your buying-to-selling ratio might be whether your packing material inventory is losing or gaining volume.)

Access Shipper Services

eBay provides a great clearinghouse for links on all the current shipping rates and services provided by USPS, UPS, and freightquote.com.

1. Click **Services** on the links bar at the top of most eBay pages.

2. Under Selling Reference, click **Shipping Center**.

Selling Reference

- Seller Central
  Get the latest and most comprehensive information about selling on eBay

- Seller Education
  Learn how to start selling - take a tour or a tutorial - it's easy!

- Seller News
  Get the latest news on upcoming events, new features, and promotions.

- Shipping Center
  Find the latest tips, and resources for shipping on eBay.

3. On the Spotlight's On sidebar, click:

- **US Postal Service Shipping Zone** to access links to use the USPS as your shipper, shown in Figure 8-10

- **UPS Shipping Zone** to access links to use UPS as your shipper, shown in Figure 8-11

Spotlight's On

- US Postal Service Shipping Zone
- UPS Shipping Zone
- Freight Resource Center

8

One of the most frustrating aspects of selling on eBay for the casual seller is determining shipping costs. You can accurately determine the cost with a little planning and a few pieces of equipment. Gather your packaging materials with your item *before* you list the item (don't seal the box or envelope in case you need to see it to respond to a buyer's inquiry). Weigh (you can find good deals on eBay for an inexpensive scale; do a title search on "postal scale") and measure (basic tape measure) the length, width, and height of the box (if you use shipper packaging, you only have to be concerned with the weight). Armed with this information, you can respond to any questions on domestic shipping costs with only the buyer's ZIP code and a few minutes on an online shipping calculator.

- **Freight Resource Center** to access links to set up a calculator buyers can use in your listing for heavier items (similar to the eBay Shipping Calculator described in Chapter 5), ship the item online, and track its progress

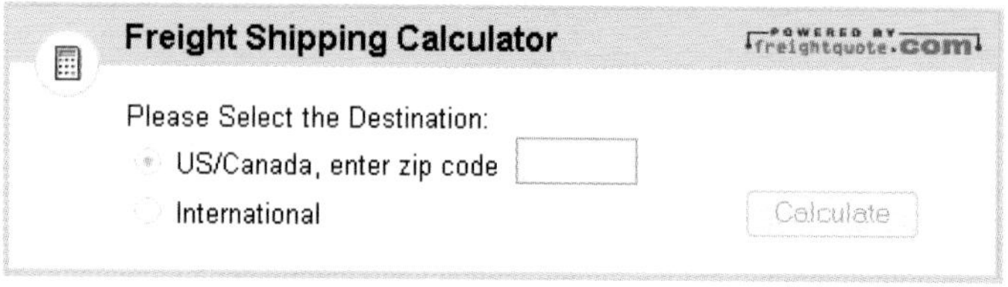

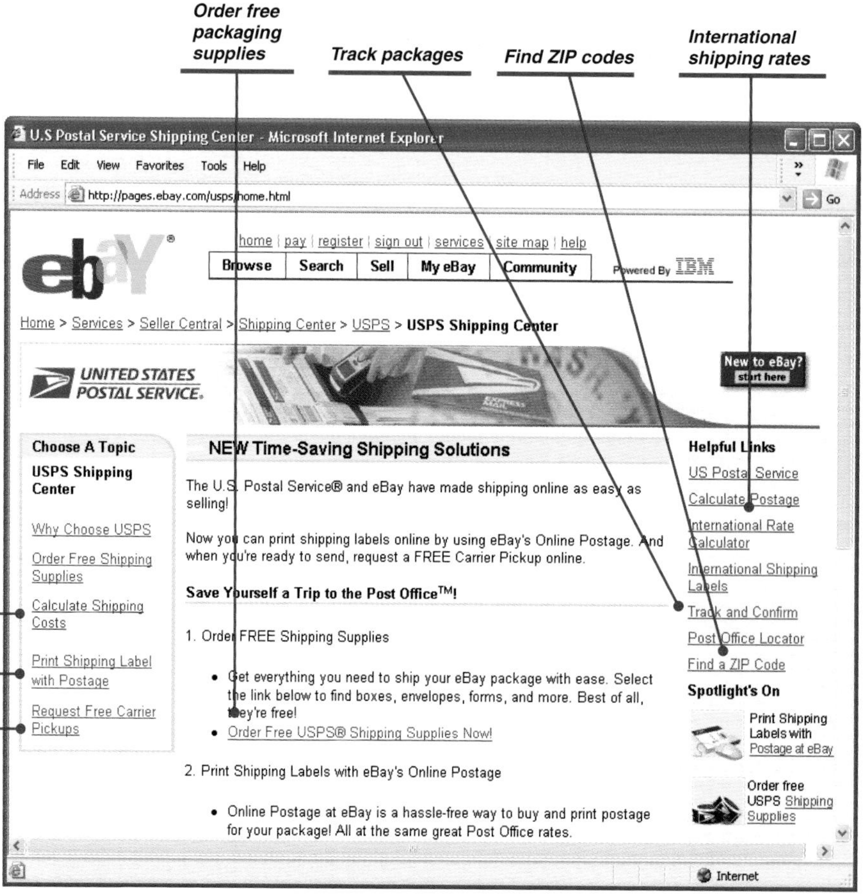

Order free packaging supplies

Track packages

Find ZIP codes

International shipping rates

Domestic shipping rates

Print a shipping label

Get free pickup service

Figure 8-10: The combined eBay and USPS Shipping Center is a great time-saver for finding the postal service you want.

Figure 8-11: The UPS Shipping Center page offers all the basic services in a condensed format.

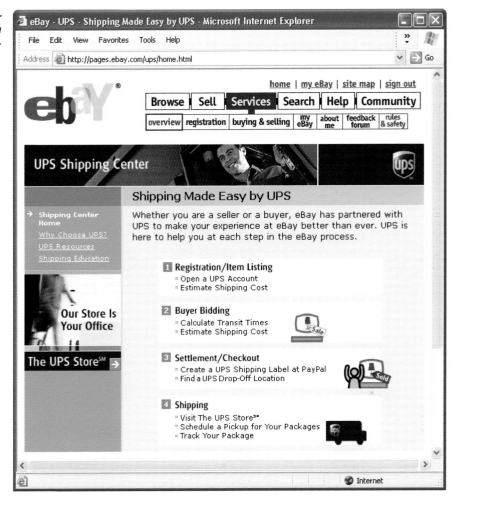

TIP

UPS provides free insurance for up to $100 of the item value for all its shipping methods. USPS offers $100 free insurance on its top-of-the-line Express Mail, but charges extra for other delivery services.

TIP

An easy way to avoid some shipping headaches is to charge an *average* fixed-rate shipping price (based on the weight of the package and closest/farthest distance the package has to travel). In the short term, you might gain or lose a little money from actual shipping costs, but things should work out to be about the same in the long run. eBay provides a chart, shown in Figure 8-12, of USPS average shipping rates for Priority, Parcel Post, and Media Mail services at http://pages.ebay.com/services/buyandsell/shipcalc_rate.html.

Figure 8-12: eBay provides average shipping costs based on minimum/maximum distances the package will travel.

Weight	Priority Mail↴			Parcel Post↴			Media Mail↴
Weight Not Over (lbs)	Minimum	Maximum	Average*	Zones 1 & 2	Zone 8	Average*	Rate
1	$3.85	$3.85	$3.85	$3.69	$3.75	$3.75	$1.42
2	$3.95	$5.75	$4.98	$3.85	$4.49	$4.32	$1.84
3	$4.75	$8.55	$7.00	$4.65	$6.32	$5.68	$2.26
4	$5.30	$10.35	$8.28	$4.86	$7.87	$7.04	$2.68
5	$5.85	$12.15	$9.58	$5.03	$9.43	$8.17	$3.10
6	$6.30	$12.30	$9.98	$5.63	$11.49	$9.01	$3.52
7	$6.80	$14.05	$10.83	$5.80	$12.83	$9.78	$3.94
8	$7.35	$15.75	$11.70	$5.98	$15.04	$10.48	$4.24
9	$7.90	$17.50	$12.55	$6.11	$17.04	$11.14	$4.54
10	$8.40	$19.20	$13.50	$6.28	$18.14	$11.76	$4.84
11	$8.95	$20.90	$14.45	$6.41	$19.15	$12.34	$5.14
12	$9.50	$22.65	$15.40	$6.54	$20.10	$$12.88	$5.44
13	$10.00	$24.35	$16.40	$6.67	$20.99	$13.40	$5.74
14	$10.55	$26.05	$17.33	$6.80	$21.84	$13.88	$6.04
15	$11.05	$27.80	$18.30	$6.92	$22.64	$14.35	$6.34
16	$11.60	$29.50	$19.23	$7.02	$23.41	$14.79	$6.64
17	$12.15	$31.20	$20.20	$7.15	$24.13	$15.20	$6.94
18	$12.65	$32.95	$21.23	$7.25	$24.82	$15.60	$7.24
19	$13.20	$34.65	$22.25	$7.37	$25.48	$15.98	$7.54
20	$13.75	$36.40	$23.25	$7.46	$26.12	$16.34	$7.84

First-Class Mail Rates↴	
First ounce	$0.37
Each additional ounce	$0.23

QUICKFACTS

SIMPLIFYING SHIPPING COSTS

The costs involved in getting an item from seller to buyer provide much fertile ground for discussion and debate among eBayers. The $64 question is, who pays? If you, the seller, pay, it simplifies things immensely as there's no need to discuss how to inform the buyer of the costs (however, most sellers do pass the shipping cost on to the buyer). Consider paying for shipping:

Shipping Service
Other (see description)

Shipping & Handling
$ 0.00

Add another shipping service

- For more expensive items; the relative cost of shipping is diminished
- Buyers appreciate a good deal (most online merchants offer some kind of free shipping)
- Eliminate 90 percent of your e-mail traffic with buyers
- Avoid any impression that you are hitting your profit target through shipping and handling charges

Create Shipping Labels Online

This feature, whether you do it from the shipper's web site or use the integrated eBay-PayPal–USPS/UPS method, is arguably the Eighth Wonder of the World. You can create USPS shipping labels with or without postage from the comfort of your home and drop packages off at a drop box or outlet near you. (You can also simply hand the package to your mailperson—a free pickup service that UPS and FedEx charge for.)

NOTE

The UPS and FedEx web sites offer services similar to USPS, but you cannot print out a label without paying for the shipping. Furthermore, you need to drop off the package at a company drop box or shipping outlet, or be charged a pickup fee.

Figure 8-13: USPS provides online printing of mailing labels for Priority and Express mail with or without postage included.

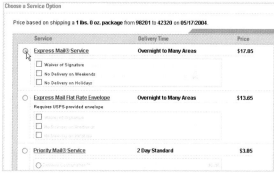

PRINT MAILING LABELS DIRECTLY FROM USPS

You can print domestic (Express Mail or Priority Mail) or international (Global Express Guaranteed or Global Express Mail) mailing labels, with or without postage (you need to establish an account to print mailing labels with postage).

1. Access the USPS home page at www.usps.com.

2. Under Send Mail & Packages, click **Click-N-Ship**.

3. On the Print Shipping Labels page, note that you may have to download software to print the labels. Click **Sign In** in the domestic or international shipping area. Sign in using your USPS user name and password, or create a new account.

Send Mail & Packages

Convenient mailing and shipping solutions.

- <u>Click-N-Ship</u>®! Print shipping labels to send packages and <u>Return Merchandise</u>.

4. You need to step through five pages to print a label:

- **Create Labels** page is used to provide return and delivery address information.

- **Choose Services** page lets you choose the level of delivery service and decide if you want to add postage (mailing labels with postage require you to add a credit card to your account).

- **Review Labels** lets you change and review any labels you have set up to print.

- **Checkout** is used to pay for postage-due mailing labels.

- **Print Labels** shows you a sample of the label to be printed, as shown in Figure 8-13.

5. Click **Yes** if you see a Security Warning dialog box that asks if you want to accept a certificate from USPS; otherwise, your mailing label may not print.

TIP

Don't tape over bar codes on shipping labels. The tape can interfere with the scanners shippers use to track packages.

PRINT MAILING LABELS FROM EBAY AND PAYPAL

You can print USPS or UPS mailing labels and pay for them from your PayPal account.

1. Open **My eBay**, and display the **Items I've Sold** view.

2. Select the check box to the left of the item you want to ship, and click **Print Shipping Labels** at the bottom of the view.

Print Shipping Labels

3. Log in to PayPal, and then choose the shipping service you want to use, as shown in Figure 8-14. Click **Continue**.

Figure 8-14: You can ship using USPS or UPS with an eBay/PayPal tool that provides integrated payment and tracking information.

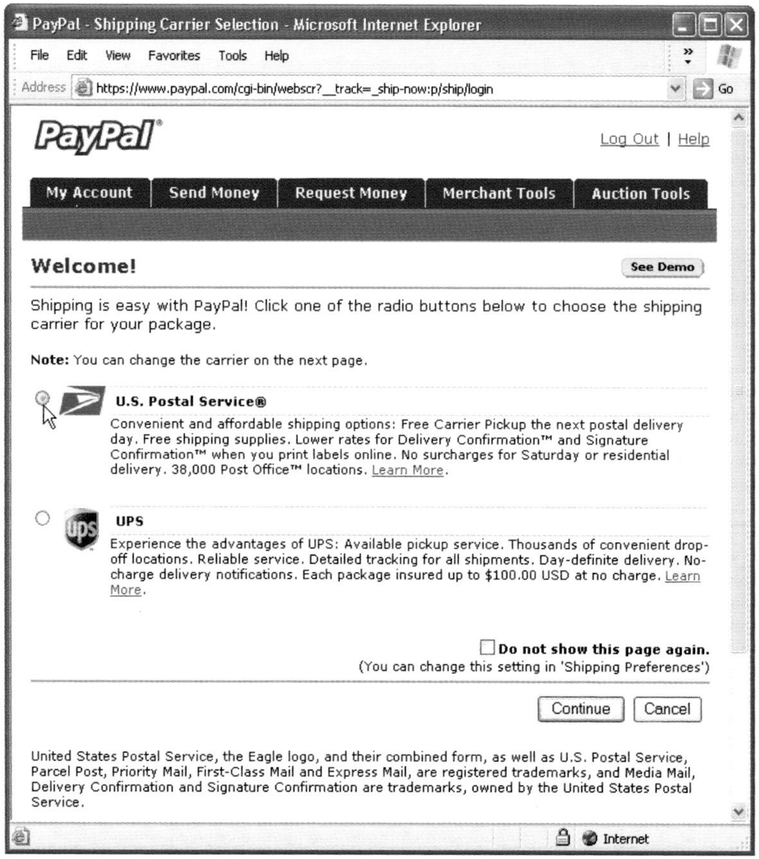

4. Choose your shipping options, and click **Continue**

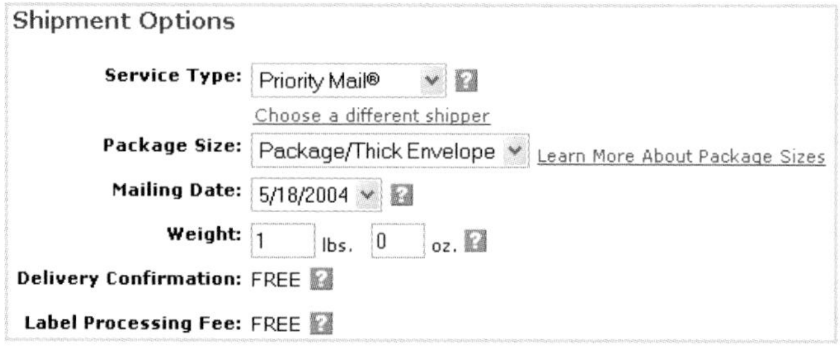

Shipment Options

Service Type: Priority Mail®
   Choose a different shipper

Package Size: Package/Thick Envelope   Learn More About Package Sizes

Mailing Date: 5/18/2004

Weight: 1 lbs. 0 oz.

Delivery Confirmation: FREE

Label Processing Fee: FREE

PayPal - Shipping Carrier Selection - Microsoft Internet Explorer

File   Edit   View   Favorites   Tools   Help

Address https://www.paypal.com/cgi-bin/webscr?__track=_ship-now:p/ship/login   Go

PayPal®   Log Out | Help

My Account | Send Money | Request Money | Merchant Tools | Auction Tools

Welcome!   See Demo

Shipping is easy with PayPal! Click one of the radio buttons below to choose the shipping carrier for your package.

Note: You can change the carrier on the next page.

U.S. Postal Service®
Convenient and affordable shipping options: Free Carrier Pickup the next postal delivery day. Free shipping supplies. Lower rates for Delivery Confirmation™ and Signature Confirmation™ when you print labels online. No surcharges for Saturday or residential delivery. 38,000 Post Office™ locations. Learn More.

UPS
Experience the advantages of UPS: Available pickup service. Thousands of convenient drop-off locations. Reliable service. Detailed tracking for all shipments. Day-definite delivery. No-charge delivery notifications. Each package insured up to $100.00 USD at no charge. Learn More.

☐ **Do not show this page again.**
(You can change this setting in 'Shipping Preferences')

Continue   Cancel

United States Postal Service, the Eagle logo, and their combined form, as well as U.S. Postal Service, Parcel Post, Priority Mail, First-Class Mail and Express Mail, are registered trademarks, and Media Mail, Delivery Confirmation and Signature Confirmation are trademarks, owned by the United States Postal Service.

Internet

5. Confirm your shipping service and cost. Click **Pay And Continue** to finish the process and print your label. Shipping confirmation and tracking data is provided to you by e-mail (see Figure 8-15) and is available on your PayPal Account Overview page.

NOTE

If you don't need postage included with your mailing label nor want to go online to print out mailing labels, you can do it the old-fashioned way—from your computer and printer.

NOTE

You can only use the PayPal shipping tool with UPS when shipping to a street address. You cannot ship to a P.O. Box address.

[Screenshot of an e-mail message window]

You created a shipping label with PayPal Shipping! - Message (Plain Text)

File   Edit   View   Insert   Format   Tools   Actions   Help

Extra line breaks in this message were removed.

From: service@paypal.com   Sent: Fri 4/30/2004 8:25 AM
To:
Cc:
Subject: You created a shipping label with PayPal Shipping!

Dear John Cronan,

You successfully created a shipping label using PayPal Shipping with U.S.
Postal Service(R). Your shipment details are below. Once you give the
package to the Post Office, your shipment will be on its way!

You can track the package online at:

http://trkcnfrm1.smi.usps.com/netdata-cgi/db2www/cbd_243.d2w/output?
CAMEFROM=OK&strOrigTrackNum=

Note: It may take up to 3 hours after the shipping label was created
for the tracking information to be available.

Take advantage of the U.S. Postal Service's Free Carrier Pickup.
Request a pickup online at www.usps.com/shipping/carrierpickup and
your carrier will pick up your package the next postal delivery day.
Or you can drop off your package at one of the convenient 38,000 U.S.
Postal Service locations nationwide.

Shipment Details

Shipped From:

Resolve Non-Sales

Much like the salesperson's mantra, "A sale starts when the customer says no," you cannot give up on an eBay listing that completed but didn't provide a sale. You have two powerful eBay features at your disposal: relisting and Second Chance Offer. Relisting an item allows you to try selling the item again at a reduced cost. Second Chance Offer comes into play when you and the highest bidder cannot come to terms and the item is offered to other auction bidders (can be also used in a few other situations). See Chapter 9 for information on actions you can take when a transaction really starts going south.

Relist an Item

eBay provides a 90-day window of opportunity to relist an item that did not sell or did not receive a bid and receive the insertion fee refund. (The same deal applies to an unpaid item, or UPI, formerly called a non-paying buyer, or NPB. See Chapter 9 for more information on actions to take for UPIs.) There are several stipulations you must satisfy:

- You are only allowed one relisting for a refund—the first time you relist.
- The relisting starting price must be less than or equal to the first listing.
- Only single-quantity, online auction and fixed-price selling formats are eligible.
- You cannot add a reserve if the original listing didn't have one. If a reserve was used the first time around, the relisted reserve must be less than or equal to it.
- The item must sell to receive the refund.

Figure 8-16: Prior to relisting an item, you should consider making changes to improve your sales the second time around.

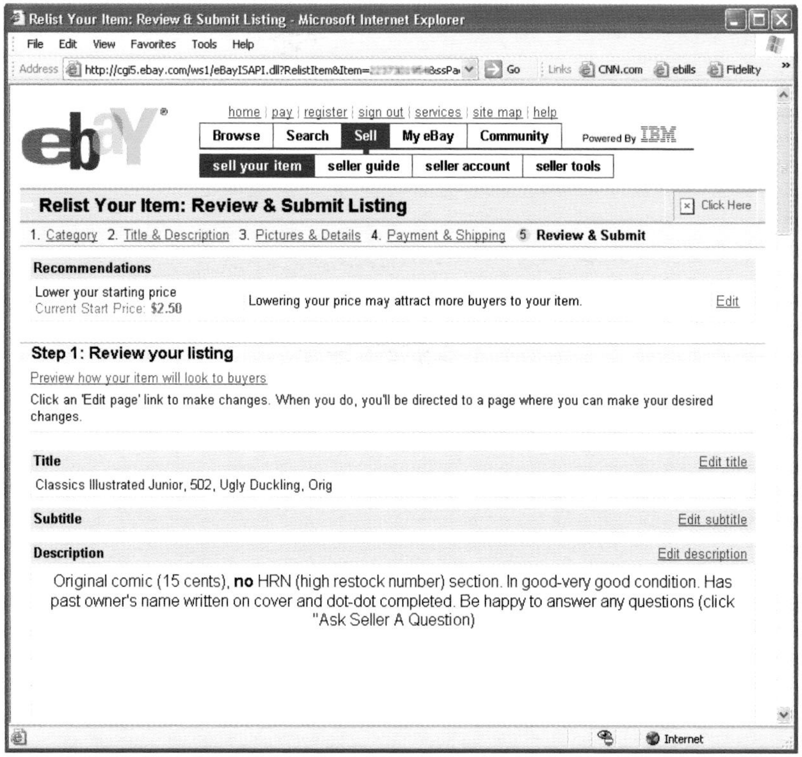

To relist an item:

1. Open **My eBay**.

2. On the My eBay Views sidebar, under All Selling, click **Unsold**.

3. In the Action column of the listing you want to relist, click **Relist**.

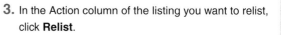
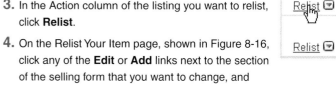

4. On the Relist Your Item page, shown in Figure 8-16, click any of the **Edit** or **Add** links next to the section of the selling form that you want to change, and review any eBay recommendations.

5. Click **Submit Listing** at the bottom of the page when you've completed any changes to the original listing.

NOTE

Second Chance Offer is also available if you have duplicate items for sale or your reserve price wasn't met. There is one other case in which it's used—unpaid items (UPIs). See Chapter 9 for information on the eBay Unpaid Item Program.

Get a Second Chance Offer

"It ain't over 'til it's over" can certainly apply to an eBay sale. If you and your winning bidder cannot come to terms to complete the sale, you can offer the item to a non-winning bidder. The Second Chance Offer is free (you pay a final value fee only when the offer is accepted), but must be selected within 60 days of a completed sale and you must have at least one non-winning bidder.

1. Open **My eBay**.

2. On the My eBay Views sidebar, under All Selling, click **Sold**.

3. Click the **Action** column down arrow for the item you want to offer to another bidder, and select **Second Chance Offer** from the drop-down list (you might need to sign in first).

   | View Payment Status ⊠ |
   | Second Chance Offer |
   | Sell Similar |
   | Relist |
   | Mark Not Shipped |

4. On the first Second Chance Offer page, click **Continue**.

5. On the second page, shown in Figure 8-17, select a duration for the offer and the bidder to whom you want to offer the item (if you have duplicate items for sale, choose as many bidders as you have items left for sale). Select **Send Me A Copy** if you want an e-mail copy of the offer sent to you. Click **Continue**.

6. On the last Second Chance Offer page, review the offer and click **Send Offer**. Your bidder will receive an offer similar to that shown in Figure 8-18.

   Send Offer >

Figure 8-17: You can offer an item to non-winning bidders if the winning bidder doesn't buy it, you have duplicate items for sale, or your reserve price wasn't met.

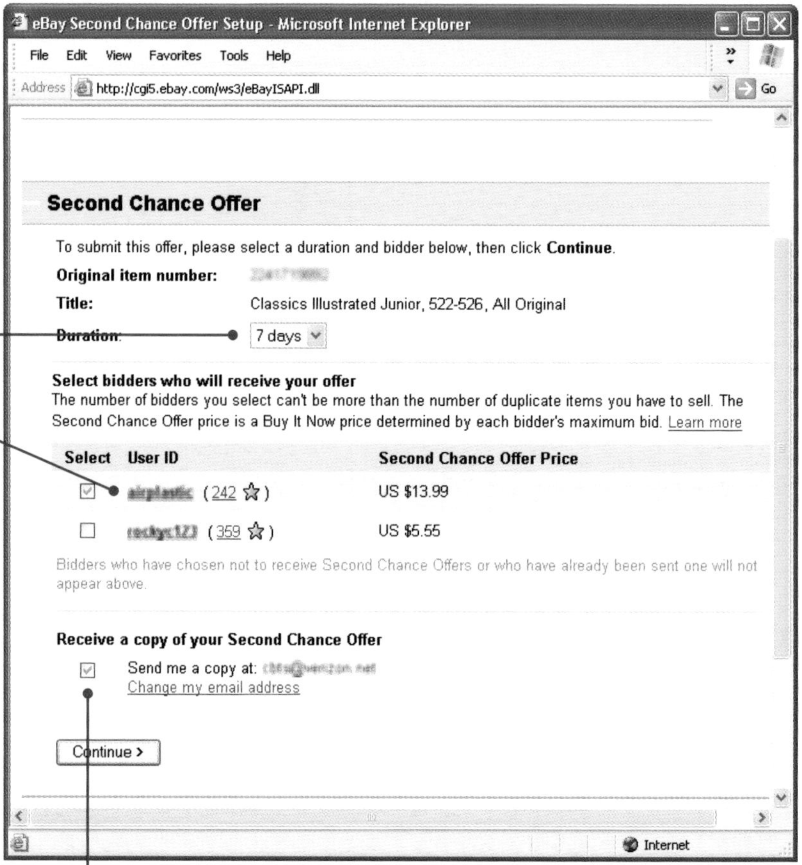

Second Chance Offer

To submit this offer, please select a duration and bidder below, then click **Continue**.

Original item number:

Title: Classics Illustrated Junior, 522-526, All Original

Choose how long the offer is good for — **Duration:** 7 days

Select bidders who will receive your offer
The number of bidders you select can't be more than the number of duplicate items you have to sell. The Second Chance Offer price is a Buy It Now price determined by each bidder's maximum bid. Learn more

Select one or more bidders to receive the offer —

Select	User ID	Second Chance Offer Price
☑	airplastic (242 ☆)	US $13.99
☐	reckyc123 (359 ☆)	US $5.55

Bidders who have chosen not to receive Second Chance Offers or who have already been sent one will not appear above.

Receive a copy of your Second Chance Offer

☑ Send me a copy at:
Change my email address

Continue >

Receive a copy of the offer

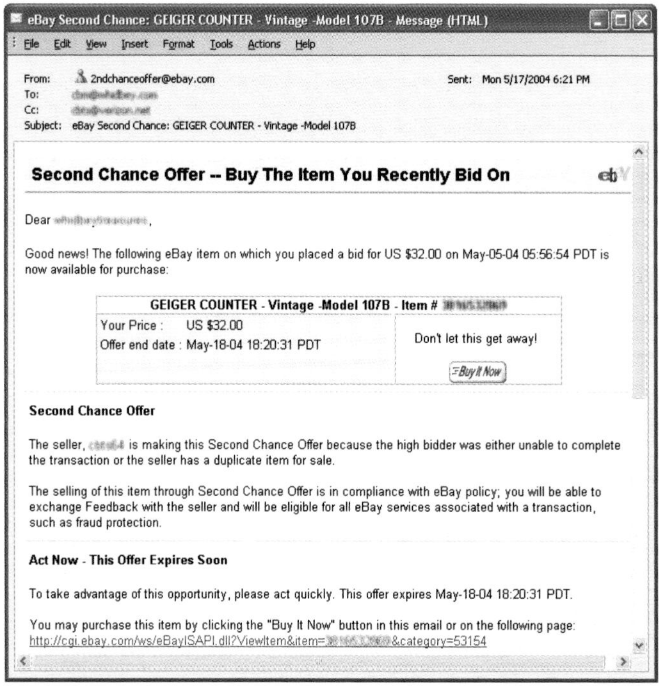

---

eBay Second Chance: GEIGER COUNTER - Vintage -Model 107B - Message (HTML)

File Edit View Insert Format Tools Actions Help

From: 2ndchanceoffer@ebay.com   Sent: Mon 5/17/2004 6:21 PM
To:
Cc:
Subject: eBay Second Chance: GEIGER COUNTER - Vintage -Model 107B

Second Chance Offer -- Buy The Item You Recently Bid On

Dear ,

Good news! The following eBay item on which you placed a bid for US $32.00 on May-05-04 05:56:54 PDT is now available for purchase:

GEIGER COUNTER - Vintage -Model 107B - Item #	
Your Price : US $32.00	Don't let this get away!
Offer end date : May-18-04 18:20:31 PDT	Buy It Now

Second Chance Offer

The seller, is making this Second Chance Offer because the high bidder was either unable to complete the transaction or the seller has a duplicate item for sale.

The selling of this item through Second Chance Offer is in compliance with eBay policy; you will be able to exchange Feedback with the seller and will be eligible for all eBay services associated with a transaction, such as fraud protection.

Act Now - This Offer Expires Soon

To take advantage of this opportunity, please act quickly. This offer expires May-18-04 18:20:31 PDT.

You may purchase this item by clicking the "Buy It Now" button in this email or on the following page:
http://cgi.ebay.com/ws/eBayISAPI.dll?ViewItem&item=&category=53154

Figure 8-18: Non-winning bidders selected for a Second Chance Offer get an e-mail that encourages them to buy the item now.

Chapter 9
Protecting Yourself and Handling Abuses

This chapter addresses how you can protect yourself as a buyer or a seller in how you set up your eBay account and handle it. From the very first step of signing on to eBay, you begin that process, first by researching buyers and sellers and the item to be bought or sold as well as you can, and then by using clear communication and straightforward transactions, always documenting your transaction activities. The second part of the chapter deals with how to handle problems when they arise. This ranges from simply contacting the other party, to arbitration, to filing charges of fraudulent behavior against the other party. The most important part of protecting yourself is making sure you are doing your homework and communicating with the other party.

Do Your Homework and Communicate

Misunderstandings about what you are buying or selling rest on the shoulders of both the buyer and the seller. Both are responsible for making clear what is being bought or sold. The buyer can't claim, "I didn't know," if a transaction goes badly, and the seller can't claim, "I didn't think she'd be interested in that!"

Communicate with Buyers

It pays for the seller to be crystal clear when describing what is being sold and under what conditions. It costs time and money to deal with misunderstandings and irate customers, and you can lose future customers as well. Your bottom line as a seller demands that you be very clear and precise. Questions to consider include:

- Does the description clearly describe the item, its condition, prior history, color, brand, size, and any other significant things about it? Is there anything about the item you are trying to hide or deemphasize that will be misleading to a buyer? If so, clarify it.

- Have you represented the item fairly as to its condition and value? Are you trying to make it sound like something it is not?

Sally, the seller, works hard at communicating with her buyer—she loves green feedback ratings.

- Does the photo clearly show all parts of the item, its blemishes as well as its strengths? Does it show only the items being sold? Is the photo potentially misleading? See Figure 9-1 for an example of a good photo.

Description

If you like black onyx, you will love this striking 3 stone, black onyx and sterling silver bracelet and ring set! The inside circumference of the cuff measures 5 inches with a 1 1/2 inch gap for your wrist to slide through for a total measurement of 6 1/2 inches. If you need to close or open the gap to adjust the size, you can do so if needed. The center cabochon stone measures 2 inches x 1 1/2 inches. The stones on the side each measure 3/4 x 1/2 of an inch. The ring's stone is 3/4 of an inch x 5/8 of an inch. The ring is a size 6 and it can be sized up to a size 9 if needed, at no extra charge. Handcrafted by a very talented artist in Gallup, New Mexico, you can't go wrong with this outstanding black onyx set! It is absolutely beautiful! If you have any questions, feel free to send an e-mail! Happy Trails! :)

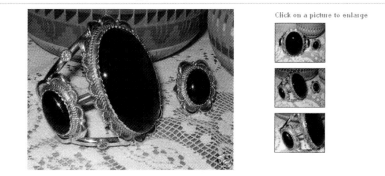

Click on a picture to enlarge

Figure 9-1: This is an example of a good photo and comprehensive description.

Shipping and payment details

Shipping and handling: US Postal Service Priority Mail: US $6.00
(within United States)

🐿 FREE shipping for each additional item you buy!*
(Shipping Discounts are offered directly from the seller.)

Shipping insurance: Included in shipping and handling cost

Will ship to United States only.

Seller's payment instructions & return policy:
I will accept PayPal, money order or cashiers check. S&H $6.00 includes insurance as well. Sorry, no sales in the state of New Mexico.

Payment methods accepted	**eBay recommended services**
💬 This seller, d*flying*cross, prefers PayPal.	Increase your PayPal sending limit. Get Verified today. 🅥
• *PayPal*®(VISA 🔲 🔲 🔲 🔲)	
• Money order/Cashiers check	
Learn about payment methods.	

Figure 9-2: This payment policy is clearly written and laid out, making it easy for the reader to follow and understand.

Bob, the buyer, wants to know that the seller is a real person who will take the time to communicate.

- Is your return policy clearly stated?

- How much do you charge for shipping and handling? Do you require insurance? Do you ship overseas? How much do you charge for international shipping? Figure 9-2 shows an example of a shipping and payment policy. Is yours as clear?

- Is your payment policy clearly stated? Have you told the buyer exactly what payment methods you accept?

- Have you stated clearly which bidders you will accept (those with 98 percent positive feedback ratings, for instance)?

- Do you require something different for new buyers with limited feedback comments?

Communicate with Sellers

The buyer, too, is responsible for the transaction. Not having enough information is not an excuse for having bought something you didn't want. Ask yourself these questions:

- Do I really know what I'm buying? Is this a prohibited or borderline product? If so, avoid it. Do I know everything I need to know about this product's history and its current condition?

- If I have questions, have I contacted the seller? Have I received a response? Has the response reassured me or raised more questions? (See Chapters 2 and 3.)

- Have I looked at the seller's feedback rating? What does it tell me? What are the customer comments?

- Do I really know how much I should be paying for this item? Have I researched what other similar products have sold for recently? (See Chapter 2.)

- Is this an unsolicited offer? (Avoid it.)

- How am I paying for it? Am I using a safe technique, such as PayPal? (Keep a record of all your purchases.)

USING FEEDBACK

eBay's feedback system helps you by providing the transaction histories of others and enabling you to build your own reputation. See Chapters 4 and 8 to see how to leave feedback as a buyer or seller.

BUILD A REPUTATION

Other buyers or sellers will know you by how you have performed in the past. See Figure 9-3 for an example of a seller with ideal feedback ratings. If past buyers or sellers have had good experiences doing business with you, you will get good feedback comments. If you have provided bad experiences, your feedback comments will reflect that. Feedback ratings are like money in the bank. They are a real currency in this cyber-economy where you can't shake hands with a business partner face-to-face. Protect your feedback rating by going out of your way to be fair and accountable.

PROVIDE FEEDBACK—GOOD, BAD, OR INDIFFERENT

Part of being a responsible buyer or seller is to give feedback. Do it fairly and in a timely manner. If the buyer or seller, is hard to deal with and you can't resolve the issue, be very specific about how you were disappointed. Do not just say, "This guy is a bum!" Be constructive, saying something like, "Two months late in shipping. Does not answer e-mail." Keep in mind that the other person can answer your negative e-mail, leaving his or her own interpretation of the experience as well as feedback for you. Be fair and accurate.

⊙ Nice product, but be sure to read about shipping charges VERY carefully.

Continued...

Take Protective Actions as a Seller

There are some tasks you can do as a seller to reduce your risk. Keeping proper paperwork is high on the list. Other actions include:

- Answer queries from a buyer immediately and fully. Always disclose anything that was not in the description. Keep the questions and answers where you can find them.

- Always save your shipping records, and ship with a tracking number and insurance. You want to be able to prove that you shipped the item, and if it arrives broken or the seller claims it is damaged, you won't be out any money. Pack the item carefully.

- If you have records on the authenticity or appraised value of your item, be sure to keep a copy for your own records in case the buyer disputes the value or authenticity.

- Contact the winning bidder and be clear about how you accept payment and how long you will wait before you consider the sale void.

Figure 9-3: An ideal feedback rating, one in the high 90s, reassures buyers and sellers of your reliability.

Member Profile: ████ (89 ★)				
Feedback Score:	**89**	Recent Ratings:		
Positive Feedback:	**100%**		Past Month	Past 6 Months	Past 12 Months
Members who left a positive:	89	⊕ positive	16	91	122
Members who left a negative:	0	⊙ neutral	0	0	0
All positive feedback received:	122	⊖ negative	0	0	0
Learn about what these numbers mean.		Bid Retractions (Past 6 months): 0		

Figure 9-4: Negative feedback is considered along with positive and neutral comments.

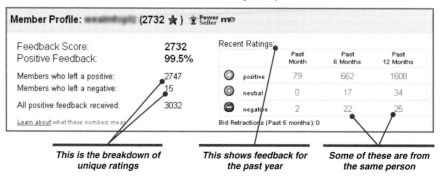

Member Profile: ████ (2732 ★) Power Seller me				
Feedback Score:	**2732**	Recent Ratings:		
Positive Feedback:	**99.5%**		Past Month	Past 6 Months	Past 12 Months
Members who left a positive:	2747	⊕ positive	79	662	1608
Members who left a negative:	15	⊙ neutral	0	17	34
All positive feedback received:	3032	⊖ negative	2	22	25
Learn about what these numbers mean.		Bid Retractions (Past 6 months): 0		

This is the breakdown of unique ratings   **This shows feedback for the past year**   **Some of these are from the same person**

USING FEEDBACK (Continued)

HANDLING NEGATIVE FEEDBACK

If you receive negative feedback, always reply to it and explain what happened. Be very clear about why the transaction was handled as it was, such as, "Tried to e-mail to explain delay, but buyer's firewall protection refused delivery." Sometimes it's easy to get carried away with indignation. If the other party was at fault, explain in a nonaggressive manner.

TOO HIGH SHIPPING
Reply by ———— Knew S&H costs before she bid, had done business before & she neg'd me then too!
Follow-up by ———— BILL CAME 10.23 WON, WITH 201.86 IN SHIPPING, NOT HANDLING. SHEESH. NO DISCOUNT.

In some cases negative feedback comments can be removed. To see whether this applies to you, select **Services** from the top links bar, and click **Dispute Resolution** under General Services, Trust And Safety. In the SquareTrade window, click **How To Remove/ Withdraw Feedback**.

EVALUATE OTHERS' FEEDBACK

Figure 9-4 contains an example of a seller with a good rating in spite of negative and neutral feedback. In this case, you can tell that some of the negative ratings were from the same person—feedback from the same person only counts as one feedback comment. Figure 9-5 shows what can happen if even one person feels he or she has been unfairly treated. For a seller with a high feedback rating, a few negative comments resulting from multiple sales to one individual are not a terrible thing; however for a relatively small seller, it can be disastrous. You can look through the feedback comments and determine if this is a consistent problem or one that just occurred with this particular buyer. You might see neutral comments that echo the same sentiment but with less passion.

Continued...

Protect the Transaction Summary

In addition to your communications with the buyer or seller and your attention to feedback and the item itself, there are other practical ways you can protect the actual transaction.

- **Protect your account** by changing your password periodically. Keep your password and personal information private.

- **Insure the item** to protect you and your buyer in case the item is damaged, broken, or lost while shipping.

- **Use PayPal** to pay for items or refund money.

- **Use ID Verify** to give others confidence in you. Look for other buyers and sellers who have been ID Verified.

- **Use credit cards** for the easiest and simplest transactions. Most credit card companies issue insurance against fraudulent transactions for additional protection.

- **Use an escrow service** for items of high value. The escrow service will make sure that the item is received and approved before releasing the money to the seller. If there is any question or the buyer is dissatisfied with the item, the escrow service continues to hold the money until the item is returned to the seller. Be aware, however, that there are fraudulent escrow services out there. Use www.escrow.com, which is recommended by eBay.

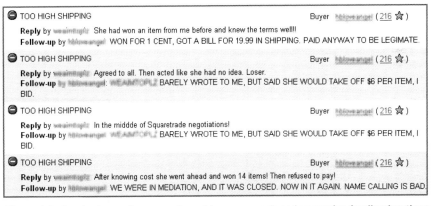

Figure 9-5: One bad experience can have big repercussions in negative feedback ratings.

USING FEEDBACK (Continued)

Or perhaps you will just see glowing comments, as seen in Figure 9-6. In this case, you can see that the sellers have given some favorable feedback to a buyer.

Things to consider when evaluating feedback ratings include:

- Become familiar with the stars, colors, and meanings (see Chapter 2).

- The rating is calculated on unique persons: +1 point for each positive comment, 0 points for neutral comments, and -1 point for each negative comment.

- Feedback comments can indicate a trend, either positive or negative.

- Check the time that negative comments were placed—recently or in the past.

- If the negative comments indicate a problem with the item, you can check the item listing to see if it is described clearly and fully.

- Do the ratings reflect the seriousness of the negative comments? That is, does the seller or buyer have too few ratings so that the results are skewed? Conversely, does the seller or buyer have so many ratings that the results are unaffected by a serious charge? Be aware of these patterns.

Deal with Buyer Problems

As a buyer, you may find several forms of fraud in eBay. Someone may pretend to be from eBay in order to access your personal information, or sellers may be fraudulent in their item descriptions. If, as a buyer, you have not been able to resolve the issue by contacting the seller and you still have not received your item after paying for it, or if the item is significantly different from what you expected, you have other choices available to you. This section addresses some of the problems you may encounter and how to resolve them.

Detect and Report Account Theft

Account theft can happen when someone else learns of your User ID or password and uses that information to steal your identity on eBay. He or she might purchase items on your credit cards, even going so far as to change your password so that you can no longer monitor your own account.

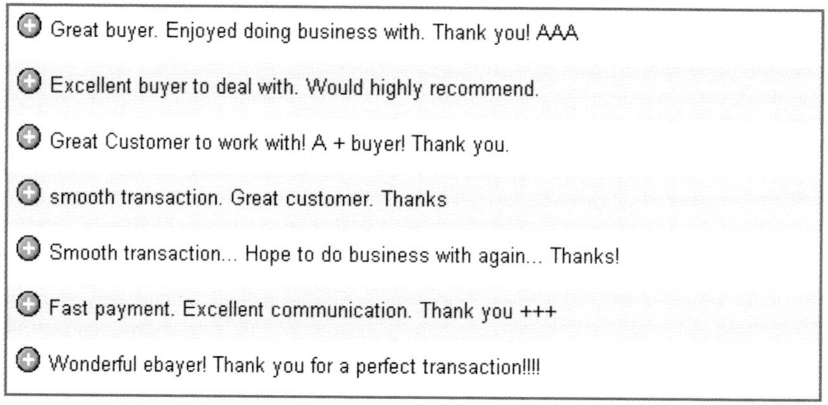

⊕ Great buyer. Enjoyed doing business with. Thank you! AAA

⊕ Excellent buyer to deal with. Would highly recommend.

⊕ Great Customer to work with! A + buyer! Thank you.

⊕ smooth transaction. Great customer. Thanks

⊕ Smooth transaction... Hope to do business with again... Thanks!

⊕ Fast payment. Excellent communication. Thank you +++

⊕ Wonderful ebayer! Thank you for a perfect transaction!!!!

Figure 9-6: All green comments tell you this seller or buyer has had good experiences.

PREVENT ACCOUNT THEFT

Ways to protect your account include:

- Never give out your eBay password, credit card information, or other personal information in response to an e-mail claiming to be from eBay. eBay promises never to ask for it in an e-mail, only online on their secure site.

- Check your account regularly to see if there are any purchases that you have not made.

- Change your password regularly, making it a maintenance routine, like brushing your teeth.

- Use the eBay Toolbar Account Guard feature. Account Guard warns you if you might be on a fraudulent web site. (See "Using Account Guard.")

SECURE YOUR ACCOUNT

You may be the victim of account theft if you cannot log on to your account because your password no longer works, you have unfamiliar charges, your PayPal account does not reflect your own activity, or you get e-mail from eBay confirming that you have purchased something you know nothing about. If any of these things happen to you, first secure your account:

- Change your password to contain both letters and numbers and also making it different from your User ID. (See Chapter 1 for information on creating strong passwords.)

- Change your secret question and answer on your eBay account.

- Verify that your address information is correct.

- Verify that your listings, purchases, and bids are yours or belong to someone who is authorized to use your eBay account (such as a spouse).

NOTE

Another method of reporting account theft is to use **Live Help**. To access it, click **Live Help** on the home page. There are two paths to finding advice here. Clicking the **Site Security** and **Account Theft** links will lead you through the maze to finding advice. Just follow the prompts. You can also chat directly with an agent online. While you are waiting for an eBay chat agent to come online, type your e-mail address. Open the **Please Select A Category** drop-down list, and click **Other**. Click **Send**. You can type your message in the lower box while you are waiting for an agent to appear. When he or she is there, click **Send** to send your message. Continue to chat with the agent until you know the solution to your problem.

REPORT TO EBAY

If you cannot access your account or find unauthorized entry onto your account:

1. Click **Services** from the top links bar.
2. Click **eBay Security Center** under General Services.
3. Click **Report A Problem** under General Marketplace Safety.
4. The Contact Us form is displayed. Select **Report Fake eBay Emails (Spoofs) And Unauthorized Account Activity** on the first level, as Figure 9-7 shows.

Report a Problem

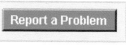

5. Select **Unauthorized Account Activity (Account Security Issues)** on the second level.

TIP

Typing http://pages.ebay.com/help/confidence/isgw-account-theft-reporting.html in your browser's address bar also will display the page that informs you about account theft and provides a way for you to contact eBay.

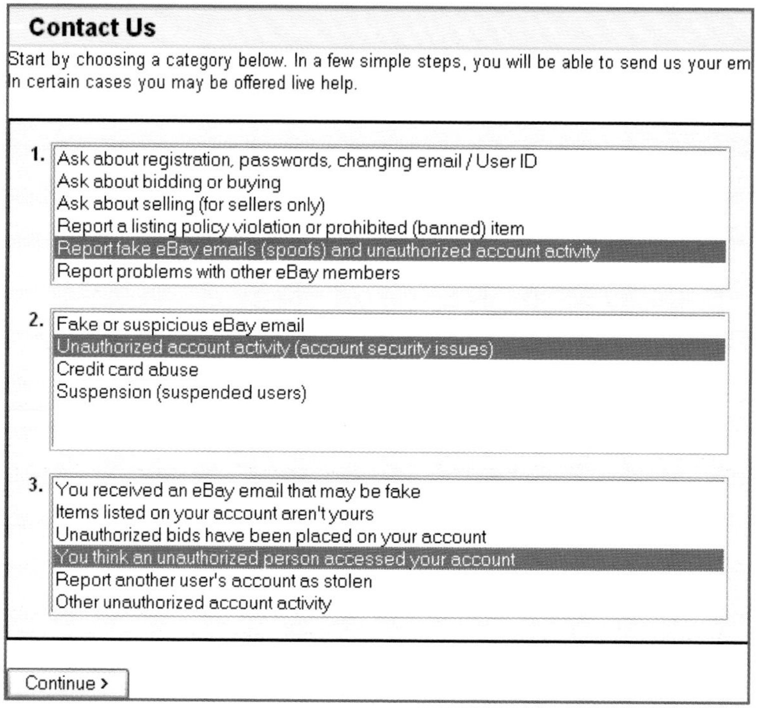
Contact Us
Start by choosing a category below. In a few simple steps, you will be able to send us your em
In certain cases you may be offered live help.
1.
Ask about registration, passwords, changing email / User ID
Ask about bidding or buying
Ask about selling (for sellers only)
Report a listing policy violation or prohibited (banned) item
Report fake eBay emails (spoofs) and unauthorized account activity
Report problems with other eBay members
2.
Fake or suspicious eBay email
Unauthorized account activity (account security issues)
Credit card abuse
Suspension (suspended users)
3.
You received an eBay email that may be fake
Items listed on your account aren't yours
Unauthorized bids have been placed on your account
You think an unauthorized person accessed your account
Report another user's account as stolen
Other unauthorized account activity
Continue >

Figure 9-7: Report your concern that unauthorized persons are accessing your account.

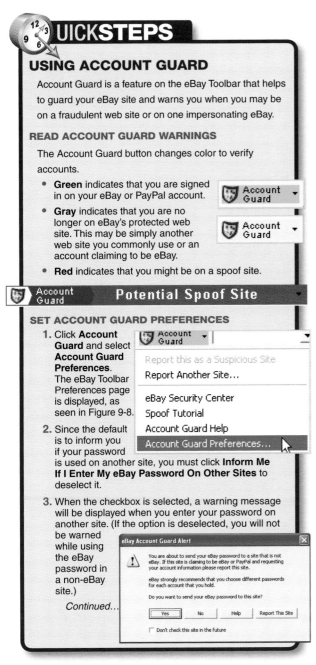

USING ACCOUNT GUARD

Account Guard is a feature on the eBay Toolbar that helps to guard your eBay site and warns you when you may be on a fraudulent web site or on one impersonating eBay.

READ ACCOUNT GUARD WARNINGS

The Account Guard button changes color to verify accounts.

- **Green** indicates that you are signed in on your eBay or PayPal account.
- **Gray** indicates that you are no longer on eBay's protected web site. This may be simply another web site you commonly use or an account claiming to be eBay.
- **Red** indicates that you might be on a spoof site.

SET ACCOUNT GUARD PREFERENCES

1. Click **Account Guard** and select **Account Guard Preferences**. The eBay Toolbar Preferences page is displayed, as seen in Figure 9-8.

2. Since the default is to inform you if your password is used on another site, you must click **Inform Me If I Enter My eBay Password On Other Sites** to deselect it.

3. When the checkbox is selected, a warning message will be displayed when you enter your password on another site. (If the option is deselected, you will not be warned while using the eBay password in a non-eBay site.)

Continued...

6. Select **You Think An Unauthorized Person Accessed Your Account** on the third level, and click **Continue**.

7. Under Customer Support Options, click **Email**. A Contact Us e-mail form is displayed.

8. Type your e-mail address, User ID, and your question or suspicion. Click **Send Email**.

Use Buyer Fraud-Protection Measures

If you think you have been defrauded by a seller, you have some choices. If you have paid for an item and have not received it, have received an item significantly different from what you thought you had ordered, received an item that was counterfeit, or returned an item but did not get the refund, you'll want to proceed in this order:

- First, within the first 15 days after the listing ends, contact the seller and try to resolve the issue between the two of you.

- Second, within 30 days, try a third-party mediator, such as SquareTrade, recommended by eBay.

- Third, within 30 days, file a claim to have your payment removed from your credit card company or file a claim with PayPal.

- Fourth, within 30 to 60 days, file a Fraud Alert to initiate eBay's Buyer Protection Program process.

Figure 9-8: Decide whether you want to be warned when using your eBay password on other sites.

USING ACCOUNT GUARD *(Continued)*

USE THE ACCOUNT GUARD REPORT FORM

To report a suspicious web site or one clearly impersonating eBay, click **Account Guard** and click **Report This As A Suspicious Site** or **Report Another Site**. An e-mail form is displayed in which you can type the circumstances for your suspicion.

TRY MEDIATION WITH SQUARETRADE

SquareTrade is a company that eBay recommends to help resolve disputes between buyers and sellers.

- A buyer or seller files a complaint with SquareTrade, filling out a form that details the issue and describes what you would like to see happen.

- SquareTrade contacts the other person by e-mail, informing him or her of the complaint and advising this person how to respond.

- The buyer and seller then directly try to come to some agreement using Direct Negotiation, a process under which both parties correspond back and forth by e-mail trying to work out a solution under the guidelines provided by SquareTrade.

- If the matter cannot be resolved directly, one of the parties may request a mediator to help out. This costs $20 from the requesting party and must be agreed to by both parties. The mediator tries to bring the two parties to some resolution that is agreeable to both sides. The mediator is not a judge or decision-maker. He or she only tries to see new possibilities and suggests them to the two parties.

To request a mediator:

1. From the top links bar, click **Services**.

2. Click **Dispute Resolution** under General Services, Trust And Safety. The SquareTrade web site opens, as shown in Figure 9-9.

Figure 9-9:
SquareTrade offers
mediation services
when buyers and
sellers cannot resolve
disputes.

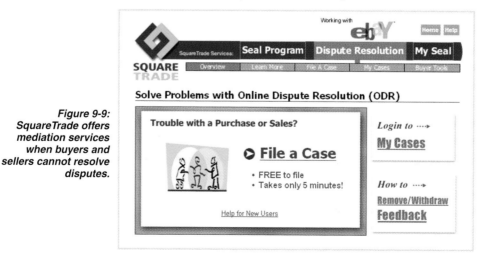

DEALING WITH SPOOF E-MAIL

Spoof e-mail is e-mail claiming to be from eBay when it is not. These are fraudulent e-mails often seeking your User ID, password, credit card information, social security number, or other private and sensitive personal information.

DETECT SPOOF E-MAIL

A spoof e-mail may have these characteristics:

- A legitimate look, with the appropriate logos and official-sounding names
- A claim that your account must be updated or changed in some way or your personal information reentered
- A request that you enter your private information (User ID and password, checking account or credit card information, social security number) either within a response to the e-mail or to a web site for that purpose
- Some type of threat that your account will no longer be accessible or that your ability to use eBay depends on your response
- The link address that you click to get to the site (which looks correct) and the URL of the site itself do not match (eBay's URL will always have an "eBay. com" before the first slash (/), such as http://pages. **ebay.com/**education/spooftutorial/spoof_3html; international sites may be slightly different)
- The Account Guard on the eBay Toolbar will turn gray or red

REPORT SPOOF E-MAIL

If you receive an e-mail that claims to be from eBay or PayPal or one of their related sites and you don't think it is, forward the e-mail to eBay.

1. In the To field of the e-mail, type spoof@ebay.com or spoof@paypal.com. Do not alter the subject line. Don't attach the e-mail to one you are sending to the security site since that destroys some of the detection capabilities that eBay has.

Continued…

3. Click **File A Case**, and continue as directed by the SquareTrade system.

You may or may not require a mediator to help with resolution. SquareTrade claims that 80 percent of disputes referred to them are handled within 10 to 14 days.

FILE A CLAIM TO BE REIMBURSED

In some cases you can file a claim to be reimbursed for purchases in which you have not received the item and have paid for it. Both eBay's Buyer Protection Program and PayPal's Buyer Protection offer these services. eBay offers up to $175 ($200 minus a $25 fee); PayPal, up to $500. The circumstances under which you might be entitled to some protection service include these limitations:

- A tangible item has been purchased on eBay. Items such as services or e-mailed information (such as e-books) are not included.
- PayPal Buyer Protection only covers payments made with PayPal. Neither program covers cash or instant money transfers since they cannot be proved.
- Both programs limit the number of claims you can make per year: eBay, to six per year; PayPal, to two.

In addition to the protections offered by eBay and PayPal, you may also be protected by your credit card policies, such as those honored when making Visa, MasterCard, Discover, or American Express purchases.

FILE WITH PAYPAL

In order to file for reimbursement from PayPal, you must file within 30 days of the transaction close and the item must be PayPal-protected.

To file a claim with PayPal Buyer Protection:

1. Verify that the item is protected by PayPal. The following logo will be displayed beneath the Seller's Information area in the View Item page.

PayPal ☑ Buyer Protection Offered
See coverage and eligibility

DEALING WITH SPOOF E-MAIL

(Continued)

2. Delete the e-mail from your e-mail account or inbox.

FIND ADDITIONAL SPOOF INFORMATION

- From the Account Guard menu on the eBay Toolbar, click **Spoof Tutorial**.

  –Or–

- Select **Services** from the top links bar, and click **eBay Security Center**. Click **Spotting A Spoof (Fake) Email**.

Account Guard
Report this as a Suspicious Site
Report Another Site...
eBay Security Center
Spoof Tutorial
Account Guard Help
Account Guard Preferences...

2. On the first bottom links bar, click **Security Center**. The Security Center page is displayed.

Announcements | Register | Security Center | Policies | Feedback Forum | About eBay

3. Scroll down and click **PayPal - Security Center** under Helpful Links.

4. On the PayPal Security Center page, scroll down, and under For Buyers, click **File A Claim**. Sign in and follow the directions to complete the claim.

For Buyers

PayPal Buyer Protection
Find out how PayPal covers eligible eBay purchases

Buyer Complaint Process
Find out how PayPal covers PayPal transactions
To dispute a transaction with your seller, you can File a Claim

Money Back Guarantee
If you covered your transaction with Money Back Guarantee and have a dispute to report File a Claim

Fraud Prevention Tips for Buyers
How to avoid fraudulent sellers

Report a Problem
Alert us to spam, or an unauthorized transaction

Helpful Links

Marketplace Rules and Policies

PayPal - Security Center

Community Discussion Board

Privacy Central

FILE WITH EBAY

The steps to filing a claim with eBay are more complex.

1. File a claim with your credit card company first to get the payment taken off your credit card account.

2. File a Fraud Alert within 30 to 60 days after the transaction. (See "File a Fraud Alert.")

3. If eBay finds that your situation meets its criteria, you will be given a link to the claim form.

4. Fill in the form, and mail it via regular mail to eBay Claims Administration along with proof of payment, a letter from the credit card company stating that they have not been reimbursed for the payment or deducted it from your account, and a letter of authenticity if you must prove that the item received is not the one listed. This absolutely must be mailed within 90 days of the transaction.

5. An eBay Claims Administrator will try to settle the claim within 45 days.

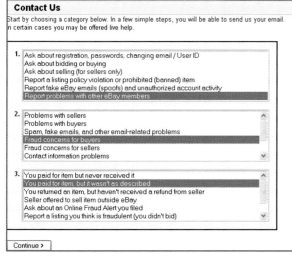

Contact Us

Start by choosing a category below. In a few simple steps, you will be able to send us your email.
In certain cases you may be offered live help.

1. Ask about registration, passwords, changing email / User ID
   Ask about bidding or buying
   Ask about selling (for sellers only)
   Report a listing policy violation or prohibited (banned) item
   Report fake eBay emails (spoofs) and unauthorized account activity
   Report problems with other eBay members

2. Problems with sellers
   Problems with buyers
   Spam, fake emails, and other email-related problems
   Fraud concerns for buyers
   Fraud concerns for sellers
   Contact information problems

3. You paid for item but never received it
   You paid for item, but it wasn't as described
   You returned an item, but haven't received a refund from seller
   Seller offered to sell item outside eBay
   Ask about an Online Fraud Alert you filed
   Report a listing you think is fraudulent (you didn't bid)

Continue >

Figure 9-10: Contact eBay with your concerns about being defrauded.

Contact Us: Send an email to eBay

To: eBay Customer Support
From:
Subject: You paid for item, but it wasn't as described   Choose a different subject

Please enter your question or concern (including details) into this form, then click **Submit**.

Item number you are reporting:

Date of payment:
--Month-- --Day-- --Year--

Payment method:
Select payment method

Have you called your seller?
Select from below

Have you used a dispute resolution service?
Select from below
Learn more about dispute resolution

Enter related information:

Figure 9-11: Send a specific e-mail to eBay reporting fraudulent sellers.

File a Fraud Alert

A Fraud Alert is a formal complaint against a seller made when you have not received an item or it is not what you thought you had purchased. It must be filed within 30 to 60 days after an item is purchased. The Fraud Alert is a required step before you can claim reimbursement from the eBay Buyer Protection Program. When a Fraud Alert is filed, eBay investigates and if the complaint is found to be valid, they have a range of actions they may take against the seller, including suspension of an eBay account.

To file a Fraud Alert:

1. Click **Help** in the top links bar. The Help page is displayed.

   home | pay | register | sign out | services | site map | help

2. Click **Contact Us** in the eBay Help box on the left. The Contact Us page is displayed.

   eBay Help
   Help Topics
   A-Z Index
   Contact Us

3. Click **Report Problems With Other eBay Members** on the first level.

4. Click **Fraud Concerns For Buyers** on the second level.

5. Choose the specific reason why you are sending the e-mail on the third level. An example is shown in Figure 9-10.

6. Click **Continue**. The next Contact Us page is displayed.

7. Click **Email**.

8. The e-mail form designed for the specific reason you're reporting is displayed, as

   Customer Support Option(s):
   Email
   Please allow up to 24 hours for a response.
   In many cases, you will receive a response sooner.

   shown in Figure 9-11. Type the information, such as Item Number, Date of Payment, and so on. Describe the specific information about the situation, and click **Send Email**. You will hear from an eBay agent in 24 to 48 hours.

USING THE UNPAID ITEMS PROCESS

The Unpaid Items Process replaces a procedure formerly referred to as Non-Paying Buyers Process (NPB). The latter process is explained in this book, as the Unpaid Items Process has just been announced. In the future, another way of dealing with nonpayments will be implemented that is designed to improve communication between buyers and sellers, since 80 percent of nonpayments are for issues dealing with communications. Some of the highlights of this future system include:

- There will be a way for buyers and sellers to communicate via a Dispute Console, which is a tool that both buyers and sellers have access to. It is primarily for sellers to manage and work with unpaid items.

- Refunds of final value fees will be expedited. If the buyer is not eligible to buy an item (out of country or unregistered buyer, for instance), the final value fee is immediately refunded.

- The seller will not have to initiate a Non-Paying Bidder Alert before filing the final value fee.

CAUTION

The first time that a bidder fails to pay, eBay issues a warning; the second time, eBay issues another warning; the third time, eBay places the bidder on indefinite suspension. The nonpayment complaints must be from different sellers before these actions can take place.

Solve Problems for Sellers

Sellers have special problems with nonpaid items. eBay considers nonpaying a serious violation of its policy and prohibits buyers from not following through with payment for items they have won in a bid or Buy It Now purchase. Sellers have several options: blocking buyers from bidding on their sales, relisting an item not paid for, making Second Chance Offers to other bidders, and requesting a refund on the costs of relisting items. A Bidder Alert may be placed on a nonpaying bidder, which is a serious thing.

Set Up a Bidder Alert

A Bidder Alert is a series of warnings and communications that enables buyers and sellers to try to come to some agreement about why a purchase is not being paid for. When a Bidder Alert is filed, eBay sends both parties e-mails notifying them of this. In order to file a Bidder Alert:

- The seller must be a registered eBay user and have sold the item.
- The Alert must be filed between 7 and 45 days of the end of the listing.
- At least one winning bidder must have met or exceeded the reserve price.

To file a Bidder Alert:

1. From the first bottom links bar, click **Security Center**. The Security Center page is displayed.

Announcements | Register | Security Center | Policies | Feedback Forum | About eBay

2. Click **Report A Problem**. The Contact Us page is displayed.

Report a Problem

3. Complete the form as shown in Figure 9-12, and click **Continue**.

4. Click **Email**. The Contact Us: Send An Email To eBay page is displayed, as shown in Figure 9-13. Type the item number and an explanation of what has happened. When the form is complete, click **Send Email**.

UNDERSTANDING THE BIDDER ALERT PROCESS

The following must take place before you can file a Bidder Alert or be reimbursed for your eBay selling fees (see the QuickFacts "Using the Unpaid Items Process" for changes to this process):

1. Within three days, contact the buyer to resolve any problems. Find out why this person is refusing to pay and see if you can work something out. Chapters 2 and 3 discuss how to contact your buyer in detail.

2. Send a payment reminder notice between 3 and 30 days of the listing close. If the person says he or she will pay and then does not, send the reminder and see if that will generate your payment.

3. Between 7 and 45 days of the listing close, file a Non-Paying Bidder Alert.

4. Within 60 days of a listing close, request a final value fee credit or for reimbursement of your fees. (You must have already completed the Bidder Alert phase.)

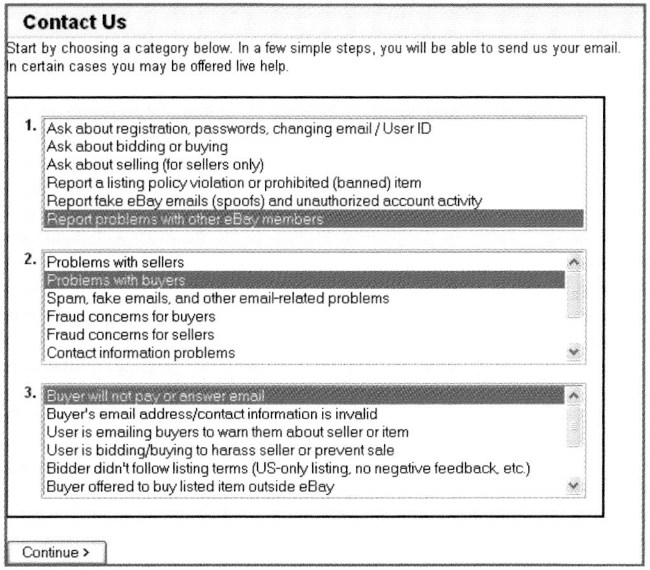

Contact Us

Start by choosing a category below. In a few simple steps, you will be able to send us your email. In certain cases you may be offered live help.

1. Ask about registration, passwords, changing email / User ID
   Ask about bidding or buying
   Ask about selling (for sellers only)
   Report a listing policy violation or prohibited (banned) item
   Report fake eBay emails (spoofs) and unauthorized account activity
   Report problems with other eBay members

2. Problems with sellers
   Problems with buyers
   Spam, fake emails, and other email-related problems
   Fraud concerns for buyers
   Fraud concerns for sellers
   Contact information problems

3. Buyer will not pay or answer email
   Buyer's email address/contact information is invalid
   User is emailing buyers to warn them about seller or item
   User is bidding/buying to harass seller or prevent sale
   Bidder didn't follow listing terms (US-only listing, no negative feedback, etc.)
   Buyer offered to buy listed item outside eBay

Continue >

Figure 9-12: To file a Bidder Alert, first report the problem.

TIP

If you, as a buyer, believe that you have had a Bidder Alert unfairly filed against you, you can appeal it. You must be able to prove that either the seller excused you from paying or that you already paid. Send the proof and the details of the transaction, such as item number and your User ID, to eBay, Inc., P.O. Box 1469, Bidder Appeal Dept., Draper, UT 84020.

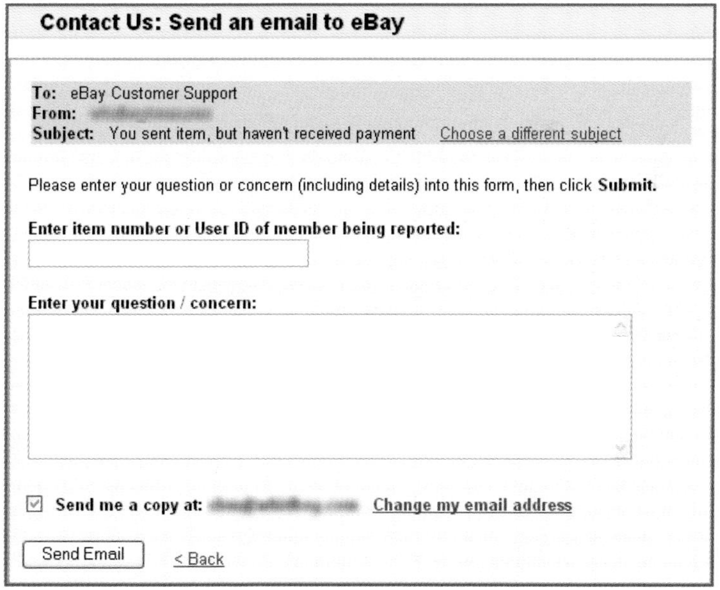

NOTE

In Dutch auctions, where multiple items are sold for the same price, you can only file one Bidder Alert for each bidder, not one for each product the person won or purchased but did not pay for.

Contact Us: Send an email to eBay

To: eBay Customer Support
From:
Subject: You sent item, but haven't received payment   Choose a different subject

Please enter your question or concern (including details) into this form, then click **Submit**.

Enter item number or User ID of member being reported:

Enter your question / concern:

☑ Send me a copy at: Change my email address

Send Email   < Back

Figure 9-13: An e-mail will be sent to eBay describing the bidder's failure to pay.

Submit a Final Value Fee Credit

A final value fee tells you the total cost of a listing, including the fees you paid to eBay. Before you can file a final value fee credit, however, you must have filed a Non-Paying Buyer Alert and tried for at least ten days to resolve the problem with the buyer. The final value fee credit must be filed within 60 days of the listing's end. (See the QuickFacts "Using the Unpaid Items Process.")

1. From the top links bar, click **Site Map**. The Site Map page is displayed.

2. Scroll down to Seller Accounts, and click **Request Final Value Fee Credit**.

Seller Accounts
Check my seller account status
Make payments toward my account
Select or choose a payment option for my eBay seller fees
Sign up/update eBay Direct Pay for seller fees
Place or update my credit card on file with eBay
Request final value fee credit
Cash out your credit balance
Change your billing currency
View my PayPal account

3. Scroll down to Number 4, and click **Request Your Final Value Fee Credit**.

| 4. Request your Final Value Fee credit | Request your Final Value Fee credit if you've: a) Filed a Non-Paying Bidder Alert 7 days or more after your listing has ended and b) Tried unsuccessfully to resolve things with your bidder 10 days after you've filed the Non-Paying Bidder Alert Form above. Your refund will be credited to your account within 48 hours. | Within 60 days of your listing's close. |
| | Worked things out with the buyer? If you have filed the Final Value Fee credit, you may use the Non-Paying Bidder Warning Removal to remove the warning for the bidder. | Within 90 days of your listing's close. |

4. Sign in again and click **Sign In**.

5. Scroll down to the bottom of the page, fill in the item number, and click **Send Request**.

Item Number	
Send Request	

You should hear back from eBay within 24 hours.

NOTE

Table 9-1 lists the circumstances under which you can claim full or partial credit for final value fees.

TABLE 9-1: REASONS FOR FINAL VALUE FEE CREDITS

Credit Type	Reason for Credit
Full Credit	• High bidder didn't contact you. • High bidder refused the item. • High bidder didn't send payment. • High bidder sent payment but check bounced or payment was stopped. • High bidder paid for the item and returned it. You issued a refund to bidder. • High bidder didn't comply with seller's terms & conditions stated in listing. • Both parties mutually agreed not to complete the transaction.
Partial Credit	• High bidder didn't complete the transaction. You sold the item to a lower bidder at a lower price. • Sale price to high bidder was actually lower than the final high bid. • One or more of your Dutch auction bidders backed out of sale. • Winning bidder in Dutch auction declined to take reduced quantity.

Block Bidders or Buyers

You can block certain people from bidding on or buying items from you. You would do this with nonpaying bidders or buyers or if you have had a bad experience with a buyer. You can build a list of up to 1,000 blocked buyers.

1. From the top links bar, click **Site Map**.

2. Scroll down to Manage My Items For Sale, and click **Blocked Bidder/Buyer List**.

3. On the Bidder/Buyer Management page, click **Continue** next to Add An eBay User To My Blocked Bidder/Buyer List.

4. In the text box, type the User IDs of the buyers/bidders you want to block from your sales. Separate the User IDs with a comma, semicolon, blank space, or by pressing **ENTER**.

5. Click **Submit**.

Buying and Selling
Manage My Items for Sale
Where is an item
Revise my item
Add to my item description
Manage/Edit my Andale.com counters
Promote your item
Fix my gallery image
Promote your listings with link buttons
Cancel bids on my item
End my listing
Relist my item
Blocked Bidder/Buyer List
Pre-approved Bidder/Buyer List
View the status of all my cross-promotions

Handle Shipping Concerns

If you have a problem with shipping—for instance, you shipped a package and it didn't arrive or it arrived damaged—you may have to deal with insurance concerns. If you did not insure the item, you cannot make a claim for it. If the item is insured, you may be reimbursed for all or part of the price of the item. In that case, contact the carrier and make the claim according to their requirements. Some possibilities are:

- www.usps.com/welcome.htm for the United States Post Office (USPS)

- www.ups.com/forms/e-mail/damage?loc=en_US for United Parcel Service (UPS)

- www.fedex.com/us/customer/claims for Federal Express (FedEx)

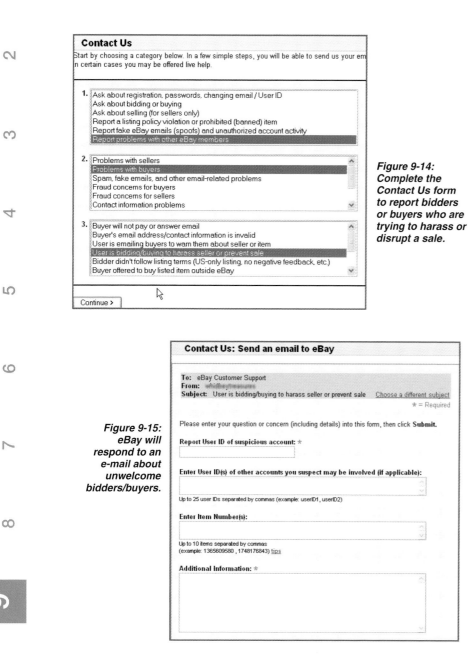

Contact Us

Start by choosing a category below. In a few simple steps, you will be able to send us your em
n certain cases you may be offered live help.

1.
- Ask about registration, passwords, changing email / User ID
- Ask about bidding or buying
- Ask about selling (for sellers only)
- Report a listing policy violation or prohibited (banned) item
- Report fake eBay emails (spoofs) and unauthorized account activity
- Report problems with other eBay members

2.
- Problems with sellers
- Problems with buyers
- Spam, fake emails, and other email-related problems
- Fraud concerns for buyers
- Fraud concerns for sellers
- Contact information problems

3.
- Buyer will not pay or answer email
- Buyer's email address/contact information is invalid
- User is emailing buyers to warn them about seller or item
- User is bidding/buying to harass seller or prevent sale
- Bidder didn't follow listing terms (US-only listing, no negative feedback, etc.)
- Buyer offered to buy listed item outside eBay

Continue >

Figure 9-14:
Complete the Contact Us form to report bidders or buyers who are trying to harass or disrupt a sale.

Contact Us: Send an email to eBay

To: eBay Customer Support
From:
Subject: User is bidding/buying to harass seller or prevent sale   Choose a different subject
                                                                                              * = Required

Please enter your question or concern (including details) into this form, then click **Submit**.

Report User ID of suspicious account: *

Enter User ID(s) of other accounts you suspect may be involved (if applicable):

Up to 25 user IDs separated by commas (example: userID1, userID2)

Enter Item Number(s):

Up to 10 items separated by commas
(example: 1365609580 , 1748176843) tips

Additional Information: *

Figure 9-15:
eBay will respond to an e-mail about unwelcome bidders/buyers.

Report Unwelcome Buyers

It's hard to imagine that there are buyers you may want to avoid, but it happens. For example, you may find buyers that are:

- Failing to meet your terms. Perhaps they are international buyers and you state that you will ship to your home country only; or you clearly state that you do not accept buyers with negative feedback ratings, and you get a bid from a buyer with a negative feedback rating.

- Using techniques that are meant to disrupt your sale. For example, someone might be bidding with no intent to pay or trying to bid even though he or she is blocked from bidding on your site or placing a bid that is so high that no one else will bid and then not paying.

To report unwelcome buyers:

1. From the first bottom links bar, click **Security Center**. The Security Center page is displayed. Click **Report A Problem**. The Contact Us page is displayed

   Report a Problem

2. Complete the form as shown in Figure 9-14.
   - Select **Report Problems With Other eBay Members** from the first level.
   - Select **Problems With Buyers** from the second level.
   - Select **User Is Bidding/Buying To Harass Seller Or Prevent Sale** from the third level.

3. Click **Continue**. On the secondary Contact Us page, click **Email**. The e-mail form shown in Figure 9-15 is displayed.

4. Click **Send Email.**

QUICKSTEPS

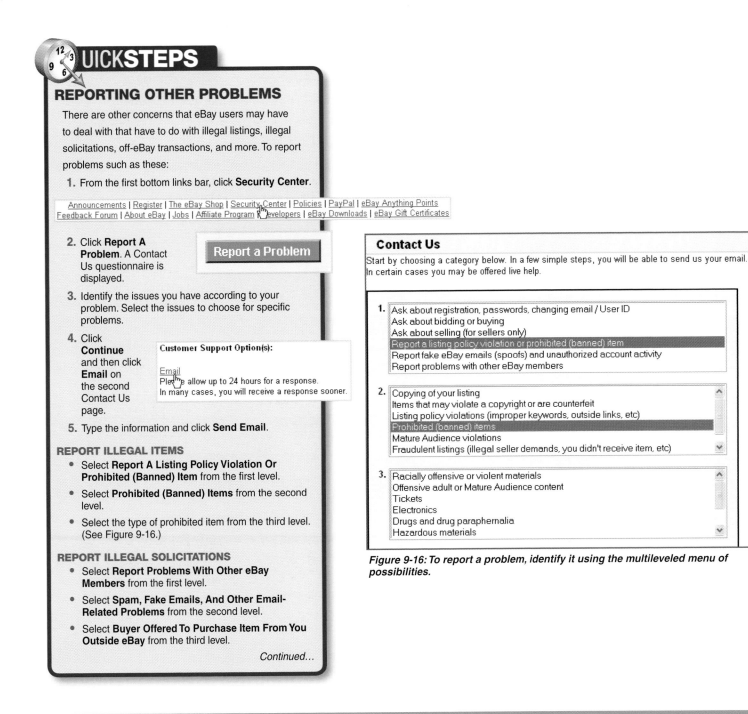

REPORTING OTHER PROBLEMS

There are other concerns that eBay users may have to deal with that have to do with illegal listings, illegal solicitations, off-eBay transactions, and more. To report problems such as these:

1. From the first bottom links bar, click **Security Center**.

Announcements | Register | The eBay Shop | Security Center | Policies | PayPal | eBay Anything Points
Feedback Forum | About eBay | Jobs | Affiliate Program | Developers | eBay Downloads | eBay Gift Certificates

2. Click **Report A Problem**. A Contact Us questionnaire is displayed.

Report a Problem

3. Identify the issues you have according to your problem. Select the issues to choose for specific problems.

4. Click **Continue** and then click **Email** on the second Contact Us page.

Customer Support Option(s):

Email
Please allow up to 24 hours for a response.
In many cases, you will receive a response sooner.

5. Type the information and click **Send Email**.

REPORT ILLEGAL ITEMS

- Select **Report A Listing Policy Violation Or Prohibited (Banned) Item** from the first level.
- Select **Prohibited (Banned) Items** from the second level.
- Select the type of prohibited item from the third level. (See Figure 9-16.)

REPORT ILLEGAL SOLICITATIONS

- Select **Report Problems With Other eBay Members** from the first level.
- Select **Spam, Fake Emails, And Other Email-Related Problems** from the second level.
- Select **Buyer Offered To Purchase Item From You Outside eBay** from the third level.

Continued…

Contact Us

Start by choosing a category below. In a few simple steps, you will be able to send us your email. In certain cases you may be offered live help.

1. Ask about registration, passwords, changing email / User ID
Ask about bidding or buying
Ask about selling (for sellers only)
Report a listing policy violation or prohibited (banned) item
Report fake eBay emails (spoofs) and unauthorized account activity
Report problems with other eBay members

2. Copying of your listing
Items that may violate a copyright or are counterfeit
Listing policy violations (improper keywords, outside links, etc)
Prohibited (banned) items
Mature Audience violations
Fraudulent listings (illegal seller demands, you didn't receive item, etc)

3. Racially offensive or violent materials
Offensive adult or Mature Audience content
Tickets
Electronics
Drugs and drug paraphernalia
Hazardous materials

Figure 9-16: To report a problem, identify it using the multileveled menu of possibilities.

Use Additional Resources

There are other resources you can contact for legal, governmental, and other
third parties.

1. From the first bottom links bar, click **Security Center**.

2. Scroll down and under General Marketplace Safety, click **Law Enforcement & Other
   Resources**. The page displayed contains several agencies and organizations from
   which you may seek assistance. (See Figure 9-17.)

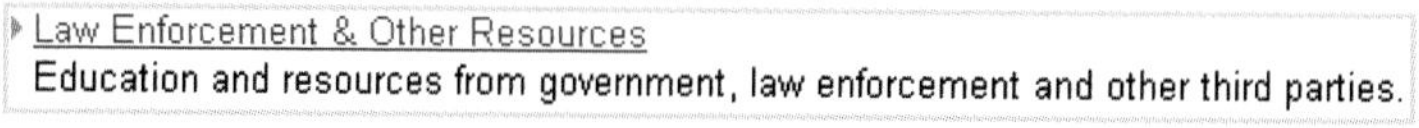

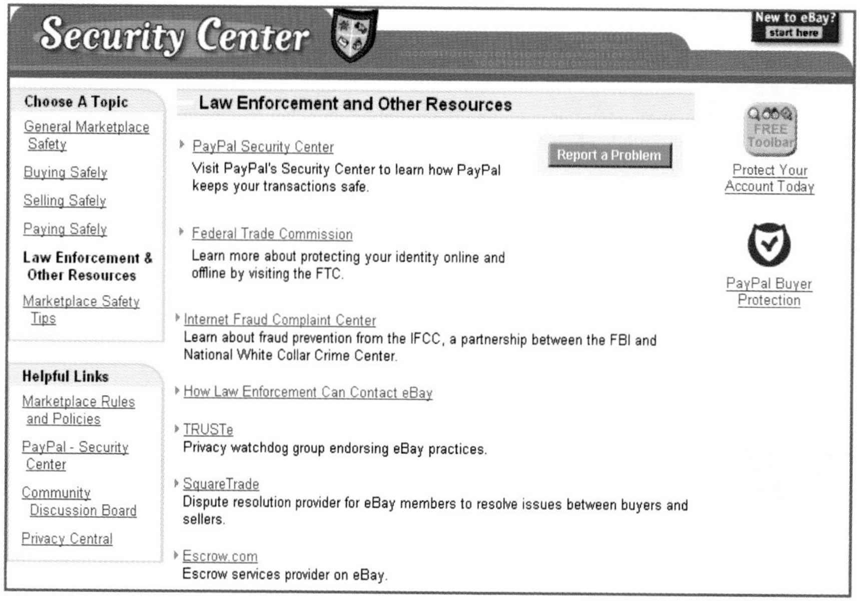

▸ Law Enforcement & Other Resources
Education and resources from government, law enforcement and other third parties.

*Figure 9-17:
Additional security
resources are a
mouse-click away.*

Chapter 10
Making eBay Your Business

In this chapter you will learn how to ramp up your selling on eBay beyond the casual sales designed to clear out a crowded cellar or garage. Selling on eBay as a business is very much both a traditional entrepreneurial undertaking and a totally unique venture. You follow basic steps, just as you would for starting any business. You will put together the necessary components of your online business, such as an accounting system, photo and shipping areas, and inventory (what you used to call "items to sell"). Once you have built the foundation of your business, you will need to actually run it—that is, decide how best to employ the programs, tools, and unique aspects of the eBay community to help you achieve your financial goals. This chapter helps you do this.

FUNDING YOUR EBAY BUSINESS

While there's nothing terribly unique about funding an eBay business, some of the types of equipment you will use (for example, computer equipment and auction management software), will be particular to selling online.

FUNDING OUTLAYS

Where your startup money is going to go:

- Equipment (computer system, camera/mini-studio, auction-related software)
- Inventory
- Operating capital (rents, payroll, phone, utilities, professional fees, shipping fees, listing fees)

FUNDING SOURCES

Where your startup money is coming from:

- Self-financing
- Investors
- Borrowing

What's Hot

Selling success often translates into being at the right place, at the right time, with the right product. Check back often to stay on top of the latest promotions and hot items on eBay.

- Merchandising Calendar
  Get advance notice of upcoming seasonal promotions and learn about which items will be spotlighted on the eBay home page.

- Hot Items by Category
  Find out which categories and products are hot--and where demand is outpacing supply! Check back often as this PDF file is updated frequently.

Plan Your Business

eBay has moved quite rapidly from being an "amateur hour," garage sale, Beanie Baby-selling dot-com to being a $21-billion-a-year enterprise. If you want to play on this playground, you'll be going head-to-head with professionals, including Fortune 500 companies. The only way to compete is to play by their rules in funding, marketing, and promoting your eBay business.

Develop Your Product

It's always best to sell a product that people want (tends to increase sales!). In order to determine what to sell:

1. **Research your customer base (eBay members) and see what people are buying.**

   - View **Completed Items** listings for products you're thinking about selling.

   - Check out **What's Hot** on eBay (**Site Map | Seller Central** (under Sell) | **What's Hot** (left sidebar)). Click **Merchandising Calendar** to see what/when items will be promoted on the eBay home page and other prominent pages. Click **Hot Items By Category** to see a report (Adobe PDF file) that lists categories by the percentage difference between bid and listing growth rates. The greater the percentage spread, the "hotter" the category, as shown in Figure 10-1.

Search Options
Show only:
☐ Items listed with PayPal
☐ Buy It Now items
☐ 🎁 Gift items
☑ Completed listings
☐ Items priced

2. **Sell what you understand.** Become knowledgeable about a product line so people come to rely on you as a source of expertise.

3. **Sell what interests you.** The passion for your product line will become evident in every facet of your business.

4. **Sell what makes you money.** The purpose of a for-profit business is just that, making a profit. If you run the numbers and determine you cannot sell the product for more than your acquisition, shipping, and overhead costs, it's time to change products.

Figure 10-1: eBay lists categories by their degree of "hotness," a measure of the percentage difference between bid and listing growth rates, to help you assess your product line.

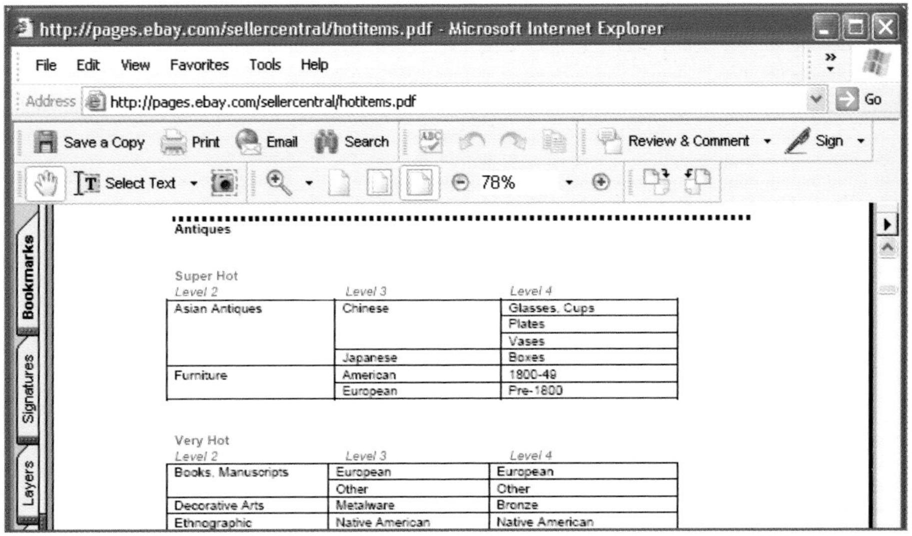

Promote Your Product

Figure 10-2: When you ascend to the loftier levels of eBay selling, you can take advantage of eBay-sponsored marketing and advertising programs.

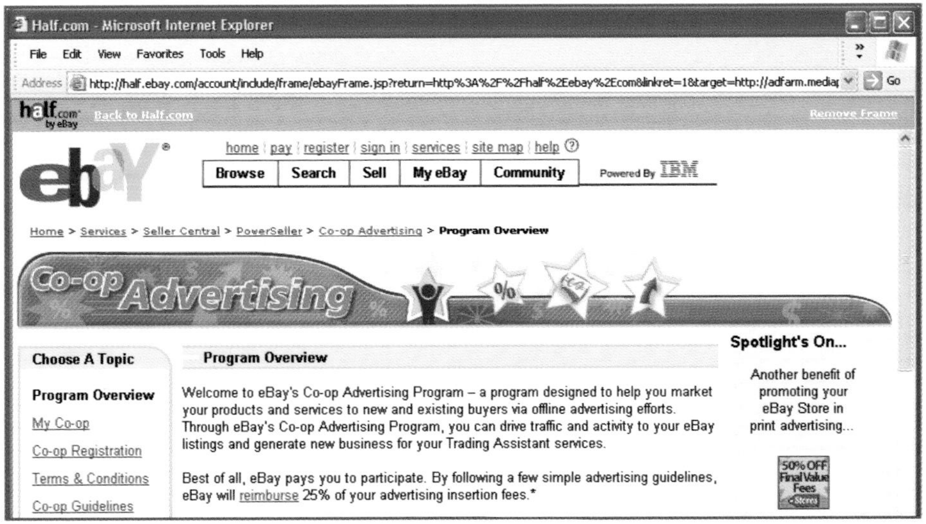

Promotion gets the word out about your product to your target audience. In eBay, you have several promotional upgrades and features you can apply to your listings (see Chapter 5). Examples of other promotional actions you can explore include:

- As a PowerSeller (see the QuickSteps "Becoming a PowerSeller"), using the cross-promotional feature available in eBay Stores to promote your auction listings along with your Store inventory items.

- Participating in eBay's Co-op Advertising Program, shown in Figure 10-2, where eBay will reimburse 25 percent of your offline advertising costs that promote your eBay selling

- Enhancing your About Me page (see Figure 10-3 and "Create an About Me Page") to provide in-depth information about you, your company, and your product

Figure 10-3: An About Me page is a great tool for cross-promoting your eBay and retail businesses.

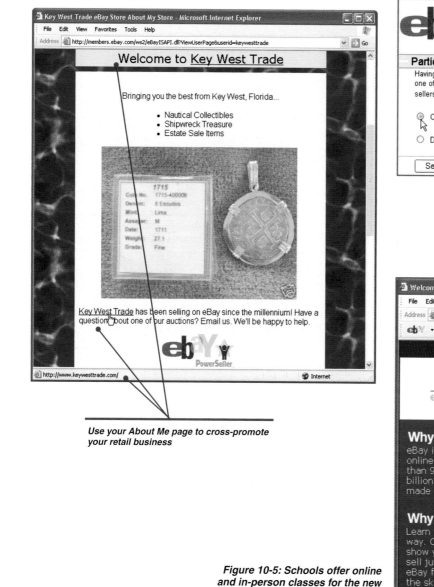

Use your About Me page to cross-promote your retail business

Figure 10-4: Let eBay help in your cross-promotional campaign.

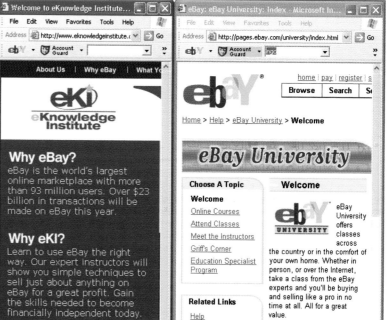

Figure 10-5: Schools offer online and in-person classes for the new and experienced eBay seller.

Create the Infrastructure

As an occasional seller on eBay, you can get away with temporary or otherwise cobbled "centers" to support your eBay selling. The increase in volume you can expect as your business takes off, however, will require a more formalized approach.

SET UP YOUR BOOKS

Keeping accurate records of your inventory costs, selling prices, shipping and handling, overhead, and associated costs is the foundation to satisfying government reporting requirements as well as keeping on top of the financial health of your business. You can get professional help to set up your accounts, use an accounting program (a popular small-business accounting software is Intuit's QuickBooks Basic/Pro/Premier—www.intuit.com), or set up your own spreadsheets, either paper-based or using a program such as Microsoft Excel.

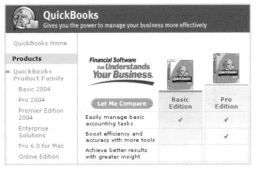

ACQUIRE INVENTORY

Chapter 5 describes the common methods of finding items to sell on eBay—at garage sales and thrift stores, for example. When selling as a business, you may need to expand your sphere of acquisitions to more traditional business sources, such as:

- Discontinued, excess, and seasonal inventory from local retailers
- Going-out-of-business sales and auctions
- Manufacturers and distributors
- Wholesalers (including eBay wholesalers)
- Importers/exporters
- Items purchased directly from foreign manufacturers

NOTE

There are several schools and universities that cater to eBay users' need for education. You'll find beginning classes that introduce you to eBay, as well as advanced classes that are relevant to building an eBay business. Classes may be online or at a site near you. Two examples of such organizations are eBay University and eKnowledge Institute, shown in Figure 10-5. eKnowledge Institute (www.eknowledgeinstitute.com), a new eBay education venue, offers classes using this book as a source of information.

About eKnowledge Institute

eKnowledge Institute was formed by business professionals and educators to instruct individuals and small businesses on eBay. eBay has revolutionized the auction world, and understanding this changing marketplace can help many individuals and businesses realize new profits.

eKnowledge Institute's 2004 eBay Experience Seminar Tour, is the largest national seminar series that instructs individuals how to use and profit on eBay. Our seminar materials were developed in conjunction with McGraw-Hill, Inc.

McGraw-Hill is one of the world's largest publishing companies, and a leader in producing educational materials including textbooks and tests. McGraw-Hill is also a leading supplier of financial and business information services. It publishes Business Week magazine and is the owner of Standard and Poor's.

CREATE PROCESSING CENTERS

Henry Ford revolutionized manufacturing by introducing the assembly line. A hundred years later, you can benefit from his wisdom by applying the same principle to move your product quickly from inventory to shipment by devoting dedicated centers to the eBay sales process. An item's typical journey through your business might include:

1. **Purchasing Center** logs a new item into your inventory database (can be a simple notebook or a database program, such as Microsoft Access) and includes sales cost, date of acquisition, and source.

2. **Photo Center** photographs the item using a studio that's set up to quickly introduce the item into a neutral background with adequate lighting. Enhance pictures to accentuate features. (See Chapter 6 for information on picture-editing techniques and programs.) Pictures are uploaded to a local computer system for ready use by your hosting method.

3. **Listing Center** describes the item, researches similar items for pricing and category selection, and submits the listing directly to eBay or your auction-management system. Listings are monitored for bidding activity and bidder/buyer inquiries.

4. **Accounting Center** processes incoming payments and releases items to shipping when funds have cleared.

5. **Shipping Center** provides materials and equipment for easy and professional packaging. Liaison and accounts with shippers are established to maximize convenience (daily pickups) and minimize costs.

LINK TO EBAY FROM YOUR WEB SITE

Having a web site is almost a given for anyone who does business today, online or offline. Even if only providing informational and customer service-oriented material, a web site adds credibility to your eBay business. Simple web sites are generally provided by your Internet service provider (ISP), and you can easily create your own with a web site-creation program, such as Microsoft FrontPage. Your ISP typically provides free web server storage space as part of your Internet connection subscription, so cost is low or minimal. To drive "outsiders" to your eBay listings, use the eBay logo to provide links to the eBay home page and your listings.

A second function of a web site is to conduct e-commerce. Unless you already have a functioning e-commerce web site, however, the added time and expense of keeping two online sales channels maintained could prove overwhelming for the small startup. Your time is probably better spent establishing your eBay presence and taking advantage of eBay's built-in marketing and advertising tools.

TIP

To change a current About Me page, follow the same steps to create one, and the forms will be pre-populated with your current settings.

1. Click **Site Map** on the links bar at the top of any eBay page.

2. Under Buying And Selling, click **Promote Your Listings With Link Buttons**.

3. Select the links you want on your web site (for example, to the eBay home page and to your listings).

☑	eBay	Links to the eBay home page
☑	SHOP eBay WITH ME!	A customized link that goes directly to a list of items you have for sale.

4. Type the URLs of your web pages that will contain the links.

```
www.acme.com/index.html
www.acme.com/catalog/cathome.html
```

5. Read the eBay Link License Agreement, and click **I Agree** (if you don't agree, you won't be able to continue).

6. On the Instructions For Installing Buttons On Your Site page, copy the HTML code for the link you want, as shown in Figure 10-6, and paste it onto your web page.

Set Up Your eBay Business

You can conduct business on eBay without doing anything more than submitting Sell Your Item forms, as you've probably done several times already. To recognize and support those who want to ratchet up their eBay involvement, eBay provides several programs that can help you take advantage of its powerful marketing and advertising engine. You can promote your business in an About Me page, create an eBay Store (effectively providing an e-commerce web site), and become a PowerSeller.

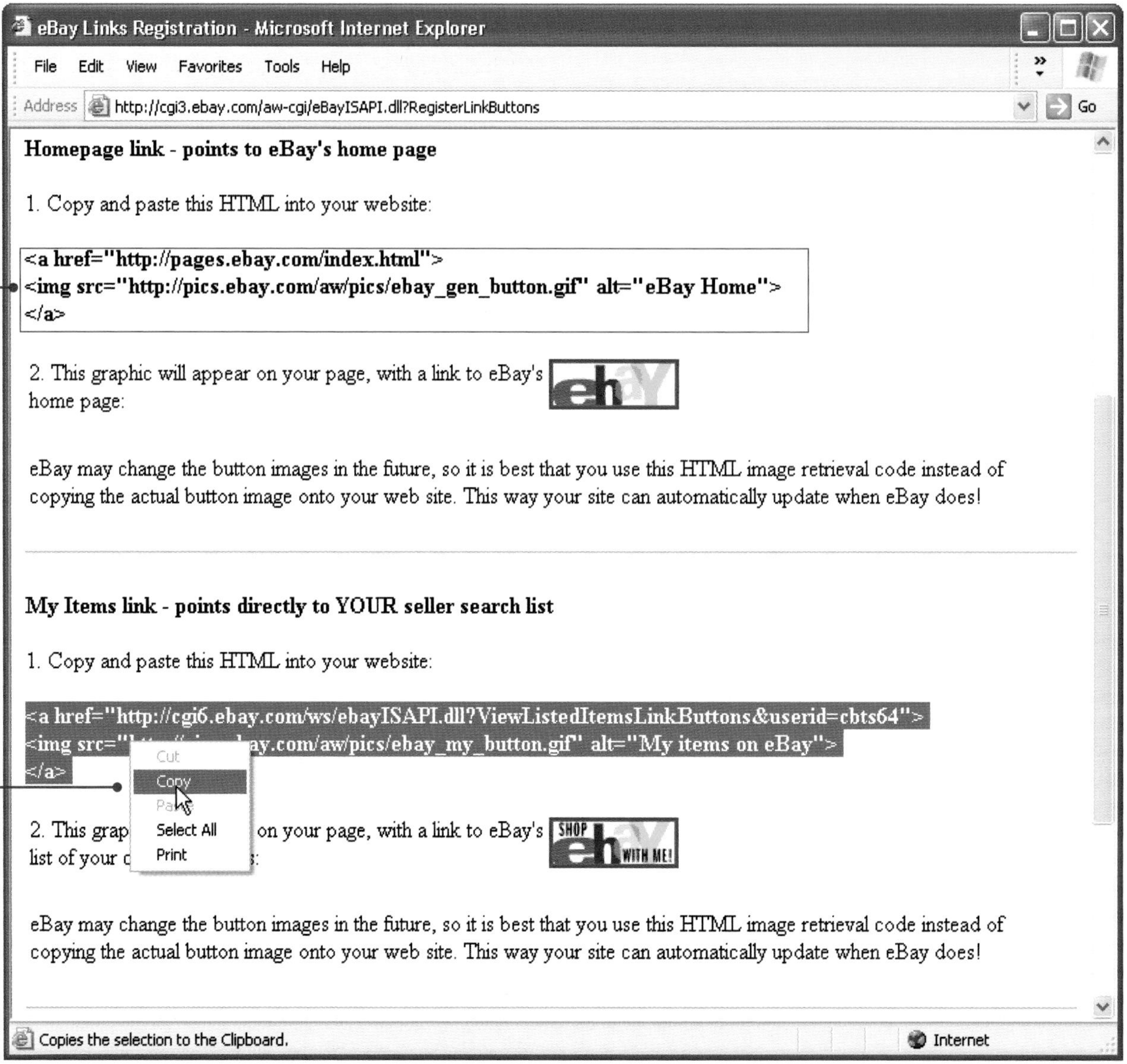

eBay Links Registration - Microsoft Internet Explorer

File   Edit   View   Favorites   Tools   Help

Address http://cgi3.ebay.com/aw-cgi/eBayISAPI.dll?RegisterLinkButtons

Homepage link - points to eBay's home page

1. Copy and paste this HTML into your website:

Copy and paste this HTML code to add the eBay logo to your non-eBay web pages

```
<a href="http://pages.ebay.com/index.html">
<img src="http://pics.ebay.com/aw/pics/ebay_gen_button.gif" alt="eBay Home">
</a>
```

2. This graphic will appear on your page, with a link to eBay's home page:

eBay may change the button images in the future, so it is best that you use this HTML image retrieval code instead of copying the actual button image onto your web site. This way your site can automatically update when eBay does!

My Items link - points directly to YOUR seller search list

1. Copy and paste this HTML into your website:

Link to your eBay listing from your web site

```
<a href="http://cgi6.ebay.com/ws/ebayISAPI.dll?ViewListedItemsLinkButtons&userid=cbts64">
<img src="http://pics.ebay.com/aw/pics/ebay_my_button.gif" alt="My items on eBay">
</a>
```

Cut
Copy
Paste
Select All
Print

2. This graphic will appear on your page, with a link to eBay's list of your current listings:

eBay may change the button images in the future, so it is best that you use this HTML image retrieval code instead of copying the actual button image onto your web site. This way your site can automatically update when eBay does!

Copies the selection to the Clipboard.   Internet

Figure 10-6: You can place HTML code that displays the eBay logo with a link to your current listings on your web pages.

Create an About Me Page

You can create a page about your business (or self) that others can reference when they research your eBay activities. If you have an About Me page, a special icon will be displayed next to your User ID and in your eBay Store header.

"Sally, the seller, creates an About Me Page to toot her own horn."

Maintained by: ▓▓▓▓▓▓ (<u>1153</u> ★) 🏆 Power Seller me ⬤

1. You can access the About Me pages from My eBay or from someone else's About Me page.

   - From the My eBay Views sidebar, scroll down to My Account, and click **Personal Information**. Under Personal Information, click **Change** to the right of About Me Page.

   –Or–

   - Open an About Me page by clicking the **About Me** icon next to a User ID in a listing or in the header of an eBay Store. At the bottom of the About Me page, click the link in **To Create Your Own About Me Page, Click Here**.

   > To create your own About Me page, <u>click here</u>.

2. The About Me introductory page introduces what the page is used for. Click the **Create Or Edit Your Page** button.

   > Create Or Edit Your Page

3. Select a layout: Centered Layout (the default), Two-Column Layout, or Multi-Column Layout. Then, click **Continue**.

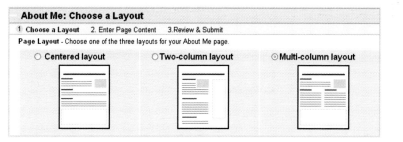

About Me: Choose a Layout
1 Choose a Layout   2. Enter Page Content   3.Review & Submit
Page Layout - Choose one of the three layouts for your About Me page.
○ Centered layout   ○Two-column layout   ⦿Multi-column layout

4. Type a page title, subtitle, and paragraph text in the text boxes provided. Be creative and give information about yourself and your business that you think others would want to know.

5. To add a picture to your page, type a label in the Label Your Picture text box. In the Link To Your Picture text box, type the URL to where the picture file is located.

6. To show your feedback on your page, click the **Show Feedback You've Received** down arrow, and select the number of feedbacks you want to display.

7. To show a product list, type a heading in the Label Your Listings text box, click the **Show Your Current Listing** down arrow, and select the number of items you want to show in your listing.

8. To add links to your page, type a name in the text box, and then type the corresponding URL for the web address. You can have up to three addresses.

9. Click **Continue** to see the page previewed, as shown in Figure 10-7. If you want to make changes, click **Back**. If the preview displays the edits the way you want them, click **Continue** again.

10. Click **Submit** to send your page to eBay.

Figure 10-7: Your About Me page is easily created using a three-step online form that can be previewed prior to posting to eBay.

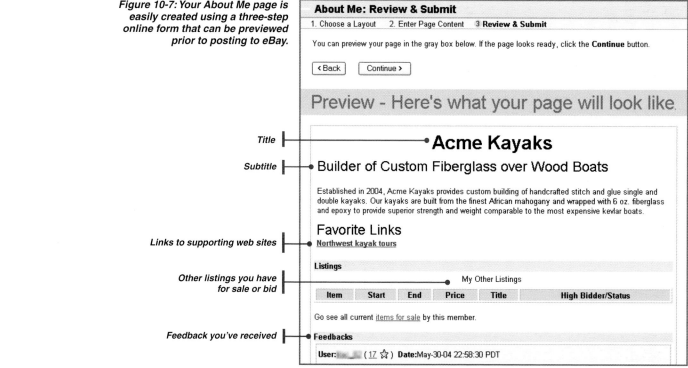

Show Feedback You've Received:

Show no comments

Show no comments
Show 10 most recent comments
Show 25 most recent comments
Show 50 most recent comments
Show 100 most recent comments

About Me: Review & Submit

1. Choose a Layout   2. Enter Page Content   3 **Review & Submit**

You can preview your page in the gray box below. If the page looks ready, click the **Continue** button.

‹ Back   Continue ›

Preview - Here's what your page will look like.

Title ├ ─•**Acme Kayaks**

Subtitle ├ ─• Builder of Custom Fiberglass over Wood Boats

Established in 2004, Acme Kayaks provides custom building of handcrafted stitch and glue single and double kayaks. Our kayaks are built from the finest African mahogany and wrapped with 6 oz. fiberglass and epoxy to provide superior strength and weight comparable to the most expensive kevlar boats.

Favorite Links

Links to supporting web sites ├ ─• Northwest kayak tours

Listings

Other listings you have for sale or bid ├ ─• My Other Listings

Item	Start	End	Price	Title	High Bidder/Status

Go see all current items for sale by this member.

Feedback you've received ├ ─• **Feedbacks**

User:▓▓▓▓ (17 ☆) Date:May-30-04 22:58:30 PDT

MAXIMIZING YOUR SALES EXPOSURE

You can maximize your selling potential by offering Buy It Now items in addition to auction items. When a buyer sees your item in the search results, it will be available in both the Auctions and the Buy It Now tabs of the search results page, thereby doubling your exposure. Additionally, many people do not like bidding in an auction; they want to get their item quickly and at a fixed, fair price. It is in your best interest to provide both paths for the buyer.

NOTE

eBay Store inventory listings do *not* appear when searching or browsing in the main section of eBay. They are restricted to searches within the eBay Stores arena. (You can search eBay Stores from within the main section of eBay by clicking the **Stores** tab on the Search | Find Items page, as shown in Figure 10-8). However, a short list of Store inventory listings does appear when a search in the main section of eBay returns fewer than ten standard listings.

Search for Stores

[   ]

◉ Stores with matching items
○ Store name and description

[Search]

More Stores search options

Start an eBay Store

eBay provides an easy-to-set-up, inexpensive feature that allows you to establish a eBay Store as a "home" within the eBay community. If you maintain a few dozen or more listings, you may find having a virtual storefront provides greater visibility to your listings by gathering them under one roof—yours.

DECIDE IF AN EBAY STORE IS FOR YOU

You can open an eBay Store under one of three subscription levels, shown in Figure 10-9. Some of the basic benefits and features of opening an eBay Store include:

- **Creating eBay Store inventory listings** (Buy It Now-type format) that run for greater lengths of time than standard listings (30, 60, 90, 120 days or Good 'Til Canceled) to help minimize relisting headaches.

- **Saving money** on eBay Store inventory listings—for example, the insertion fee for a 120-day listing is only $0.08 (standard final value fees and similar upgrade fees also apply).

- **Displaying standard auction listings within your Store** along with your Store inventory listings.

- **Organizing your Store items** in up to 20 custom categories.

- **Obtaining your own URL** that you can provide to potential buyers, both in and out of eBay.

- **Cross-promoting listings** by displaying similar or complementary listings that appear in the Sell Your Item form and in bidding and purchase e-mails your customers receive. (See the QuickSteps "Enlisting eBay to Help You Cross-Promote.")

- **Customizing your Store's presence** by selecting themes or using your own HTML design, inserting your own logo and graphics in the Store header, and including additional pages

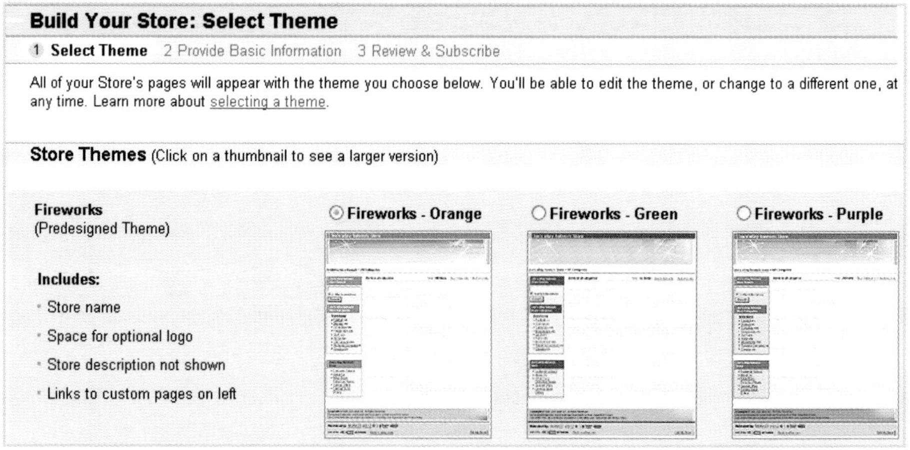

TIP

Use a web-authoring/HTML-editing program, such as Microsoft FrontPage, to design a custom look to your eBay Store. See Chapter 6 for information on creating your own eBay pages using FrontPage and HTML.

Build Your Store: Select Theme

1 **Select Theme**   2 Provide Basic Information   3 Review & Subscribe

All of your Store's pages will appear with the theme you choose below. You'll be able to edit the theme, or change to a different one, at any time. Learn more about selecting a theme.

Store Themes (Click on a thumbnail to see a larger version)

Fireworks
(Predesigned Theme)

Includes:
- Store name
- Space for optional logo
- Store description not shown
- Links to custom pages on left

○ **Fireworks - Orange**   ○ **Fireworks - Green**   ○ **Fireworks - Purple**

- **Obtaining monthly sales reports from eBay**, breaking out your sales into several metrics, such as the number of unique buyers, how buyers got to your listing, and bids per listing.

Figure 10-8: eBay Store listings don't generally appear when searching the main section of eBay, but you can search for just Store listings by using the Stores tab.

home | pay | register | sign out | services | site map | help

Browse   **Search**   **Sell**   **My eBay**   **Community**   Powered By IBM

find items   **find members**   **favorite searches**

Basic Search   Advanced Search   By Seller   By Bidder   **Stores**

Search keywords or item number (required)

[   ]   [All of these words ▼]   [Search]   Learn more

☐ Search title **and** description
☐ Search Store Inventory items only

Figure 10-9: You can open a basic eBay Store for a minimal fee and upgrade to more advanced features as your business grows.

	BASIC	FEATURED	ANCHORED
Additional fully customizable pages in your Store	5 Pages	10 Pages	15 Pages
FREE subscription to Selling Manager Pro **Coming Soon!**		✔	✔
Advanced Store traffic reporting (includes visitor path analysis and bid and buy-it-now tracking)		✔	✔
Advanced Store sales reports (includes eBay marketplace data to benchmark your Store)		✔	✔
Increase exposure on eBay		✔ on eBay Stores Pages	✔ on eBay Stores Pages
Promotional dollars to spend on the eBay Keyword Program		✔	✔
24-hour dedicated live Customer Support			✔
Monthly Subscription Fee	$9.95	$49.95	$499.95

OPEN AN EBAY STORE

To open an eBay Store:

1. Ensure that you meet the minimum requirements: maintain a seller's account with a credit card on file and have a feedback rating of 20 or higher or be ID Verified.

2. Click **Services** on the links bar at the top of any eBay page.

3. Under Advanced Seller Services, click **eBay Stores**.

4. On the Open An eBay Store page, follow the links to read additional information on Stores, or click **Open An eBay Store Now!**.

5. Log in and review (as necessary) the agreement. Then click **I Accept The eBay User Agreement**.

6. Set up your Store by completing the three-page form where you select a theme, provide your store name and description, and select a subscription level, as shown in Figure 10-10.

7. Click **Start My Subscription Now**.

Start My Subscription Now >

Figure 10-10: *To open an eBay Store, all you need to do is pick a theme, give it a name and description, and choose a subscription level.*

QUICKSTEPS

BECOMING A POWERSELLER

So you've been selling a lot of items on eBay and covet that slick icon you see next to a seller's User ID. Becoming the big dog of eBay selling is not a trivial matter, however, and eBay only hands these icons out after you've earned your eBay stripes. (You are invited to join when eBay determines you've met their criteria.) To check to see if you qualify to become a PowerSeller:

1. Click **Services** on the links bar at the top of any eBay page.

2. Under Advanced Seller Services, click **PowerSeller Program**.

3. Under the Welcome description, Why Become A PowerSeller?, click **Check Here**.

4. Sign in and chances are you will see the message shown in Figure 10-11. Unless you are qualified to be a PowerSeller (described in the following), eBay politely declines your offer to become one.

BE A PROLIFIC SELLER

• Start now and keep selling for at least 90 days.

• Submit at least four listings a month for the three months prior to your consideration for PowerSeller status.

• Sell at least $1,000 per month in average gross sales for three months for entry-level PowerSeller status (Bronze).

Continued...

Sally, the seller, working hard trying to become an even bigger PowerSeller

Figure 10-11: *You have to be a steady, prolific, and upstanding eBay seller before you can be designated a PowerSeller.*

BECOMING A POWERSELLER

(Continued)

- Keep selling and increase your three-month average gross sales to achieve higher PowerSeller levels: $3,000 (Silver), $10,000 (Gold), $25,000 (Platinum), $150,000 (Titanium).

BE A GOOD EBAY CITIZEN

- Maintain outstanding feedback with at least 100 entries at a 98 percent positive rating.
- Do not run afoul of eBay policies.
- Pay your eBay bills on time.

KEEP IT ONCE YOU GET IT

- Respond to high bidders within three business days.
- Stay in compliance of eBay policies.
- Maintain and honor an appropriate return policy.

QUICKSTEPS

SELLING LIVE

If you have an established auction business (licensed auction house or those auctions using a licensed auctioneer), you can partner with eBay and offer its members the opportunity to place absentee bids and even live bids during the conduct of your auction.

1. Visit www.ebayliveauctions.com and click **Sign Up As A Seller**.

2. Contact eBay by e-mail, or complete and submit an online form, as shown in Figure 10-13.

Chapter 4 describes how to bid on live eBay auctions.

Offer Anything Points

eBay provides an incentive program called Anything Points that you can use to attract buyers to your items and to reward them for using PayPal as a payment method. You can choose how many points to provide successful buyers (between one and ten points per dollar of final value fee paid through PayPal). You are charged $0.01 for each point given. Assign points to your current listings using Offer Manager.

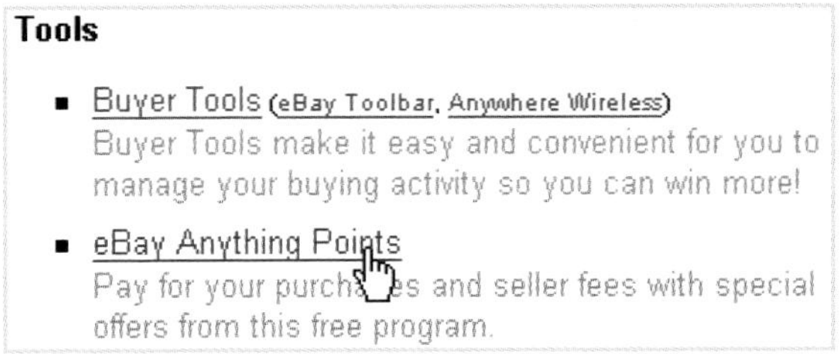

Tools

- Buyer Tools (eBay Toolbar, Anywhere Wireless)
  Buyer Tools make it easy and convenient for you to manage your buying activity so you can win more!

- eBay Anything Points
  Pay for your purchases and seller fees with special offers from this free program.

Log-in to Offer Manager

1. Click **Services** on the eBay menu bar.

2. Under Tools, click **eBay Anything Points**.

3. On the Anything Points page, click **Sellers–Offer Points** on the Choose A Topic sidebar.

4. Read over the FAQs and details of the program, and click **Log-In To Offer Manager** when ready to assign points to your listed items. You will need to sign in first.

5. Follow the instructions in Offer Manager to assign points to the listings you want. Your buyers will see a graphic added to the item description, as shown in Figure 10-12.

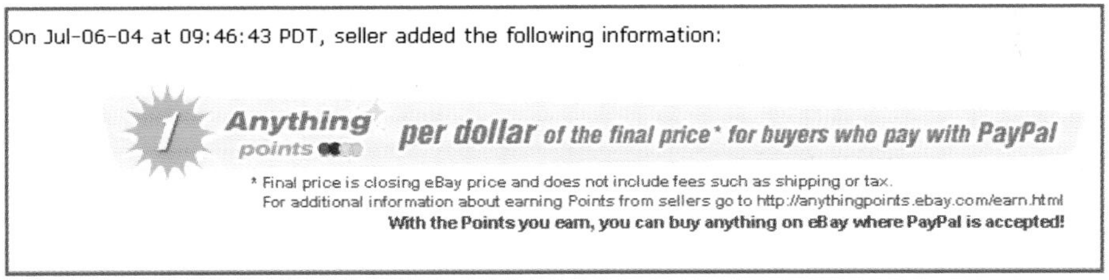

On Jul-06-04 at 09:46:43 PDT, seller added the following information:

1 Anything points **per dollar** of the final price* for buyers who pay with PayPal

* Final price is closing eBay price and does not include fees such as shipping or tax.
For additional information about earning Points from sellers go to http://anythingpoints.ebay.com/earn.html
With the Points you earn, you can buy anything on eBay where PayPal is accepted!

Figure 10-12: You can offer buyers from one to ten Anything Points on your listings.

Figure 10-13: Leverage your auction business by offering eBay members a chance to place live or absentee bids.

NOTE

A company called AuctionDrop brings an interesting twist to the trading assistant and drop-off store concept. In partnership with The UPS Store, AuctionDrop allows an owner to sell an item on eBay by simply dropping off the item at any UPS Store (the item must be on an approved AuctionDrop list). The UPS Store packages the item and sends it to AuctionDrop, which then opens the package, writes a description, takes pictures, and lists the item on eBay. When the item sells, they ship the item to the buyer and send the owner a check, minus their and eBay's fees. (According to AuctionDrop, for example, an item that sells for $200.00 would net the owner approximately $111.85.)

Sell for Others

You can leverage your experience and knowledge of eBay selling by offering to sell items for others. Selling on *consignment* pays you for your services (which can be anything you and the consignee agree upon) by collecting a fee or a percentage of the selling price or both.

Consign Items

One of the hottest trends for using eBay as a business is the concept of listing items for others; that is, becoming a *trading assistant*. Many folks don't care to join eBay, get involved with the mechanics of creating a Sell Your Item form, or deal with the customer service interaction of current and completed sales. You typically purchase a software program that allows you to set up accounts for multiple consignees and provides other related features, such as allowing each consignee to view his or her listings (under your eBay User ID). Trading assistants sell a myriad of items for a variety of clients:

- Individuals (best served with a retail outlet; see "Open a Drop-Off Store")
- Charitable and fundraising organizations
- Retail businesses that have excess inventory or returns
- Other eBay sellers who have just too many items to sell themselves

To become a trading assistant:

1. Set up your business infrastructure (see "Create the Infrastructure").
2. Procure suitable software.
3. Advertise your business. (Join the eBay Trading Assistant Program to gain potential exposure among the millions of eBay users.)

Join the eBay Trading Assistant Program

eBay provides a clearinghouse for successful sellers and potential customers to come together but doesn't get directly involved in the terms or arrangements—these are left to the participants to work out. Pricing, shipping, relisting decisions, and how you get paid are among the details that should be worked

out before you list an item for someone. If you would like to offer your selling services to others (you can also offer to *buy* for others), you need to demonstrate some selling prowess and that you're a good eBay member. To be a trading assistant:

- You must have sold four or more items in the past 30 days.
- Your feedback rating must be 50 or better and at least 97 percent of it must be positive.
- You must be in good standing with eBay.

To start the process of becoming a trading assistant:

1. Click **Services** on the links bar at the top of any eBay page.

2. Under Listing Solutions, click **Trading Assistants**.

Open a Drop-Off Store

One idea for capitalizing on the eBay juggernaut is to open a brick-and-mortar storefront and accept items off the street to sell on eBay. Basically a consignment business, you typically charge an upfront insertion fee (different from and greater than eBay's fee) and then pay the consignee when the item sells, minus shipping costs and a commission fee. You can open your own store or join one of the rapidly growing national franchises iSold It (www.i-soldit.com) and QuikDrop (www.quikdropfranchise.com).

Use Auction-Management Services

As your eBay business grows, you will quickly find yourself needing more auction-management features than those provided by My eBay.

Try eBay Tools

Access selling tools provided by eBay by clicking **Site Map** on the links bar at the top of any eBay page. Under Selling Tools, click one or more of the following:

Figure 10-14: Turbo Lister lets you create listings offline and upload them when you are ready.

QUICKFACTS

INVESTIGATING SERVICES AND PROGRAMS

There is no shortage of auction-management programs for you to check out. Do a Google search for a sense of the number.

Programs that came up with positive comments in discussions by eBay members include:

- **Sold!** (www.timbercreeksoftware.com)
- **Auction Sage** (www.auctionsagesoftware.com)
- **Auctiva Basic** (www.auctiva.com)
- **Easy Auctiontools** (www.auctiontools.net)
- **Auction Hawk** (www.auctionhawk.com)
- **SpareDollar** (www.sparedollar.com)
- **Microsoft Office Excel 2003** (www.microsoft.com/office) Some assembly required! (See *Microsoft Office Excel 2003 QuickSteps*, published by McGraw-Hill/Osborne.)

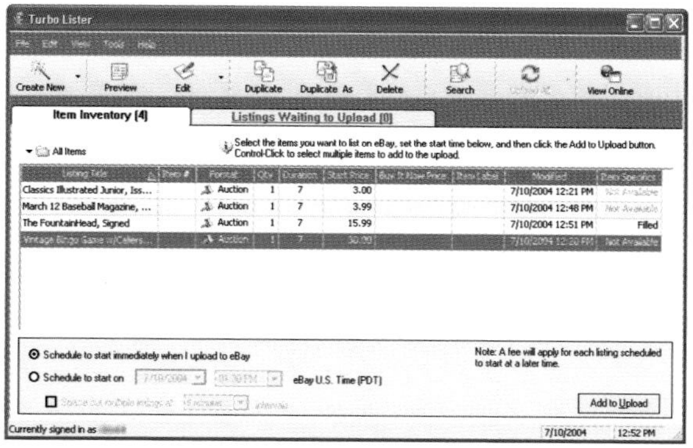

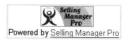

- **Turbo Lister** (free) is not specifically a management tool, but it does ease your workload by allowing you to more easily create, organize, and submit multiple listings while working offline. The main Turbo Lister window is shown in Figure 10-14.
- **eBay Selling Manager** ($4.99 per month) had a lot of its selling thunder stolen from the latest upgrade to My eBay, although it continues to offer greater post-sale support.
- **eBay Selling Manager Pro** (($15.99 per month) is touted for "high volume and business sellers" (translation: PowerSellers) and includes bulk listing, reporting, and many automated features (it offers the most features of the eBay-provided services). As with Turbo Lister and Selling Manager, logos appear in your listings that are uploaded to eBay.

  Powered by Selling Manager Pro

- **Seller's Assistant Basic** ($9.99 per month), like eBay Selling Manager, is primarily geared toward creating listings and has essentially been usurped by upgrades to the selling form, such as being able to add templates and layouts, and by the latest My eBay. (Add eBay Selling Manager for the same monthly subscription fee.)
- **Seller's Assistant Pro** ($24.99 per month) is a companion service to Selling Manager Pro for the higher-volume seller. (Purchase both services for the same higher monthly fee.)
- **PayPal Merchant Tools** is a tool that provides a collection of tools to help you accept and manage payment and shipping. Click the **Merchant Tools** tab at the top of any PayPal page.

Employ Preferred Solution Providers

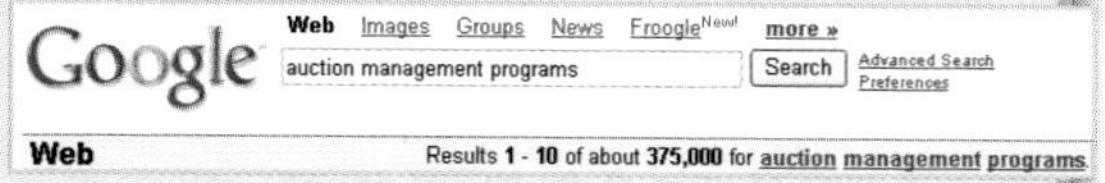

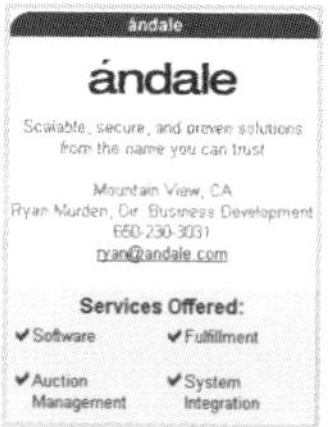

When you've outgrown the capabilities provided by off-the-shelf programs and need a custom approach to your eBay sales, consider employing one of eBay's Preferred Solution Providers. These companies (an example is Andale, the provider of free hit counters for Sell Your Item forms, described in Chapter 5) have been reviewed by eBay and provide complete solutions to your eBay business, including custom software development, auction management, hosting, order fulfillment, and complete system integration.

1. Click **Services** on the links bar at the top of any eBay page.
2. Under Advanced Seller Services, click **Preferred Solution Provider Program**.
3. Contact one or more of the providers via e-mail, phone, or snail mail.

G

gift
  certificates, 16
  finding a, 38, 47
grading services, 69
graphics. *See* pictures

H

HalfZone, 6
Help, eBay, 27-28
hit counter. *See* counter
home page, 3
  finding the eBay, 4
  making My eBay your, 158
  using the eBay, 5-9
HTML (hypertext markup language)
  adding background images with, 153
  formatting text with, 99, 102, 104, 151
  hyperlinks, 153-154
  linking to pictures with, 152
  tips, 152-153
  using WSIWYG editors for, 150

I

icons
  describing listings, 36
  describing users, 42
  used in My eBay, 32
ID Verify, 13-14
inserts, 102
inventory. See items
invoices, 6, 181, 183-184
items
  acquiring for sale, 90, 221
  acronyms for condition of, 51
  creating titles for, 92, 97, 98
  damaged, 200, 213
  describing, 99-102, 149-154, 164
  evaluating descriptions of, 54-55,... 70, 76
  finding, 3, 39-41
  investigating, 69-70
  packaging, 186-188
  pricing, 103-105
  promoting, 218-220, 222-224, 228
  selling similar, 165-166
  See also Featured Items

L

legal resources, 216
listings
  canceling, 170-172
  editing, 162-164
  fees for, 90-91, 174-176
  finding, 160-161
  notes in, 21

  pricing for, 103-105
  rescheduling, 159
  scheduling, 105
  upgrading a, 109-110
  See also auctions
logos. See pictures
lots, 84

M

mediation, 206-207
Member Spotlight, 30
Microsoft
  Alerts, 74
  FrontPage, 150
MissionFish. *See* charity auctions
money orders, 82, 91, 96
multiple-item auctions. *See* Dutch Auctions
My Account, 13, 20-22
My eBay, 16-22
  Favorites, 32-34
  making your home page, 158
  preferences, 181
  tracking items with, 77-79
  tracking sales with, 176-177
My Favorite Categories, 32-34
My Summary, 17-19, 21

R

read-only, deselecting, 30, 50
registering, 9-11
reimbursement claims, 207-208
relisting, 193-195
reporting
   account theft, 203-204,
   problem buyers, 214
   specific problems, 206, 209-211,
   214-216
   spoof e-mail, 207-208
reserve prices, 62, 68, 104-105
retracting bids, 90, 91

S

sales
   evaluating your, 174-179
   resolving non-, 193-196
   starting, 91-92
   steps to successful, 175-176
   tracking completed, 176-179
   views for managing, 156-158
   without bids, 163
   See also listings
sales tax, 181
scanners, 130-132
scheduling listings, 105, 156, 159
searches
   Advanced, 37-39
   Basic, 36-37
   favorite, 34-35
   specialized, 8
   See also finding
Second Chance Offer, 193, 195-196

seller accounts, 88-89
Seller Central, 88
sellers
   asking questions of, 56-57
   communication tips for, 198-199
   contacting, 90-91
   favorite, 33, 35
   finding, 39-40
   finding feedback about, 39-40
   reducing risks for, 200
   resolving problems for, 210-216
   return policies for, 111
   services for, 229, 230, 234
   stars for, 47
selling
   acquiring items for, 90, 221
   calculating costs for, 174-176
   views, 156-158
   with minimum effort, 90
selling form
   completing the, 93-118
   preferences, 158,
   the parts of the, 92
   See also categories, titles,
descriptions, pictures, payment,
shipping
shill bidding, 63, 91
shipping
   acronyms, 52
   cost calculation, 112-115, 187-190
   data in the description, 175
   flat-rate, 114
   insurance, 189, 201, 213
   items, 186-193
   information for sellers, 110-116
   labels, 190-193
   problems with, 213

sign-in,
   automatic, 22
   for live auctions, 88
   options, 22
   preferences, 168
sniper bidding, 62-64
software
   auction management, 234
   consignment, 232
   custom, 234
Specialty Sites, 3, 5
SquareTrade, 206-207
standard auctions, 7
stores. See businesses
subtitles, 98-99

T

tax. See sales tax
threads, discussion, 23-25
time
   considerations for bidding, 60-64
   limitations for bidding, 62
   official eBay, 61
   See also duration
timeshares. See real estate
titles, item, 97-98
themes, 108
Toolbar, eBay
   installing the, 70-71
   setting preferences on the, 77-78
   using the, 72, 78, 161
tracking
   bids in multiple windows, 62-63
   categories, 32-34
   items, 77-79

live auctions, 86
trading assistant, 232-231
transactions, 2
   closing out, 176
   fees for, 174
   protecting, 201
   viewing, 175-176, 178

U

Unpaid Items Process, 210
UPS, 186, 187, 189, 190-193, 213
User Agreement, 11, 14-15
User ID
   changing a, 20-21
   creating a, 10, 11, 12
   tracking a, 44
USPS, 187-192, 213

V

vacation homes. See real estate
vehicles, 5
   fees for selling, 174
   finding, 47-48

W

web site
   link to eBay, 222-224
   link to another, 226
wireless alerts, 72-74
workshops, 28

International Contact Information

AUSTRALIA
McGraw-Hill Book Company Australia Pty. Ltd.
TEL +61-2-9900-1800
FAX +61-2-9878-8881
http://www.mcgraw-hill.com.au
books-it_sydney@mcgraw-hill.com

CANADA
McGraw-Hill Ryerson Ltd.
TEL +905-430-5000
FAX +905-430-5020
http://www.mcgraw-hill.ca

GREECE, MIDDLE EAST, & AFRICA
(Excluding South Africa)
McGraw-Hill Hellas
TEL +30-210-6560-990
TEL +30-210-6560-993
TEL +30-210-6560-994
FAX +30-210-6545-525

MEXICO (Also serving Latin America)
McGraw-Hill Interamericana Editores S.A. de C.V.
TEL +525-1500-5108
FAX +525-117-1589
http://www.mcgraw-hill.com.mx
carlos_ruiz@mcgraw-hill.com

SINGAPORE (Serving Asia)
McGraw-Hill Book Company
TEL +65-6863-1580
FAX +65-6862-3354
http://www.mcgraw-hill.com.sg
mghasia@mcgraw-hill.com

SOUTH AFRICA
McGraw-Hill South Africa
TEL +27-11-622-7512
FAX +27-11-622-9045
robyn_swanepoel@mcgraw-hill.com

SPAIN
McGraw-Hill/Interamericana de España, S.A.U.
TEL +34-91-180-3000
FAX +34-91-372-8513
http://www.mcgraw-hill.es
professional@mcgraw-hill.es

UNITED KINGDOM, NORTHERN,
EASTERN, & CENTRAL EUROPE
McGraw-Hill Education Europe
TEL +44-1-628-502500
FAX +44-1-628-770224
http://www.mcgraw-hill.co.uk
emea_queries@mcgraw-hill.com

ALL OTHER INQUIRIES Contact:
McGraw-Hill/Osborne
TEL +1-510-420-7700
FAX +1-510-420-7703
http://www.osborne.com
omg_international@mcgraw-hill.com